D0148617

POLITICAL STABILITY
AND
DEMOCRACY IN MEXICO

Political Stability and Democracy in Mexico

THE "PERFECT DICTATORSHIP"?

Dan A. Cothran

Westport, Connecticut
London

Library of Congress Cataloging-in-Publication Data

Cothran, Dan A.
    Political stability and democracy in Mexico : the "perfect
dictatorship"? / Dan A. Cothran.
      p. cm.
    Includes bibliographical references and index.
    ISBN 0-275-94345-3
    1. Political stability—Mexico. 2. Mexico—Politics and
government—20th century. I. Title.
JL1281.C7   1994
972.08'35—dc20   93-23679

British Library Cataloguing in Publication Data is available.

Copyright © 1994 by Dan A. Cothran

All rights reserved. No portion of this book may be
reproduced, by any process or technique, without the
express written consent of the publisher.

Library of Congress Catalog Card Number: 93-23679
ISBN: 0-275-94345-3

First published in 1994

Praeger Publishers, 88 Post Road West, Westport, CT 06881
An imprint of Greenwood Publishing Group, Inc.

Printed in the United States of America

The paper used in this book complies with the Permanent
Paper Standard issued by the National Information Standards
Organization (Z39.48-1984).

10 9 8 7 6 5 4 3 2

To my wife, Cheryl, and my daughters, Leslie and Amanda.

To my brothers and sisters, Jerry, Lowell, Duvon, Paul, and Joy.

To the memory of my parents, Marvin and Retha Cothran,
and my sister, Clara.

Contents

Figures and Tables

FIGURES

TABLES

Preface

This book is not a general description of the Mexican political system, but an attempt to explain one of the most remarkable characteristics of that system—its stability for a period that surpasses that of any other Latin American country. It is, therefore, an interpretive essay that seeks to answer one central question: why has Mexico been governed by the same political regime since 1920 while all other Latin American countries have experienced violent overthrow of governments since World War II? The book argues that Mexico's political stability has been a result of six factors: institutionalization, effectiveness, adaptability, elite unity, location, and coercion.

The reader will note that democracy is not in my list of factors. In the past, democracy was not essential for stability in Mexico. The Peruvian writer Mario Vargas Llosa said in 1990: "The Mexican political system is not democratic—let's not kid ourselves. It is a unique system that has no equivalents in the world, that has managed to keep a party in power by adapting to circumstances with a versatility that no other authoritarian system has managed" (*Proceso*, no. 723, September 10, 1990, quoted in Andrew Reding, "Mexico: The Crumbling of the 'Perfect Dictatorship,' " *World Policy Journal* 8 (2) Spring 1991, p. 257). He called the Mexican system "the perfect dictatorship," by which he meant that it was a system of veiled authoritarianism that perpetuated a party in power, rather than a person, allowing some criticism as long as it did not fundamentally threaten the system. However, the regime was willing to use all means, "including the worst," to suppress criticism that might threaten its rule. Thus Mexican political stability has been made possible in part because of one-party rule. As we approach the end of the century, however, it may be that political stability in Mexico is no longer possible without democracy. The challenge of the future, therefore, is whether the Mexican political system has the versatility to transform itself peacefully by adapting to the demands of the twenty-first century.

The opportunity to teach Latin American politics at Northern Arizona University allowed me to renew an interest in Mexico, and summer grants from NAU's Organized Research Committee provided some financial support for the research, especially for chapters 2, 4, and 5. My thanks to the committee and to Dean Henry Hooper for that support. Warm appreciation to Gerald Hughes for introducing me to the wonders of the Macintosh computer. Thanks to Cara DeAngelis for help with the index.

The opportunity to exchange ideas over the years with Sheryl Lutjens, Eldon Kenworthy, David McKell, Magdaleno Manzanárez, Glenn Phelps, Samuel Schmidt, Franklin Tugwell, James Wilkie, and others helped to crystallize my thoughts on the subject of political stability and change. My thanks to Professors McKell, Phelps, Manzanárez, and Schmidt for reading all or parts of the manuscript. Very special thanks to Cheryl Cole Cothran and Fred Thompson for reading the entire manuscript and for help over many years that went far beyond the call of duty. Our conversations for two decades have had the character of a perpetual seminar. My appreciation to Jim Dunton, Richard Sillett, and D. Teddy Diggs of Praeger Publishers for their editorial help.

For facilitating my research in Mexico, my sincere thanks go to Marieclaire Acosta, Luis Alvarez, Samuel del Villar, Julio Faesler, Saul Figueroa, Ifigenia Martínez, Isabel Molina, Porfirio Muñoz Ledo, and many others who took the time to enlighten me about political affairs in their country. Special thanks to Leticia Calzada for putting me in contact with so many knowledgeable people. My appreciation to Joe Keenan, American journalist in Mexico, for giving me the opportunity to write several articles for the *Mexico Journal* in 1988. I also thank Alan Robinson, Cindy Anders, and Jim Weddell of the *Journal* for sharing their insights with me. Although Alan and I never wrote the book together that we planned, I hope he will consider this one the next best thing. In particular, I would like to thank Cuauhtémoc Cárdenas for graciously sharing his vision of Mexico with me.

The analysis of Mexican political stability owes much to those mentioned above, who helped to clarify my thinking or improve my language but who cannot, of course, be held accountable for the shortcomings of the book.

My family has helped me in this research in many ways. Joy and Lowell Cothran added to my archives with voluminous clippings on Mexico. My wife, Cheryl Cole Cothran, has provided inspiration in many ways for many years. Without her help, this book would have taken much longer to finish. Finally, my daughters, Leslie and Amanda, have helped me to see the limits of regime coercion and the necessity of adaptability if authority is to be legitimate and stable. Perhaps now they will understand why their father was "always sitting at his desk."

POLITICAL STABILITY
AND
DEMOCRACY IN MEXICO

1

Mexican Political Stability

OVERVIEW OF THE ARGUMENT

Stability is an important concept in political science. One of the most fundamental questions in the discipline is why a political system persists or, conversely, why it is transformed, whether peacefully or violently. The literature
that deals in one way or another with stability, usually through asking about
instability, is so vast as to be almost coterminous with the literature of political
science itself. However, stability is not very often studied directly. To the contrary, it is usually dealt with indirectly by studying its precedents, such as
legitimacy, or its absence, as in revolution.[1] But whether examined directly or
indirectly, stability is a crucial variable in political science.[2]

Stability is also an important goal of political development. By the 1970s,
political stability had clearly emerged as one of the major goals of most developing societies.[3] Yet political stability has been an elusive quality in the twentieth century. Britain and its former colonies are exceptions in a world generally
characterized by regimes of short duration and irregular executive succession.
As a region, Latin America has been particularly susceptible to unscheduled
removal of governments. For example, every one of the twenty republics of
Latin America except Mexico has experienced a violent overthrow of government since 1945.

In this context, the political stability of Mexico is all the more unusual.
While Latin America suffered a wave of military takeovers in the 1960s and
1970s, Mexico retained its civilian-dominated, semiauthoritarian political system. When the rest of Latin America experienced a trend toward democratization in the 1980s, Mexico again stood apart in retaining the same political
regime that has governed it since the 1920s.[4] In fact, Mexico is the only Latin
American republic to avoid violent change of government from 1920 to the
present. During these decades Mexico labored under severe political strains that

might have toppled other governments, and yet the Mexican regime remained intact. Therefore, in a region characterized by political volatility, Mexico stood out, for good or ill, as a case of unusual political stability.

Any regime that lasts so long must possess fundamental qualities that account for its endurance. This book will examine the sources of the remarkable stability that has characterized the Mexican regime for over sixty years. Its thesis is that Mexico's political stability has largely been a result of the interaction of six factors: the highly *institutionalized* nature of the regime (rare in Latin America), the *effectiveness* of the country in achieving economic growth, the *adaptability* of the regime in responding to the changing demands of society, the *cohesion of the political elites* to a degree unheard of in Latin America, the *location* of Mexico next to the United States, and the systematic use of *coercion*. The book will examine four periods in Mexican political history when these qualities were most starkly demonstrated: the 1930s, the period from 1940 to 1970, the 1970s, and the period surrounding the 1988 election. It will then use the framework to analyze the efforts of Carlos Salinas to reinvigorate the regime after the severe setbacks of the 1980s. Finally, the book will examine the probability of continued stability in the 1990s as well as the likelihood of a transition to greater political democracy.

Every political regime periodically faces challenges to its authority and stability, sometimes in spectacular ways. The Communist regimes of Eastern Europe saw how shaky their authority really was when the coercive component of that authority was withdrawn in 1989. After the Soviet government declared that it would not maintain communism in Eastern Europe by force, the Communist regimes collapsed with shocking speed. The Soviet regime itself then evaporated in 1991 after many of its political elites lost confidence in the ideological basis of the system.

In recent years Mexico too has experienced a severe crisis of regime. In the 1980s, the country suffered a decade of dismal economic performance characterized by massive capital flight, unprecedented foreign debt, record unemployment, and rampant inflation. Largely because of this abysmal economic performance, the regime faced an electoral challenge in 1988 in which the ruling party lost more seats in the national congress than at any other time in its history and nearly lost the presidency itself. That challenge continued after 1988 as the opposition won governorships for the first time and many more positions in state and local governments. The opposition parties were better organized and more determined than ever before.

It is difficult to say whether the Mexican political system will remain semiauthoritarian, evolve toward greater liberal democracy, or become convulsed in violence. However, because of the prospect that Mexico might lose the stability that has been the hallmark of its political system for so long, this is an appropriate time to consider the sources of the remarkable stability that characterized the country up to now. Whatever happens in the future, Mexico has had a record of political stability unmatched in the Third World. In fact, the ruling group of Mexico has been in power without interruption (1920–93) longer than any other group in the twentieth century except the Communist Party of the Soviet Union (CPSU), which was banned after the unsuccessful coup attempt in August 1991 after seventy-four years in power (followed by the collapse of the Soviet Union itself in December 1991). In 1994, the Mexican ruling group will surpass even the record of the CPSU (1917–91).[5]

Rather than a complete history of Mexican politics, this is an interpretive essay that seeks to explain an important quality of the Mexican regime. The four periods examined in the book demonstrate the fundamental strengths of the regime. The years of Lázaro Cárdenas in the 1930s produced the institutionalization of the Mexican regime that laid the foundation for future political stability. During the period from 1940 to 1970, Mexico experienced the rapid economic growth that helped to endow the regime with greater legitimacy. The years of Luis Echeverría and José López Portillo (1970–82) illustrate well the flexibility of the regime in responding to the dominant pressures of the era, first from the left and then from the right. Then the period surrounding the critical election of 1988 demonstrates the fourth fundamental characteristic of the Mexican regime, the unity of its elites. Despite the most severe challenge in seventy years, most of the political and military elites remained loyal to the regime. The regime was characterized by most of the qualities during each period, but each period illustrates one of the qualities in bold relief: the 1930s and institutionalization, 1940–70 and economic effectiveness, the 1970s and adaptability, and 1988 and elite unity.

In addition to these four qualities that are best illustrated by certain periods, two other qualities have been continuously important in contributing to Mexican political stability. These are the *location* of Mexico next to the United States and the ability and willingness of the Mexican regime to use *coercion* to maintain itself in power. These will be discussed where appropriate throughout the book.

The location of Mexico has been an important determinant in that country's history in many ways other than fostering stability in the twentieth century. Its location next to the expansionist United States helps to explain the loss of half of its national territory in the nineteenth century. Then Mexico's economic growth after 1875 was aided by huge amounts of capital and technology that flowed in from the United States. The encouragement and support of U.S. government and business helped to sustain the long reign of Porfirio Díaz from 1876 to 1911. Later the relatively open border made it easier for the revolutionaries in 1910 to marshal their forces for the attack on the Díaz regime. Partly because of pressure from the U.S. ambassador, the revolutionary government of Francisco Madero was overthrown in 1913 and Mexico was hurled into the most violent four years of its revolution. U.S. policy then contributed to the overthrow of President Victoriano Huerta in 1914. Desire for U.S. recognition influenced the policies of the Mexican government from 1920 onward, and U.S. support helped to sustain that government in power on several occasions from 1923 to 1940. The United States virtually always put its influence on the side of the Mexican regime whenever that regime was challenged because it has almost always preferred the status quo in Mexico to any other alternative, including democracy. In the twentieth century large amounts of immigration contributed huge quantities of funds to the Mexican economy and acted as a safety valve for political tensions that might otherwise have built up as a result of the high levels of unemployment in Mexico. Thus the position of Mexico next to the United States has almost continuously affected the fortunes of Mexico and its government.

Another factor that affects stability in any political system is coercion, which every regime uses to put down internal challenges. Although coercion beyond a certain point can be destabilizing, some coercion has been necessary for the continued survival of most regimes. At various points throughout the analysis of the interaction of these four fundamental factors, therefore, it will be shown how the use of coercion (defined here as physical force and electoral fraud) has waxed and waned with the severity of the challenge to the Mexican regime. As so many regimes did, this one came to power through violence, used significant amounts of violence to consolidate its power in the early years, and then continued to use varying amounts of coercion to maintain itself in power until the present. Generally, the level of coercion has declined since 1920, but there have been periodic bursts of repression.

The rest of this chapter will elaborate in greater detail the theoretical framework used in this book to explain Mexico's remarkable political stability. It argues that these six qualities contributed to political stability by affecting the calculations of political actors. That is, relevant political actors—especially elites—were presented with incentives to accept the political system rather than try to replace it.

Chapter 2 will analyze the construction of the modern Mexican state during the administration of Lázaro Cárdenas in the 1930s. One of the major factors that helps a polity move from instability to stability, or "order," is the institutionalization of political processes. That is, political processes and power must be depersonalized or separated from any particular individual and attached to positions which can be filled by various individuals. The institutionalization of political processes has been one of the primary strengths of the Mexican regime since 1920. Chapter 2 will explain how regime institutionalization was achieved and how it has contributed to political stability. Cárdenas accumulated enormous personal power and then contributed that power to the political system in order to build a strong state and achieve long-term political stability.

Chapter 3 will look at the period of rapid economic growth from 1940 to 1970, a period known as the Mexican economic miracle. During that time, Mexico had one of the highest economic growth rates in the world. The growth was sustained long enough to provide some satisfaction to numerous groups that formed a part of the ruling coalition, especially business and organized labor. However, the rewards were unevenly distributed, and by the end of the

1960s, serious tensions had accumulated, forcing the regime to respond to a different set of demands in the 1970s.

Chapter 4 will examine the crisis of the 1970s, the most severe challenge to the Mexican regime between the 1930s and 1988. It will show how the adaptability of the regime allowed it to respond to the growing demands for greater social justice. This contributed to the maintenance of the regime at a time when many Latin American political systems were experiencing military coups or continuing personalistic dictatorships. Instead of suffering the fate of so many Latin American governments during times of stress, the Mexican regime adapted to the dominant pressures of the moment. President Echeverría (1970–76) responded with populist policies and rhetoric in an effort to defuse discontent on the left. When that strategy provoked a reaction from business and the middle classes, the next president (López Portillo, 1976–82) responded with efforts to placate those sectors. Once again, therefore, the regime adapted to the demands of the times and retained enough support to continue in power. This chapter will deal with the Echeverría government in some detail and the López Portillo administration more briefly.

Chapter 5 explores the fourth factor that has kept the Mexican regime so stable, elite cohesion. Although one cannot deny the importance of mass action in affecting politics, elite behavior is often more decisive. Elite "settlements," or agreements that establish a framework within which elites agree to conduct politics, can be a crucial force for stability. Although important defections have occurred from 1920 to the present, the governing elite remained unified enough to retain power. The political elites remained relatively cohesive and retained enough support from military, labor, business, and intellectual elites to fend off challenges. This chapter looks especially at the crisis of 1988, when numerous members of the political elite defected from the regime and mounted the greatest political challenge in decades. In 1988, at a time of grave economic crisis, Cuauhtémoc Cárdenas, son of the former president, broke with the ruling party and ran as an independent candidate for president. He was conceded a larger share of the vote than any other opposition candidate for president in the regime's history, but the cohesion of the elites allowed the regime to withstand the severe pressures of the Cárdenas challenge for the time being.

Chapter 6 shows that Carlos Salinas employed the classic methods to try to reestablish the authority of the regime. He tried to demonstrate that a new president can bring a fresh approach to government, took various measures to stimulate economic growth and redistribute income, and sought to reconsolidate the regime by responding to some extent to the demands for democracy. For this purpose, he enacted a new electoral law, recognized some opposition victories, and addressed some of the complaints about human rights abuses. In short, he tried to use all the fundamental characteristics of the Mexican regime to restore the authority that had been weakened during the 1980s.

Chapter 7 uses the framework developed in the book to assess the prospects for continued stability as well as the potential for a transition to a more democratic political system. It argues that the Mexican political system will remain stable only if the regime applies the traditional qualities to the demands of the modern era. The half century of political stability and economic growth produced a more educated, middle-class, and urban society in which people insist on more meaningful participation in the decisions that affect their lives. Therefore, the regime must be institutionalized, effective, adaptable, and unified in new ways, and it must recognize the limits of coercion and U.S. support in the present era.

CONDITIONS OF POLITICAL STABILITY

Political stability is a result of a regime's authority, or ability to govern. Authority is composed of adequate legitimacy to elicit support for the regime's claim that it deserves to be in power and adequate coercive ability to entice the acquiescence of those who do not believe that it deserves to be in power. Support and acquiescence in turn are a result of individual political actors' calculations that are made in the context created by the qualities of a regime— institutionalization, effectiveness, adaptability, elite unity, coercive ability, and the "location" of the regime in its international context. These relationships can be depicted in this way:

Figure 1.1
Regime Qualities and Political Stability

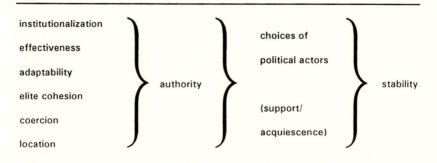

The context within which political actors make decisions affects their calculations and hence their choices. A political system that is highly institutionalized, effective, and adaptable, with unified elites who are willing to use coercion judiciously to maintain their rule, and that is favored by powerful international forces will tend to be stable because those conditions will structure the self-interested calculations of political actors in ways that will provide support for, or at least acquiescence in, the continued rule of the regime. People will tend to see it in their interest to accept, and even participate actively in, the regime because the rules of the game are predictable, the regime is effective in providing the valued things that people want, it is flexible enough to change course when demands build up, and the unity of the elites and their willingness to use coercion provide little hope of a replacement of this regime with another.

But political stability is precarious because of the existence of potential challengers who would like to supplant a regime, or at least replace the rulers of the moment. To remain in power, therefore, rulers must establish their authority through some combination of coercion and legitimacy (the perception by the public that a particular set of rulers deserves to be in power). The more legitimate the regime is in the eyes of all the population, the better for stability, but all other things being equal, it is more important that the regime be seen as legitimate by *elites* than by nonelites because the former, by definition, have more of the resources that can either sustain or weaken a regime, such as institutional position, followers, coercive ability, or money.

The two components of authority—legitimacy and coercion—are related to each other in complex ways. Regimes often come to power through a combination of legitimacy and coercion and then use both of these qualities to maintain themselves in power. Up to a point, the two are positively related. Enough coercion must be employed against those who are widely seen to behave in unacceptable ways (e.g., "criminals" or "terrorists") to maintain order or the regime will begin to lose its legitimacy even in the eyes of those who previously considered it legitimate. Beyond that point, coercion becomes inversely related to legitimacy. If a regime uses "excessive" force (as defined by each observer), that act is both an indicator and a cause of eroding legitimacy. To the degree that large numbers of political actors (individuals, groups, and especially elites) accept and support the regime, it will tend to be stable.

Two types of explanations that have competed with one another in social science can broadly be characterized as structural and choice types of theories. Structural theories emphasize the determining effect of impersonal qualities of the environment in which human behavior takes place—qualities such as wealth, social class, international position, and so on. Structural theories emphasize the constraining influence of such impersonal factors and relegate human choice to a relatively small role in determining social outcomes. Choice types of explanations, on the other hand, recognize these environmental constraints but emphasize (or at least explore) the degree of choice available to human actors.

In the past few years, scholars seemed compelled to choose categorically between the two types of explanation. More generally, it was widely believed during this time that one had to commit to a single explanatory approach rather than to combine elements of several approaches because it was thought that important advances in knowledge tended to come in large jumps, often involving the complete rejection of previous ways of seeing reality. In one of the most influential works written on the philosophy of science, Thomas Kuhn argued that scientific knowledge does not progress in the cumulative way most people assumed, that is, with bits of knowledge piled one upon another to produce a better and better understanding of the world. Rather, Kuhn argued, science proceeds for a while within a particular theoretical perspective, or "paradigm," until the anomalies in the observed world accumulate to the point that the paradigm itself is called into question. Then a scientific "revolution" occurs in which a new theoretical paradigm replaces the outmoded one.[6] Three of the most notable instances of such scientific revolutions were the replacement of the view that the sun revolved around the earth by the opposite view, the substitution of evolution for creation, and the supplanting of Newtonian physics by Einstein's theory. For several decades, many political scientists were enthralled by this notion of scientific revolution and took the position that if a theoretical approach had shortcomings, then it should be completely replaced by a new approach.

In the 1950s and 1960s, modernization theory sought to explain why economic growth and political stability occurred in some societies more than in others.[7] But eventually modernization theory was shown by numerous scholars to have flaws, and so, under the influence of Kuhn's idea of scientific revolution, many scholars abandoned modernization theory and searched for new approaches. Such new "paradigms" included dependency theory, rational choice theory, and others. For example, one author criticized the "ideology of developmentalism" and the philosophy of science upon which modernization theory appeared to be based—the "notion that knowledge is built up through patient, piecemeal accumulation of new observations, which has reached its triumphal culmination in the modern data bank."[8] She and other scholars argued that modernization theory was outmoded and should be discarded in favor of an entirely new construct.[9]

In recent years, however, many political scientists seem willing to slow down the proliferation of "new" theories and, instead, to consider the possibility that the most fruitful approach for explaining political phenomena might be a theory that consolidates the various components of existing theories. Whereas in the past this would have been condemned as mushy-headed indecisiveness, more scholars are now willing to consider the possibility that a relatively complete and accurate explanation of reality might have to borrow components from various theoretical traditions. For example, after describing four approaches that had been used to explain Latin American politics—pluralism, clientelism, authoritarian-corporatism, and class analysis—one scholar came to the conclusion that although each was useful in pointing out certain important realities, "no single theoretical framework can encompass the totality of the social processes that must be taken into account in analyzing political change in Mexico."[10] Indeed, Kuhn himself soon eased off of his earlier claim that competing theories were mutually exclusive.[11] Likewise, other scholars agreed that the development of theory usually does not proceed by sudden, all-or-nothing shifts, but continuously and in incremental steps. Thus scientific inquiry is more evolutionary than revolutionary. This is not to say that the scientific enterprise always proceeds in a piecemeal, cumulative way. Sometimes an existing view is flatly wrong (e.g., that the sun revolves around the earth), and hence sometimes theory does advance by jumps. Most of the time, however, it advances by accretion. A logical implication of the return to an evolutionary view of science is the acknowledgment that many theories are partially valid and that we might be able to construct an even better theory by selecting what appear to be the most sustainable parts of various explanations. That is what seems to be occurring in recent years.

For several decades, and perhaps at least since Karl Marx, social science has been dominated by what might be called "structural" explanations. To correct for earlier superficial "great men" theories of historical causation, which saw history as the story of choices and actions of such leaders as Martin Luther, Henry VIII, Louis XIV, and Napoleon, Marx and other scholars sought explanations at a more profound level. Whether they focused on the mode of production (Marx), experiences in infancy (Freud), or values (Weber), explanations were sought at a level broader than the individual. As different as they are in most ways, even the two dominant attempts to explain development and underdevelopment since World War II share the characteristic that they are both predominantly "structural" theories. Although dependency and modernization theories use different explanatory variables, they both see development largely as a result of contextual variables outside the control of individuals and leaders. Whereas dependency theory might see the international capitalist system as the prime determinant of economic and political developments, modernization theory might emphasize the role of the availability of capital, the amount and type of investment and education, the level of literacy, the size of the middle class, and so on. The implication is that people, including leaders, who operated within these structural conditions had very little room for individual choice that would make much difference in broad outcomes.

Other approaches to explaining political events have emerged in recent years, approaches that ascribe considerably more importance to the role of human choice in affecting political outcomes. Theories of rational choice have been around at least since Thomas Hobbes, but they have developed rapidly in the past few years.[12] Different authors may disagree on how "rational" people are, to what extent they calculate costs and benefits, what they consider to be costs and benefits, and the extent to which social "norms" affect behavior, but choice approaches are all premised on the assumption that people behave in ways calculated to obtain desirable results. However, if "rational choice" is pushed too far, it becomes almost indistinguishable from structuralist theories in that people make virtually inevitable choices within the constraints that they face. That is, given the structure of incentives that confront them, people really have almost no choice in their course of action. Although few scholars would deny the overwhelming influence of contextual factors on behavior, much recent research in social science has focused on the range of choices within those prevailing constraints, as well as on how choices may change as constraints change. For example, leaders and elites have increasingly been acknowledged as playing a role in political change.[13]

One important stream of scholarship shows the importance of elite agreements in overcoming a tradition of political turmoil and violence. Robert Alexander explained the successful transition from dictatorship to democracy in Venezuela in 1958 by reference to the greater willingness of Rómulo Betancourt and other members of the political elite to compromise than they had exhibited a decade earlier. In his writings, Albert Hirschman always stressed the importance of choice. The very titles of his books emphasized the importance of believing in the possibility of progress and taking action to make it happen: *Journeys toward Progress, A Bias for Hope,* and *Exit, Voice and Loyalty.* After the collapse of civilian governments in Latin America in the 1960s and 1970s, various scholars began to notice the importance of explicit decisions and actions taken by political elites which may have contributed to the breakdown of democracy in Latin America in that period. Though not denying the importance of structural conditions such as economic difficulties, pressures from emerging classes, and the like, these scholars also could not dismiss the importance of specific choices made by political leaders. In 1978 several articles in a book edited by Juan J. Linz and Alfred Stepan emphasized the behavior of political leaders in bringing about the establishment of democracy in some countries and the breakdown of democracy in others. John Peeler's 1985 examination of Colombia, Venezuela, and Costa Rica demonstrated the critical role that skillful and moderate political leaders had played in the establishment of lasting civilian rule in these countries.[14]

After 1975, as authoritarian regimes throughout the world began to give way to more democratic civilian regimes, political scientists increasingly noted the role of political leaders in bringing about the transition. Certain key leaders such as Juan Carlos, Mario Suárez, Lech Walesa, Mikhail Gorbachev, and Ronald Reagan were given some credit for encouraging the movement toward democracy, though no one argued simplistically that they could have done it single-handedly.[15] Mentioning Gorbachev and Reagan points up that structure and choice are integrally related. As political leaders on the international level, they contributed to a change in the structural context within which national leaders acted. When Gorbachev announced that the Soviet Union would no longer protect Communist regimes in Eastern Europe with force, national leaders such as Lech Walesa and Vaclav Havel were suddenly freer to pursue courses of action that they had previously been prevented from undertaking. When Reagan pressured the Sandinista government in Nicaragua to hold elections, anti-Sandinista politicians were able to pursue their favored course within the new context. Thus recent events have dramatically demonstrated the interactive relationship between structure and choice. Even scholars such as Guillermo O'Donnell and Philippe Schmitter, who previously took a largely structuralist view of dictatorship and democracy, have begun to focus more on the behavior of political elites in crafting arrangements with which the various social forces could live.[16] Although a recent study of democracy in developing countries offers political leadership as only one causal factor among ten,[17] even that is an increase over much of the earlier analysis in the field. Scholars perceived that "political learning" had taken place during the period of authoritarian rule; elites learned that they were not doomed to repeat the patterns of the past; cycles of violence did not have to recur endlessly.[18]

Therefore, events of recent decades have chastened both political leaders and political scientists. Both groups are more aware of the complexity of reality and the virtues of compromise, whether in ideology or theory. Political leaders, at least in Latin America, seem to be more aware of the virtues of agreeing on a few fundamental premises and then proceeding incrementally from there, rather than insisting on the whole package at once. (This is not to say that everyone in the region has been won over to a conciliatory, incremental view; Fidel Castro, the Shining Path guerrillas, and conservative Haitian elites were among the holdouts in the early 1990s.) In like fashion, more political scientists seem to agree that social behavior has neither the predictability of a clock nor the indeterminacy of a cloud.[19] Some social action is characterized by pattern and predictability, as in the physical sciences, but much is characterized by chance, creativity, and choice.[20] Thus there seem to be fewer calls today for completely discarding one theoretical approach in favor of another and a greater willingness to combine usable concepts from various explanations.

This book unapologetically employs an eclectic explanation that combines structural and choice approaches. It recognizes that most of the theoretical traditions in political science have something to tell us about the important questions. Dependency theory, for example, correctly emphasizes the importance of the international system in creating the context within which smaller countries operate, especially with regard to the vulnerability of the less-developed states. For example, every one of the factors in our explanation has been affected to some degree by the position of Mexico as a relatively poor country on the periphery of the world capitalist system, located next to a much richer and militarily more powerful neighbor. Certain aspects of dependency theory were validated by Mexico's rapid economic growth during World War II when a drop in the availability of certain manufactured imports from the United States and Europe forced Mexico and the rest of Latin America to produce many products that they had previously imported.

However, most aspects of the economic boom that began with the war can be seen as a validation of modernization theory, with its emphasis on the benefits for developing countries of integration into the international economic system. For example, Mexico's exports of textiles, manufactured food, drink, tobacco, and chemicals increased dramatically during the war. As Raymond Vernon says, "The war created a new external demand for Mexico's exports, doubling the total between 1939 and 1945."[21] Thus Mexico's economic growth, like that of most rapidly growing countries, was export-led, not autarkic. In this sense, modernization theory—properly updated—seems to be a better explanation of Mexico's economic development than does dependency theory. Indeed, in a broad sense the apparent triumph of democracy and capitalism over authoritarianism and socialism throughout much of the world seems largely to validate the modernization type of explanation for development. In 1990 Lucian Pye, one of the fathers of modernization theory, argued that events since the 1950s have largely vindicated modernization theory, except that the magnitude of the changes has been greater and the pace faster than most modernization theorists predicted.[22]

The approach employed in this book also makes use of the concept of choice, whether we want to call it "rational" or not. Because of the wide range of hypotheses in the political science literature about degrees of choice available to people, it is necessary to clarify what is meant by the term. I begin from the premise that people are generally motivated by their perceived interests (whatever they are interested in achieving).[23] People pursue their interests according to their calculation of the costs and benefits and in terms of their perceptions of the probability that any particular event will occur. This does not mean, however, that structural conditions are unimportant. They are still extremely important, and the degree of choice should not be exaggerated. In fact, the unifying theme in this book is the interaction of choice and constraints. Moreover, to say that people choose, even within constraints, does not mean that they always make "rational" choices from the point of view of an observer with a good understanding of the relationships between available means and the decision makers' ends. People may make "irrational" choices that do not seem likely to lead toward their stated goals. Nor does "choice" imply only intended consequences. A particular choice may have consequences that are intended and desirable, intended and undesirable, unintended and desirable, or unintended and undesirable. All I am claiming is that it *was* a choice and that it may have been rational or not. The point is that choices are made *within* constraints; choices are not *dictated* by constraints, as often seems to be assumed in more thoroughly structural explanations.

A recent effort to synthesize structural and choice models of politics has been called a "strategic choice model." This approach reminds us of "possibilism" and of the "opportunities for constructive change" in the tradition of Albert Hirschman.[24] The danger, of course, is that one will overemphasize choice and underestimate the degree to which choices are constrained by structural factors. Yet to explore the range of choice that exists in no way need blind one to the real constraints. Thus the approach employed in this book is a blend of choice and structural theories in which the situation frames the choices to a large degree but in which actors retain some latitude for making choices within that situation.

The factors that contributed to Mexican political stability were all related to the cost-benefit calculations of political actors, and that relationship was the mechanism by which they contributed to stability. The regime had a virtual monopoly on the use of coercion, and it was willing to use that coercion to maintain itself in power; potential challengers had to take that fact into account. The highly institutionalized nature of the regime meant that certain things would predictably happen, such as the inauguration of a new president after the next election. Therefore, people took that likelihood into account when deciding on their course of action. For most of the past half century, the Mexican economy grew at a healthy rate and, although that growth disappeared in the 1980s, Mexicans should not be considered irrational if they believed that better times would return once again. The flexibility of the regime in the past also made it reasonable for Mexicans to assume that the government would continue to adapt to emerging demands. For all these reasons, therefore, elites and non-elites could be considered rational if they acted as if their self-interest would best be served by continuing to accept the existence of the regime.[25]

Thus institutionalization, perceived effectiveness, adaptability, elite cohesion, location, and coercion all reinforced each other in their contributions to regime stability. They did so mainly through influencing the incentives of political actors to support the regime. The more that those factors leaned in one direction (institutionalized procedures, effective policies, flexible strategies, cohesive elites, moderate use of coercion, and continued support from the United States) rather than the other, the more likely that each political actor would see his interest in supporting, or at least not opposing, the regime.

This chapter has laid out the framework for an analysis of Mexico's political stability. Chapter 2 will analyze the construction of the modern Mexican state during the administration of Lázaro Cárdenas in the 1930s.

NOTES

1. For example, the index to Robert Dahl, *Modern Political Analysis,* 4th ed. (Englewood Cliffs, N.J.: Prentice-Hall, 1984), an overview of the field of political science, contains four references to *revolution* but none to *order* or *stability.* Likewise, the index for Ronald Chilcote, *Theories of Comparative Politics: The Search for a Paradigm* (Boulder, Colo.: Westview Press, 1981), an overview of the field of comparative politics, lists *revolution* twenty-one times but *stability* none. This does not mean that they do not deal with stability, only that it did not loom large enough in their thinking to list it as a separate concept in the index. To some extent, this is a function of the theoretical paradigm of the author. For example, Samuel Huntington, *Political Order in Changing Societies* (New Haven: Yale University Press, 1968), has numerous references in the index to *political order* and *stability,* as well as to *instability* and *revolution.* Similarly, Myron Weiner and Samuel Huntington, eds., *Understanding Political Development* (Boston: Little, Brown and Company, 1987), lists *revolution* in the index eight times and *stability* six times.

2. A classic treatment of stability and instability that summarizes much of the literature up to that point is Huntington, *Political Order.* A good survey of the literature on violent instability is Thomas Greene, *Comparative Revolutionary Movements,* 3d ed. (Englewood Cliffs, N.J.: Prentice-Hall, 1990).

3. Samuel Huntington, "The Goals of Development," in Weiner and Huntington, *Understanding Political Development*, pp.3–32.

4. Not that the "wave of democratization" of the 1980s has been unilinear. For example, by 1992, Haiti, Peru, and even Venezuela had experienced setbacks. The attempted coup in Venezuela in November 1992 was not successful in overthrowing President Carlos Andres Pérez, but it demonstrated how fragile democracy was in much of Latin America. See Samuel Huntington, *The Third Wave: Democratization in the Late Twentieth Century* (Norman: University of Oklahoma Press, 1991), for a discussion of how democratic trends are often followed by reversals.

5. That is, if the regime is dated from 1920, when the forerunners of the present ruling group came to power through military rebellion against their own revolutionary comrades. One could actually date the regime from an earlier time—say 1914, when revolutionary leader Venustiano Carranza became the head of the government that would eventually emerge as the revolutionary regime, or from 1917, when Carranza's position as president was regularized. The conventional date is 1929, when the governing party was organized, but that understates the longevity of the Mexican regime by at least nine years and perhaps as much as fifteen years. Whichever date is chosen, the Mexican regime has been in power longer than any other in Latin America.

6. Thomas Kuhn, *The Structure of Scientific Revolutions* (Chicago: University of Chicago Press, 1962).

7. For example, Walt Rostow, *The Stages of Economic Growth* (Cambridge: Cambridge University Press, 1960); Cyril Black, *The Dynamics of Modernization: A Study in Comparative History* (New York: Harper and Row, 1966); Lucian Pye, *Aspects of Political Development* (Boston: Little, Brown and Company, 1966); Huntington, *Political Order;* and Gabriel Almond and G. Bingham Powell, *Comparative Politics: A Developmental Approach* (Boston: Little, Brown and Company, 1966).

8. Suzanne Bodenheimer, "The Ideology of Developmentalism: American Political Science's Paradigm-Surrogate for Latin American Studies," *Berkeley Journal of Sociology* 15, 1970, quoted in Chilcote, *Theories of Comparative Politics*, p. 285.

9. Of course, some scholars continued to believe in the explanatory power of modernization theory, although it was modified to take account of new observations and new insights from other theoretical approaches. For example, see Samuel Huntington, "Political Development and Political Decay," *World Politics* 17 (3), 1965, pp. 386–430; Dankwart Rustow, "Transition to Democracy: Toward a Dynamic Model," *Comparative Politics* 2 (3), 1970; and G. Bingham Powell, *Contemporary Democracies: Participation, Stability, and Violence* (Cambridge: Harvard University Press, 1982).

10. Viviane Brachet-Márquez, "Explaining Sociopolitical Change in Latin America: The Case of Mexico," *Latin American Research Review* 27 (3), 1992, pp. 91–122.

11. Thomas Kuhn, *The Structure of Scientific Revolutions,* 2d ed. (Chicago: University of Chicago Press, 1970).

12. For example, Kenneth Arrow, *Social Choice and Individual Values* (New York: John Wiley, 1951); Peter Blau, *Exchange and Power in Social Life* (New York: John Wiley, 1964); Gary Becker, *The Economic Approach to Human Behavior* (Chicago: University of Chicago Press, 1976); Robert Axelrod, *The Evolution of Cooperation* (New York: Basic Books, 1984); James S. Coleman, *Foundations of Social Theory* (Cambridge, Mass.: Belknap, 1990).

13. For example, James MacGregor Burns, *Leadership* (New York: Harper and Row,

1978); Robert Tucker, *Politics as Leadership* (Columbia: University of Missouri Press, 1981); Guillermo O'Donnell, Philippe Schmitter, and Laurence Whitehead, eds., *Transitions from Authoritarian Rule,* (Baltimore: Johns Hopkins University Press, 1986); and Bryan Jones, ed., *Leadership and Politics* (Lawrence: University of Kansas Press, 1989).

14. Juan J. Linz and Alfred Stepan, eds., *The Breakdown of Democratic Regimes: Latin America* (Baltimore: Johns Hopkins University Press, 1978), and John Peeler, *Latin American Democracies: Colombia, Costa Rica, Venezuela* (Chapel Hill: University of North Carolina Press, 1985).

15. This is not to say that their influence was always toward democracy everywhere or was fast enough for everybody. One can question whether Reagan's primary commitment was to democracy or merely *against* radical reform, as in his support of the Contras in Nicaragua. Likewise, Gorbachev was unseated and the Soviet Union dismantled when he did not move rapidly enough for some reformers.

16. For example, contrast the structural approach in Guillermo O'Donnell, *Modernization and Bureaucratic Authoritarianism* (Berkeley: Institute of International Studies, 1973), with the greater emphasis on individual decision making in G. O'Donnell, "Introduction to the Latin American Cases," in O'Donnell, Schmitter, and Whitehead, *Transitions from Authoritarian Rule: Latin America,* pp. 3–18.

17. Larry Diamond and Juan Linz, "Introduction: Politics, Society, and Democracy in Latin America," in Larry Diamond, Juan Linz, and Seymour Martin Lipset, eds., *Democracy in Developing Countries: Volume 4, Latin America* (Boulder, Colo.: Lynne Rienner Publishers, 1989), pp. 1–58.

18. Nancy Bermeo, "Democracy and the Lessons of Dictatorship," *Comparative Politics* 24 (3), 1992, pp. 273–91.

19. Gabriel Almond and Stephen Genco, "Clouds, Clocks, and the Study of Politics," *World Politics* 29, 1977, pp. 489–522.

20. Gary Mucciaroni, "The Garbage Can Model and the Study of Policy Making: A Critique," *Polity* 24 (3), 1992, pp. 459–82.

21. Raymond Vernon, *The Dilemma of Mexico's Development: The Roles of the Private and Public Sectors* (Cambridge: Harvard University Press, 1963), p. 95.

22. Lucian Pye, "Political Science and the Crisis of Authoritarianism," *American Political Science Review* 84 (1), 1990, pp. 3–19.

23. The concept of "interest" should not be understood simplistically. Interests may be "altruistic" (helping others while receiving only psychic rewards for ourselves), "enlightened" (helping others while helping ourselves), "selfish" (hurting others while helping ourselves), or "destructive" (hurting both ourselves and others).

24. David Collier and Deborah Norden, "Strategic Choice Models of Political Change in Latin America," *Comparative Politics* 24 (2), 1992, p. 240.

25. This analysis is valid up to the present. However, the conditions in which these factors for stability operate appear to be changing, and therefore the continued stability of the regime is uncertain. This will be discussed further in chapter 7.

2

The Institutionalization of the Mexican State

An important factor that accounts for much of Mexico's political stability is the institutionalization of the regime. Although this was a long process that took many years and involved the contributions of many people, choices made by Lázaro Cárdenas during his presidency (1934–40) and afterward were crucial to the stabilization of the regime and to the building of a strong Mexican state. In fact, the career of Cárdenas is a textbook case of how an individual leader accumulated personal power and then contributed it to the political system in order to build a state that would endure beyond his own time in office. Other leaders who did this were George Washington, Kemal Atatürk of Turkey, and Rómulo Betancourt of Venezuela.[1] Some who did not were Ferdinand Marcos of the Philippines, Anastasio Somoza of Nicaragua, and perhaps Fidel Castro of Cuba.[2]

In late 1934 when Cárdenas became president of Mexico, he inherited a situation that had been stabilized to some extent but still had explosive potential. This chapter describes how he built elite and popular support, transformed the ruling party to channel that support, defeated competing regional warlords, incorporated labor and peasants into the regime, and then proceeded to transfer his personal power to other men and institutions and to watch over them until the new pattern was firmly in place.[3] In 1940 he handed over to his successor a regime with the essential characteristics that would remain until the present. Mexico has had an unbroken succession of presidents every six years since 1934, without serious military rebellion, and no president has stayed in office more than one term. Such depersonalization of power is rare in developing countries, but it is necessary if a stable political system is to outlast the time of an individual leader. Unlike most previous Mexican leaders and many other political leaders in Latin America, Cárdenas, despite being the most popular Mexican leader of the century, generally behaved in ways that moved Mexico away from the personalistic rule of caudillos and toward greater reliance on institutions. This chapter lays out the broad range of actions by Cárdenas that stabilized the modern Mexican state. In particular, it emphasizes the accumulation of personal power and the systematic transferal of that power to the regime.

INSTITUTIONALIZATION AND POLITICAL STABILITY

If a regime is to consolidate its power beyond the time of one strong man, it must institutionalize itself; that is, it must create regularized patterns of interaction that maintain people in relatively consistent relations over time. It must structure political behavior so that people interact peacefully rather than through violence.[4] It does this through creating rules, beliefs, and relationships, many of which will be fostered by and expressed through formal organizations. If the state is to be strong and dominated by civilians rather than soldiers, then strong civilian political institutions must be created. Almost by definition, an institution will tend to outlive any particular individual leader or member. An institution establishes relationships and structures incentives that prompt people to have certain expectations and therefore to behave in certain ways. Karl Deutsch defined it this way:

An institution is an orderly and more or less formal collection of human habits and *roles*—that is, of interlocking expectations of behavior—which results in a stable organization or practice whose performance can be predicted with some reliability. . . . To *institutionalize* a practice, process, or service is to change it from a poorly organized and informal activity into a highly organized and formal one.[5]

New institutions may emerge either spontaneously or deliberately.[6] Such new patterns emerge because they serve some human need, and then the new behavior becomes habitualized by being rewarded. George Homans emphasized the distinction between primary, or material, rewards and secondary, or social, rewards such as social esteem or national pride. He argued that institutions do not persist just because they are enshrined in norms but because they provide payoffs for individuals. If primary or material rewards decline, the institution may coast for a while on the strength of the secondary rewards such as social approval. However, if primary rewards are not forthcoming for a long time, eventually people will depart from the institutional channels. In short, institutional behavior does not continue merely because it is a rule (formal or informal) but because it continues to be rewarded.

We are particularly interested in the development of a new pattern of behavior in which political actors in Mexico came to interact peacefully rather than violently. That transformation took place over a period of twenty years from 1920 to 1940, but especially from 1935 to 1940. Gradually, violence came to seem less rewarding because of the creation of a strong and legitimate state that could dispense both rewards and punishments, a tightly constructed political party within which the struggle for office could occur peacefully, a military that became increasingly convinced that revolt would be unrewarding, and a resolution of the most vexing political problem of all, the presidential succession.

From its emergence as a separate discipline in the nineteenth century until about 1950, political science was dominated by an institutional orientation. It tended to describe the formal institutions of government and politics such as parties, legislatures, executives, and the judiciary. Although some students asked if the real behavior behind the institutions was different from the formality, the predominant orientation was toward the formal institutions themselves. The state was seen as an independent force in collective life. After 1950, however, a "behavioral revolution" swept political science, directing attention away from formal institutions, which were often dismissed as empty shells, and toward the behavior of individuals and groups as they engaged in conflict and cooperation over political power and public policies. For the next twenty years or so, institutions receded in importance as political scientists tended to see them merely as arenas where behavior was shaped by more fundamental forces such as class, culture, geography, economy, demography, technology, ideology, and religion.[7] Behavioralists tended to see the state as a resultant of such fundamental forces, rather than as an independent factor acting on these forces and on public policy. Then, increasingly after 1970, political scientists began to see political institutions themselves as important factors in influencing the outcomes of politics. In fact, the state itself might have an independent effect not only on public policies but also on the other factors, which previously tended to be seen as independent of politics. One group of authors argued for "bringing the state back in" to the analysis of politics and "taking the state seriously" as a causal factor.[8] Other scholars urged social scientists to "rediscover institutions."[9]

The "new institutionalism" is, however, different from the old. It urges scholars to look not only at formal institutions but at *real* institutions—the actual rules and norms that influence people's behavior. To focus on institutions as an important variable is to ignore neither the larger social context of politics nor the motives of individual actors. Thus a particular outcome, whether political democracy, one-party dominance, or some other, "depends not only on economic and social conditions but also on the design of political institutions. Bureaucratic agencies, legislative committees, and appellate courts are arenas for contending social forces, but they are also collections of standard operating procedures and structures that define and defend values, norms, interests, identities and beliefs."[10] James March and Johan Olsen seem to posit institutions as factors almost in opposition to individual choice as a way that decisions are made. They recognize that much behavior is "consequential" or instrumental (rational self-interest is one important criterion for instrumental choice but is not the only possible one). In reasoning from consequentiality, "the question, 'why did you do that?' elicits an answer in the form 'I did it because I expected it to have consequences that I value.' '' Institutional or norm-based behavior, on the other hand, would elicit an answer like "I did it because that is what was appropriate of someone in my position in that situation." [11] Jurisprudence is a field that is firmly based in institutional theory. Norms (legal categories) are established, and then jurisprudence asks which category a particular case fits into. Jurisprudence is not supposed to reason from consequentiality; it does not ask, What will be the consequences for society of labeling this behavior as first-degree or second-degree murder? It simply asks, Into which category does this action seem to fit most appropriately? Although March and Olsen may overestimate the degree to which norm-influenced behavior ignores specific consequences, they perform a service in alerting us to the potential power of norms over behavior. However, one could criticize their approach as "all norms and no calculation." By contrast, I see human decision making as occurring in a context in which both norms (expectations of certain behavior by those in certain roles) and calculations coexist.

In fact, norms are one important factor entering into our calculations. We obey these norms in large part because we believe that to do so will likely lead to consequences that we value. Those consequences may include the approval of others, the maintenance of institutional arrangements that we value, and so on. The most extreme case of institutional, norm-based behavior that seems relatively independent of a calculus of consequences is the actions of soldiers who in wartime charge the enemy at the risk of their own lives—apparently a clear case of behaving "appropriately" rather than behaving consequentially. However, even that action can be seen as largely consequential. If the soldiers did not behave in that way, they would likely suffer opprobrium and perhaps even a court-martial. It is difficult to believe that they are acting in that way solely, or even largely, because they believe that such behavior is appropriate in that situation. Thus I see institutions and norms as helping to structure the total situation within which individuals calculate the likely consequences of their behavior, rather than as the—at times—sole determinant of that behavior. After all, the norms are not always clear-cut. Quite different behaviors might be seen as appropriate in a given situation. In addition, even where the "appropriate" behavior is clear, individuals frequently violate the expectation. It would seem that other factors besides norms are affecting their behavior.

Thus the argument that I make in this chapter is not that the creation of certain political institutions in Mexico made any particular behavior inevitable thereafter but that it made certain behavior more likely, not only by creating behavioral norms but also by structuring the situation in such a way as to make certain behavior appear more promising in its consequences than other behavior. Specifically, the creation of a broadly based regime led by a strong presidency that regularly changed hands restructured the incentives of important political actors so that most of them, most of the time, saw it in their interest to remain within the regime rather than to wander outside of it. As Jon Elster says, "Institutions can affect behavior by altering the bargaining context for individuals."[12] Ultimately, if institutions have any effect on society, it is through affecting the behavior of individuals. Moreover, "Talk about individuals is just shorthand for talk about individuals who interact with one another and with people outside the institutions. Whatever the outcome of the interaction, it must be explained in terms of the motives and the opportunities of these individuals."[13]

The Mexican regime is institutionalized in many ways. The official party consists of formal sectors (labor, peasants, middle-class groups) that make decisions in more or less prescribed ways (usually top-down). Local and state governments relate to the federal government in relatively predictable ways (usually top-down). But perhaps the most important aspect of the Mexican political system that has been regularized is the matter of presidential succession. The institutionalization of presidential succession is important not just because it exists, in the sense that an election occurs every six years. Rather, the important quality is the nature of the succession—that it *always* brings in a new president without fail and that there is no reelection. Thus, decades ago, Mexico resolved one of the thorniest problems with which all political systems must come to grips, a problem that has particularly vexed Latin American political systems. Irving Louis Horowitz calls this "the 'highest stage' of revolution-making: solving the riddle of succession."[14] The regular turnover of the Mexican presidency means that most actors in the political system have some interest in perpetuating the system. Members of the elite can hope that they might flourish in a future administration or that they might even be selected for the presidency. Thus institutionalization of the succession contributes to elite cohesion. Likewise, nonelites can believe that even if things have not gone well under the present administration or even under the last several, the certainty of a new president offers at least the *hope* that things will improve. The new president might bring in new policies or at least greater attentiveness and skill in the implementation of present policies.

Institutionalization, especially of the succession, also makes perceived effectiveness easier to achieve, in two ways. People will tend to be more tolerant of a given degree of effectiveness because however short of perfection it falls, the possibility always exists that the next administration will do better. Second, the fact of a regular turnover also often produces real change. There is some likelihood that the turnover will produce new officials who have at least slightly different points of view on policy and who will be willing to try something different. If the same officials—from president on down—stay in office indefinitely, there is a higher probability of continuing given policies despite the problems with these policies. Thus the institutionalization of the succession not only provides the hope of change but may even provide for change itself. Thus a depersonalized regime will tend to be more flexible and adaptable. This affects the cost-benefit calculations of elites and nonelites alike.

Institutionalization contributes to the legitimacy and hence the stability of a regime in another important way. Legitimacy is not based merely on regime effectiveness but is generally based on "legitimizing principles" that preceded the regime itself. For Mexico, the overarching legitimizing principle has been the Revolution, the amorphous process that includes not only the events of 1910 to 1917 but also all governmental activities since then that recalled the Revolution, such as land distribution, oil expropriation, or even the ceremonial laying of a wreath at the tomb of Emiliano Zapata. The Revolution meant many things to different people, but the most common themes were political liberalism, social justice, and Mexican nationalism. Every administration from that of Venustiano Carranza (1914–20) to the present has claimed that it was trying to make progress on all three of these revolutionary principles, although the emphasis changed somewhat with each presidential administration.[15]

The regime early on sought to institutionalize the legitimizing principle of the Revolution through the creation of a revolutionary party as well as the institutionalization of other aspects of the political system, such as the succession. The evolution of the party is illustrated by the changes in its name. It always had the word *revolution* in it, but the other major word changed. When former president Plutarco Calles created the party in 1929, he called it the National Revolutionary Party, as if to underscore the government's efforts to unite a fragmented set of feuding regional caudillos into a national structure for resolving political conflict. In 1938 President Lázaro Cárdenas restructured and renamed it the Party of the Mexican Revolution, emphasizing the revolutionary theme of nationalism, as exemplified by his government's expropriation of foreign oil companies carried out only weeks earlier. Then in 1946 the party was renamed the Institutional Revolutionary Party to emphasize that revolutionary goals had been permanently imbedded in the political structure. All Mexicans could confidently pursue those goals through the political system and the official party, rather than look outside the "proper channels" (a phrase that the government frequently used during the 1988 election campaign to criticize the activities of the opposition).

Thus the Mexican political elite institutionalized legitimacy by claiming to be the heirs of the Revolution. To accomplish this, the elite sought to institutionalize various political processes to allow it to claim an unbroken connection with both the leaders and the participants of the Revolution. The unbroken circle of revolutionary presidents goes back not only to Calles but also to Alvaro Obregón, the major military leader of the Revolution and the first postrevolutionary president. In fact, the present regime traces its origins even to Francisco Madero, the liberal democrat who started it all in 1910, and to Carranza, the chief political leader of the revolutionary forces from 1913 to 1920.

Two things about the institutionalization of legitimacy by the revolutionary elite should be pointed out. First, many of their actions—such as creating a national party and carefully observing the one-term limitation in the presidency—were intended to put an end to violence and to achieve political stability rather than to create "legitimacy," although this emerged as a by-product of their actions.[16] Second, nothing said so far should be taken to mean that

Mexican political elites behaved in a purely cynical way to create an "image" of legitimacy with little reality behind it. It seems likely that men who risked their lives and property in the Revolution believed to some degree in what they were doing. As for later leaders, there is evidence that they also believed, to one degree or another, in the values of the Revolution and the virtues of the regime, apart from their own self-interest.[17]

The institutionalization of political legitimacy gave the regime an enormous advantage, providing it with much greater room for maneuver. As Joseph Rothschild has said, "A perception on the part of its public that a system is legitimate can compensate—for astonishingly extended periods of time—for erroneous, inefficient, and ineffective performance."[18] This substitution of legitimacy for real effectiveness in the achievement of material goals is especially important for the intelligentsia. Whereas the working classes may look for specific material benefits, intellectuals are often concerned about non-material values such as nationalism.

MEXICAN POLITICS BEFORE 1935

Mexico did not always have a stable polity. In fact, after achieving independence from Spain in the 1820s, the country had one of the most unstable political systems in Latin America. Military coups were commonplace in the 1830s and 1840s as Santa Anna and other predatory generals toppled governments with regularity. As one account puts it, "Mexican history from 1833 to 1855 constantly teetered between simple chaos and unmitigated anarchy."[19] Martin Needler points out: "There were 30 presidents in 50 years, rigged elections alternating with revolts in dreary succession. Governments were ineffectual, the economy decayed, the social order crumbled; generals and politicians plundered the treasury, foreign loans were floated at ruinous rates of interest, and half the national territory was lost to the United States."[20] The most notable type of leadership during this time was personalistic and charismatic. As Frank Tannenbaum wrote of General Santa Anna: "His hold over the people of Mexico partakes of the unreal. His gifts were those of a ventriloquist or a magician, and his power over the Mexicans had something of the pathological in it."[21] Whether from a lack of desire or of skill, or because conditions were not favorable, Santa Anna did not transfer his personal power to the political system. He left the Mexican polity as chaotic as he found it.

In the 1850s and 1860s, Mexico was wracked by intermittent civil war and governed by various liberal and conservative heads of state, sometimes simultaneously, including Emperor Maximilian von Hapsburg and Benito Juárez. Not until Porfirio Díaz seized power in 1876 and ruled for the next thirty-five years was stability achieved. In fact, there are remarkable similarities between the present regime and the prerevolutionary regime of Díaz. Both were highly centralized, relatively authoritarian, and characterized by the use of corruption as a motivational device and by the ritual use of elections to renew loyalty rather than to select leaders.

But perhaps the most important way in which the present Mexican regime differs from the *Porfiriato* is in its degree of institutionalization, especially in the depersonalization of power and in the rotation in office of government officials. Díaz amassed an enormous amount of political power, but virtually all of it remained personalistic. He made little effort to transfer it to the system by creating strong and stable political institutions—political parties, an independent legislature, or merely a systematic and peaceful way of selecting presidents—that would have persisted no matter which individuals filled them. After sitting out the 1880–84 term, he was reelected regularly from 1884 to 1910, but as he got older the struggle to succeed him debilitated the regime.[22] As Mexican scholar Lorenzo Meyer has written:

The main political problem of the old system was not so much its authoritarian character as its resistance to depersonalization, and depersonalization would have been the only way to handle the transmission of power in an orderly fashion. . . . The constant re-election of the President, as well as many of the governors, made it difficult to renew political personnel and closed off the careers of many young and ambitious people.[23]

It was competition among members of the elite in the struggle to succeed the aging president that eventually did the system in. Thus the downfall of Díaz was partly a result of the fragmentation of the elite. The struggle among elite factions began to tear the regime apart and left it too weak to confront the Madero rebellion.[24] As Theda Skocpol argues, violent revolution is most likely to occur in personalistic ("neo-patrimonial") regimes in which power and other resources are monopolized by a tiny elite and in which the principle of succession is unclear.[25]

In 1910, revolution broke out, and almost three decades passed before the country settled down to the pattern of stable government that has held ever since. In fact, as late as the 1930s, Mexico's political future was anything but certain. Since 1940, however, Mexico has been the most stable country in the region. How did such stability come about? What role did institutions play in the stabilization of the Mexican political system?

By the time Cárdenas became president in December 1934, some progress had been made toward the creation of a stable Mexican state. After almost twenty-five years of revolution, an old regime had been destroyed, but a new one had been only partially created in its place. A new constitution was written in 1917, but large parts of it remained unimplemented by 1934. Some stability had been achieved in presidential succession since 1920. In addition, a broad coalition party was created in 1929 when Calles founded the Partido Nacional Revolucionario (PNR). Another accomplishment by 1934 was the changing role of the military. During the 1920s and early 1930s, the army was increasingly professionalized and removed from direct intervention in politics. Presidents Obregón and Calles must be given major credit for reducing the size and budgets of the military, transferring zone commanders periodically so that they had less time to build personal loyalties with their troops, and in general making the military a force for defending the government rather than for overthrowing it.

Therefore, by the time Cárdenas became president, considerable progress had been made toward the creation of a strong and stable government,[26] but much remained to be done. Many observers have concluded that the primary contribution of Cárdenas was his efforts to fulfill the social and economic promises of the Revolution through measures that would improve the lives of the poor. On the contrary, the more enduring legacy of Cárdenas was the political dimensions of his policies; he acted to institutionalize and thereby to stabilize the new regime. He defined the problems facing Mexico, made difficult choices within severe constraints, and skillfully mobilized resources to pursue what he saw as the solution to the problems that he had defined. At crucial junctures, both during and after his presidency, Cárdenas made choices and provided an example that strengthened formal and informal political institutions, thereby helping Mexicans to develop new habits of political behavior. This is not to say that some of his actions were not divisive or that they all had positive effects. It is to say, however, that he was instrumental in constructing a strong, institutionalized state that would endure.

Cárdenas's contributions to political institutionalization and state building were many, but they can be organized into four categories: support building, party building, taming the military, and presidency building. There is considerable overlap in these categories, and many actions could easily be placed in more than one category, but they are still a useful way of organizing the state-building implications of Cárdenas's actions.

CÁRDENAS INSTITUTIONALIZES THE REGIME

Building Support for the Regime

By the end of Calles's presidential term (1924–28), he and former president Obregón were the undisputed leaders of the revolutionary coalition. They had the constitution amended to allow a president to be reelected after sitting out a term, whereupon Obregón was reelected in July 1928 to a second term, which had been lengthened to six years. A few days later Obregón was assassinated. Calles decided not to impose himself again as president but instead ruled from behind the scenes for the next six years as the *jefe máximo* of the Revolution. With the acquiescence of a pliant Congress, he selected an interim president (Emilio Portes Gil) until a new election could be held the next year. His hand-picked candidate for the election of 1929 (Pascual Ortiz Rubio) had little political experience and quickly fell into a pattern of following Calles's orders. However, Calles finally decided that Ortiz Rubio was either too weak or too independent, and Calles persuaded him to resign the presidency in 1932. Congress selected another close Calles associate (General Abelardo Rodríguez) to fill out the remainder of the six-year term to which Obregón had originally been elected. The next question, then, was who to put forward as the revolutionary coalition's next candidate for president in 1934.

It is not altogether clear why Calles decided to select Cárdenas. Whereas Calles himself had become increasingly conservative on issues such as land distribution and labor militancy, other members of the revolutionary group had decided by 1933 that the regime needed to move to the left. Cárdenas was a relatively popular choice among these elements of the revolutionary elite, and support for him appears to have increased to the point that Calles apparently felt he had little choice. Besides, Cárdenas had generally been a loyal supporter of Calles, and the *jefe máximo* probably thought he could control Cárdenas the way he had controlled the three presidents from 1928 to 1934.

Virtually all accounts of Cárdenas mention his extensive travels during the 1934 campaign. Even though the election had all the predictability of a bull-fight, Cárdenas campaigned with a fervor that was unprecedented. (The closest was perhaps Madero's extensive electoral campaign of 1909–10.) He visited all twenty-eight states and traveled more than seventeen thousand miles, going by train, automobile, horse and foot. Such campaigning was something new for a presidential candidate, and like so many things Cárdenas did, his travels set a standard for later candidates.

Moreover, he pursued not only mass support for the regime but elite consensus as well, a factor that is a key determinant of regime stability.[27] Other things being equal, the more that elites agree on procedures for interaction, as well as on the substantive policies pursued within that framework, the more stable a political system is likely to be. A major source of Cárdenas's political strength was his keen awareness at the time he came to the presidency of where much of the power lay in the Mexican political system—with regional caudillos and local notables. Probably a major reason that he traveled so widely in the 1934 campaign was to become better acquainted and to forge alliances with local leaders.[28] Cárdenas continued to travel widely after becoming president. He spent several weeks in the Laguna region in the northwest and then several weeks on the east coast, especially the Yucatán, to oversee the distribution of land in those areas. His presence served the dual purpose of giving greater impetus to the policy of land distribution and of monitoring how well the policy was being implemented. His local appearances contributed greatly to Cárdenas's popularity, but like many of his actions, they increased the popularity of the presidency and of the regime at the same time.

The great trio of policies usually associated with the Cárdenas years include encouragement of labor, land distribution, and oil expropriation. Soon after taking office, Cárdenas's government began to encourage the unionization of labor. Labor support for the government had been channeled through the Confederación Regional Obrera Mexicana (CROM) from Carranza to Rodríguez. But CROM was conservative and corrupt, and the rest of labor was fragmented. Cárdenas found the labor movement a "chaos of factions." He threw state support into an effort to unify the movement in one labor central and announced that the government would deal with only this group.[29] Cárdenas gave his support to a young Marxist organizer, Vicente Lombardo Toledano, and within a year the latter had persuaded "tens of thousands of workers to organize unions, to join government-sponsored unions, to bring previously independent syndicates into federation with one another, and finally to affiliate with the government-sponsored Mexican Workers Confederation," or CTM.[30]

Cárdenas not only encouraged unionization and the centralization of labor but also tolerated and even encouraged labor militancy. There was a great increase in strikes in the first years of the Cárdenas government, from 202 in 1934 to 642 in 1935, although many of the early strikes were jurisdictional disputes among labor factions rather than primarily between labor and management.[31] Such actions almost certainly did not endear Cárdenas to business, but they did greatly increase his support from certain factions of labor, which later proved to be important in several challenges to his presidency and to the regime. However, he did not take two further steps strongly advocated by Lombardo Toledano—the widespread arming of workers' militias and the uniting of urban workers and rural campesinos into one huge confederation. Such actions might have provoked a military effort to overthrow Cárdenas and put Mexico on a far more rightist track, as was occurring in so many Latin American countries in the 1930s. One author correctly says that Cárdenas "sought the strengthening of the working class but did not wish this class to dominate the state."[32] In reality, it was probably not likely that the working class would "dominate the state." However, it was possible that organized workers could have become far more influential in Mexico, as they did in Argentina after 1945. Cárdenas apparently did not favor even that degree of working-class influence, which might have been an independent threat to the government.

Another policy designed to pursue social justice and strengthen political support was the distribution of land. Cárdenas distributed more land than all previous revolutionary presidents combined. Presidents from Carranza in 1915 to Rodríquez in 1934 distributed just under eight million hectares, while Cárdenas distributed over twenty million hectares in six years, or over twice as much as in the previous twenty years. For our purposes, the land distribution was important because of the increased support that it generated for the regime. Whatever its socioeconomic effects, the effort to help the campesinos increased regime legitimacy, especially among peasants and intellectuals. The total number of people living on *ejidos* (communal farms) doubled in the Cárdenas years. By 1940, *ejidos* owned 47 percent of Mexico's crop land.[33] There was great inefficiency in *ejido* production, owing partly to the government's neglect of irrigation, fertilizer, and other necessary technical inputs. Nonetheless, as Alma

Maria Garcia Marsh argues, "For the former rebellious peasants, the return of their land, even if it was in the form of small, unprofitable strips, served to foster a sense of 'winning' tangible gains."[34]

The peasants were thus made stronger supporters of the regime and less likely to try to overthrow it in the future. As Albert Michaels wrote, "By stabilizing and enlarging the scope of the ejido . . . Lázaro Cárdenas accomplished more both for national unity and political stability than had all his predecessors."[35] More than one regime (e.g., France) has discovered that giving land to the peasants can transform them from radical opponents to strong supporters of the regime.[36] The support of the peasants was further structured and consolidated by the organization and incorporation of the peasants into the official party in 1938, as discussed below.

Perhaps the most spectacular act of the Cárdenas administration was the expropriation of oil. As with land distribution, the short-term economic consequences of expropriation of foreign oil companies were disastrous. Mexico suffered from a lack of technical expertise in oil drilling and from a closing of the U.S. market after the expropriation. The quantity of oil pumped and sold fell precipitously, and it was almost ten years before oil production reached preexpropriation levels. Whether the expropriation was a wise decision in the long run is open for debate and depends in large part on the values that one wishes to emphasize, such as economic efficiency or nationalism. But whatever the economic consequences, the effects on national unity and regime popularity were dramatic. Mexicans of most classes applauded the oil expropriation, and March 18 is still a national holiday to celebrate Mexico's economic independence. As Michaels says of Cárdenas and the oil expropriation: "By this one act he had united the nation behind him *as no other single move could have done.*"[37] Nationalism, especially when directed at the United States, has almost always been a powerful weapon that Mexican presidents could use to galvanize support for the regime.

Therefore, the three main "revolutionary" policies usually associated with the Cárdenas years—encouragement of labor, land distribution, and oil expropriation—may or may not have had positive socioeconomic effects; scholars still debate that question today. It seems unequivocal, however, that these actions greatly increased political support for Cárdenas, for the presidency, and for the regime. They contributed significantly, therefore, to the stabilization of the political system.[38]

Another way that any government seeks to build support is to dispense benefits to individual supplicants. The Cárdenas files of the Archivo General de la Nación in Mexico City are full of letters from individuals and groups throughout the country asking for something. Local governments asked for a road or a military detachment to guard against bandit raids. Newspapers asked for larger subsidies, especially *El Nacional,* whose publisher pointed out in a letter of October 1935 that the paper devoted a lot of space to making government activities known. The same newspaper was still complaining of the paltry subsidy in November 1940. Individuals asked for help getting their pensions and other benefits. A teacher in Coahuila created a youth band and requested a monthly federal subsidy for it.[39] Apparently, when he traveled around, President Cárdenas made promises to individuals and groups. Many of the letters in the presidential files reminded him of his promises and asked him to pay up. In most cases, he and his private secretary referred the letters to the appropriate department with a request that the department inform the presidency of their disposition of the matter.

Of course, Cárdenas's policies did not appeal to everyone. Business disliked the prolabor policies and land distribution, and some elements of business even opposed the oil expropriation. However, it is possible that the anti-Cárdenas attitude of business has been exaggerated. The worst of Mexico's depression was from 1926 to 1932. In 1933, the Mexican economy grew 9 percent in real per capita terms and then grew an average of 5 percent a year from 1934 to 1938. This was partly a result of the recovery of the world economy and an increase in the prices of some of Mexico's leading exports such as oil and silver, but it was also partly due to the stimulatory fiscal policies of Cárdenas. The government spending on infrastructure such as roads and on social programs such as education and public health probably contributed significantly to the economic growth that Mexico experienced during the 1930s. Stephen Haber argues, "As the present analysis of investor confidence and new capital spending shows, Mexican manufacturers did not perceive the reformist government of Cárdenas as particularly inimical to their interests."[40] For example, the Cárdenas government nationalized few firms except foreign oil companies and some foreign-owned landholdings. He did not follow these expropriations by nationalizing other foreign-owned industries such as mining, despite the fact that the Mine and Metalworkers Union pressed the government to nationalize the industry. Mining accounted for 60 percent of Mexico's exports, and it was over 95 percent foreign-owned. Unlike the petroleum industry, "the major market for mineral exports was the U.S., a market which would have been effectively closed if the mining companies had been expropriated."[41] Thus one could argue not only that Cárdenas's economic policies were good for business but that his contributions to political stability were even more important in laying the foundation for the economic takeoff that Mexico would experience after 1940.[42] Meanwhile, however, in 1938 the Mexican economy slipped into recession again, partly in response to the U.S. recession of 1937–38. This and the overall conservative reaction to Cárdenas's policies led to the creation of the Partido de Acción Nacional (PAN) in 1939, which would become the leading opposition party over the next five decades.

Cárdenas's policy of "socialist" education also alienated some Mexicans from the regime. Even if the poor in the countryside liked the new rural schools, the Catholic church persuaded many peasants that the antireligious education was from the devil. Thus Cárdenas's educational policies alienated the church and some segments of the peasantry. In fact, there was considerable

turmoil in the late 1930s in some parts of Mexico over the question of education. However, after fifteen years of an intensive antichurch stance and a three-
year civil war between conservative Catholics and supporters of the government
(1926–29), the Cárdenas government brought about a considerable improvement in church-state relations by backing away from the more extreme aspects
of the antichurch education and other forms of perceived persecution of the
church.

Thus Cárdenas built support for his government and for the regime by such
actions as land distribution, labor organization, oil expropriation, and traveling
about the country and meeting with elites and masses. Although these policies
no doubt cost him some support among parts of the population, they almost
certainly gained him more support than they lost. Cárdenas was building support not merely for himself but for the presidency as an institution and for a
regime that would endure beyond his own time in office.

Cárdenas continued to be popular after he left the presidency. In a survey of
members of the regime in the 1980s, Cárdenas and José Vasconcelos (a political leader and intellectual) were the two most frequently mentioned leaders of
the early period whose examples were responsible for the decision of young
people to go into government or politics.[43] Cárdenas also continued to be an
influential political figure after leaving the presidency, having more associates
in important positions in government from 1940 to 1975 than any other ex-president.[44]

Building the Party

The building of popular support took specific institutional form in the mass
organizations that Cárdenas encouraged, organizations such as the Confederation of Mexican Workers (CTM) and the National Confederation of Peasants
(CNC). That support was then channeled through a restructured political party.
One of the major shortcomings of the revolutionary regime before 1929 was
the lack of any institutional means by which the political elite could interact in
a regular way, without violence, according to rules that were generally accepted. Conflict within the elite was endemic and generally resulted in a military rebellion once the sitting president announced his choice of a successor.
That no rebellion occurred in 1940 or thereafter was due in large part to the
greater institutionalization of the regime, including the reconstruction of the
official party, under Cárdenas.

One author has estimated that in 1928 there were eight thousand identifiable
political "parties" in Mexico.[45] Each regional, economic, ideological, and personalistic group created its own party as a vehicle for an ambitious politician
or particular point of view. Party creation was hectic at election time and then
died down between elections. After Obregón's reelection and assassination in
July 1928 Calles, in his last "state of the union" address on September 1,
called for the creation of a single party to represent all revolutionaries. Accord-

ingly, regional strongmen, military caudillos, businessmen, labor and peasant leaders, intellectuals, and others gathered in March 1929 to create the Partido Nacional Revolucionario (PNR). Such a structure, with Calles at its center, could provide a regular channel of communication both up and down the political system. It enabled Calles and his close associates to receive comment and support from others in the revolutionary coalition more systematically; the leaders could also issue directives on policy and succession in a more coherent way and thereby maintain much of their own political power while not actually in office. Most important, it provided a forum for conflict resolution among contending forces, especially the revolutionary generals. It may be true, as many have charged, that one of Calles's primary motives in establishing this party was to perpetuate his own power.[46] Moreover, one author argues that leaders who want to create and perpetuate their own political power yet lack charisma tend to build such institutions; hence Calles built the PNR because he did not have charismatic authority over elites or masses.[47] Whatever Calles's motives, the major long-term effect of the creation of the party was the further consolidation and stabilization of the new regime. Thus the creation of the PNR in 1929 was an important step in the process of institutionalized state building.

However, because it was mainly a coalition of elites, the party was subject to shifting alliances among those elites and hence instability over time. This is a particularly severe shortcoming in a political system in which elites are accustomed to interacting through violence. It lacked strong connections with the majority of the labor, peasant, and middle-class populations. Cárdenas remedied that deficiency by organizing these groups and then incorporating them into a new party. As we saw above, he first sponsored the reorganization of urban labor into a new labor central, the Confederation of Mexican Workers, in 1936. At the same time, he sponsored the organization of peasants into state-based confederations, which were unified in 1938 into one national peasant organization, the National Confederation of Peasants. While encouraging labor and agrarians to unite internally, he prevented their consolidation into one large proletarian organization—thus employing the classic control principle of "divide and rule"—a move that suggests that Cárdenas's primary goal was to accumulate political power for the regime rather than to empower the masses. In early 1938 the party was restructured along corporatist lines and renamed the Party of the Mexican Revolution (PRM). It consisted of discrete labor, agrarian, military, and middle-class-bureaucratic sectors. Such a corporatist framework, of course, was popular in the 1930s, especially in Southern Europe and Latin America. The Mexican version of corporatism has lasted longer than most, however. As Cárdenas created and used it, the party had two major functions in the Mexican political system: to mobilize support for the regime and to act as a defining instrument, a "delineator of loyalty."

As many observers have argued, Cárdenas was undoubtedly motivated by a desire for workers and peasants to have a greater voice in their own affairs and in recommending policy to the government, but an equally strong motive for

their mobilization and organization into the restructured party was the support
that they offered to his regime, as evidenced by the fact that he allowed the
organizations little autonomy. The greatly expanded worker and peasant organizations within the party gave him tremendous resources to use in his battle
against those who threatened his government, and they were also a bulwark
against any potential military rebellion. (These organizations were mobilized in
the struggle with Calles in 1935–36, as we shall see below.) The party, with
its organized but divided working class, was also Cárdenas's answer to the call
for a "popular front" movement as advocated by the pro-Soviet left in Mexico
in the 1930s. Thus Cárdenas was able not only to defeat Calles's threat to his
government but also to preclude a popular front led by someone like his fiery
Marxist labor leader. With the CTM, Lombardo Toledano tried very hard to
organize the peasants and ally them with urban labor. He recognized that Cárdenas was keeping the workers and peasants apart in order to play them off
against one another.[48] However, given Cárdenas's substantive policy preferences on land distribution and labor rights, it would not be accurate to say that
Cárdenas merely wanted labor and peasants to organize for the support they
could give him at this time. Rather, he wanted to build up labor and peasant
groups as specific counterweights to business, landowners, and the military.
This not only would give the peasants and workers a stronger voice in the
regime but would also give the regime greater room for maneuver and thereby
greater autonomy relative to all organized social forces. Then his and future
governments would be in a better position to pursue their policy preferences
somewhat more independently of the various social forces. Therefore, the major function of the corporatist party was to mobilize support for the regime and
then to control that support.[49]

The second function of the party was as a delineator of loyalty or gauge of
support for the "revolutionary" regime. If a person or group left or was expelled from the party, they were effectively removed from further consideration
for high government office. Personal loyalties to particular clique leaders were
thereby supplemented by the broader loyalties to an institution.[50] The official
party in Mexico is as broad as two parties in most political systems. To remain
in the party, therefore, does not necessarily imply a commitment to particular
substantive policy positions (although there are a few that have been unassail-
able, such as the oil expropriation). Rather, it implies a commitment to a particular process of conflict resolution. It means that the person is committed to
pursuing goals within a controlled framework that includes much bargaining,
highly elite decision making, generally rigged elections, and an acceptance of
the results of the process. Even if one is personally disadvantaged within the
party, it is best to remain rather than to appeal to a wider set of referees such
as the army, mass organizations, or the public in general. To bolt the party, as
did various leaders such as Joaquín Amaro, Juan Andreu Almazán, and Lombardo Toledano at various times, meant that one had rejected the procedural
consensus and was no longer a part of the regime. Thus the party as touchstone

was a powerful enforcer of loyalty to the regime. To stay within the party was to stay in the political game and to retain a chance to serve in the government; to leave the party was to become an outsider, a permanent member of the opposition, and to forfeit all chances of exercising political power.

Such an umbrella party greatly expanded the range of the regime's ideological and behavioral tolerance and therefore made the regime more flexible.[51] No longer was loyalty to a particular leader the ultimate test, the failure of which cast the miscreant into the outer darkness to become a potential enemy of the regime; now, as long as a person or group worked within the party, even if not looked on favorably by the current group in office, that group or person could look forward to the possibility of a brighter political future the next time around. Therefore, Cárdenas's broadening of the party to include most major social forces had enormous implications for political stability. Since such a broad-based party was to have a virtual monopoly of political power, it meant that the benefits of cooperation were greatly increased and the potential benefits of violent conflict were greatly decreased. That is, the structure of incentives facing political actors changed dramatically. Sectors of the population—the military, workers, peasants, and bureaucrats and other middle-class groups—were balanced against each other within the governing coalition.

The Mexican Revolution was one of the great mobilizing processes of the twentieth century. Millions of people participated in it, and many of those expected to participate in the political process that followed. Samuel Huntington argues, "The stability of any polity depends on the relationship between the level of political participation and the level of political institutionalization."[52] If an increase in participation outpaces the building of institutions for structuring that participation, the result is likely to be the raw, direct pressure of the participating groups on government. In one of the most colorful descriptions of political instability ever written, Huntington describes such "praetorian" societies: "Each group employs means which reflect its peculiar nature and capabilities. The wealthy bribe; students riot; workers strike; mobs demonstrate; and the military coup."[53]

A major reason for the creation and expansion of the Mexican revolutionary party from 1929 to 1940 was to mobilize and control elite and mass support so that such raw pressure on government could be reduced. As we shall see in the next two sections, Cárdenas's state building especially sought to insulate the presidency from the praetorian pressures of the army and personalistic caudillos.

This does not mean that the preexisting political system of patrimonialism, or patron-client relations, was completely replaced by a new institutionalized bureaucratic system—far from it. The new structure overlay and gave definition to the old system of clientelism. Mexican politics continued to be characterized to a large extent by clientelism, or "a logic of political organization that emphasizes personal loyalties and vertical relationships as the central principle of political organization."[54] Thus the success of the newly institutionalized system still depended on the distribution of rewards such as offices, land titles, wage settlements, and exceptions to business regulations as a means of maintaining political support. The major difference was that the distribution now took place through a single party and a corporatist state, rather than through more strictly personalistic relations as in the past.

Taming the Military

As indicated earlier, Mexico had a history of military interference in politics. Edwin Lieuwen wrote in 1960:

Probably no country in Latin America has suffered longer and more deeply than Mexico from the curse of predatory militarism. More than a thousand armed uprisings plagued this unfortunate republic in its first century of nationhood. . . . Yet Mexico has been able to rid itself of the plague of militarism. A quarter-century ago no Latin American army was more political than the Mexican; today the armed forces are virtually out of politics. Mexico has moved from one extreme to the other.[55]

One of the important sources of violence and instability from 1911 on was the large number of revolutionary and military leaders with their own armies loyal to them personally and pursuing their own purposes. Before Cárdenas became president in 1934, the army had been partially tamed. Presidents Obregón and Calles had done much to make it more attractive for military men to support the regime than to oppose it. Cárdenas finished the job.

In 1920 Carranza tried to impose a civilian successor as president. Because Carranza had chosen a conservative civilian, and partly in opposition to Carranza's conservative labor and agricultural policies, much of the army, with labor and peasant support, rebelled and overthrew him. It was the last successful military uprising in Mexican history. Obregón, the leader of the rebellion and the greatest military hero of the Revolution, became president and set about building a ruling coalition and bringing the army under government control. As Lieuwen wrote of Obregón, "He was the first to visualize and to implement successfully an entirely new set of control techniques."[56] Unlike Carranza, who had largely rejected labor's support, Obregón first turned to labor and encouraged the expansion of CROM, the labor central that had supported his revolt to overthrow Carranza. Not wanting to depend solely on urban labor, however, Obregón also courted agrarians by encouraging their organization and by distributing nine times as much land as Carranza had. Obregón also received the support of the political parties that labor and agrarians organized during this time. Thus for the first time since 1910, Mexico had a stable ruling coalition composed of civilian, political, labor, agrarian, and the military elements. Remaining outside the coalition were business, hacienda owners, the church, and those factions of the military that had rebelled against the Obregón government.

In addition to the policy of building up other social forces and incorporating them into the regime as a counterweight to the military, Obregón and Calles also used many of the same direct-control techniques used by Díaz to render the military less of a threat to the regime. The army was purged of generals who had supported Carranza or who subsequently were suspected of plotting rebellion; some were executed, some were exiled, some were merely retired. The remainder were bought off either by direct payments or by being allowed new opportunities at money-making. Pancho Villa, for example, was paid about one million pesos from 1920 until his assassination in 1923. In fact, almost half of the central government budget under Obregón went to the military.[57] When Obregón became president, the army numbered about one hundred thousand men; by 1924 it had been reduced to sixty thousand men. In addition to reducing its size and cost, Obregón also tried to reduce the independence and autonomy enjoyed by regional commanders. He carved up military zones into smaller units so that each commander had fewer resources at his disposal. He often shifted commanders around while leaving their troops behind, in an effort to break the personalistic bonds between generals and "their" troops. He appointed fewer military men to the cabinet and to governorships. He and his war minister, General Joaquín Amaro, professionalized the military by modernizing the curriculum of the Military College, reorganizing the army general staff, and trying to base promotions somewhat more on technical merit than on political connections.

Calles continued the process of reducing the political power of the military. He brought urban labor more fully into the regime than had Obregón, partly as a counterweight to the military in the potential use of physical force. CROM was heavily subsidized by the government, and its leader, Luis Morones, became minister of industry, commerce, and labor. Through his minister of war Calles also improved the recruiting standards, living conditions, and equipment of the military. By 1930 Amaro had cut the size of the army to fifty thousand men and had reduced the military budget from 107 million to 70 million pesos.[58] The military share of federal expenditures declined from 44 percent under Obregón to 31 percent under Calles. A major part of the strategy during these years was to create a layer of younger, more professionally oriented soldiers under the revolutionary generals, soldiers who would presumably be loyal to the government even if their commanding generals tried to rebel. Ironically, the more professionalized army that Calles and Amaro helped to create would be one of the major factors that allowed President Cárdenas to survive the challenge of Calles in 1935.

The extent of the achievement of Obregón and Calles in subduing the military is indicated by the fact that the 1934 election was the first in fifteen years to take place without a military rebellion. However, much remained to be done, and Cárdenas oversaw the further depoliticization of the military. He served as war minister for about a year before becoming president, as president for six

years, and as defense minister for three years almost immediately after leaving
the presidency. He was, therefore, in formal control of the military for much
of the time between 1933 and 1945.

Almost all of Cárdenas's actions were aimed at getting the military out of
politics. First, he built up labor and peasant organizations as direct counterweights to the revolutionary generals, and as in the previous fifteen years,
unions and agrarian leagues were periodically called out to demonstrate their
force and capabilities. The organized physical support of workers and peasants
was probably one of the most important factors in deterring the revolutionary
generals from launching further rebellions. Such a strategy was dangerous, of
course. The mobilization of workers could have resulted in a conservative-
military reaction and civil war, as happened in Spain in the 1930s, or in fierce
repression, as occurrred in Chile in the 1970s. That it did not is perhaps attrib-
utable to the rest of Cárdenas's strategy.

The increasing importance of unions and agrarian organizations as political
forces was matched by the declining size and importance of the military. The
number of revolutionary generals declined both with time and with each unsuccessful revolt. With each rebellion, a few more were killed, exiled, or retired.
According to Lieuwen, by the 1930s, Mexico was ruled by an uneasy clique
of five generals—Calles, Amaro, Almazán, Saturnino Cedillo, and Cárdenas.[59]
After becoming president, Cárdenas systematically engaged in actions to dis-
pose of all four of his competitors. Calles challenged Cárdenas in 1935–36 and
was sent into exile. Amaro, who was closely associated with Calles, fell from
power at the same time; when he tried to run for president in 1940, Cárdenas
threatened to put him on trial for his part in the 1935 Calles conspiracy. General Cedillo, the last of the regional caudillos, resigned from Cárdenas's cabinet
in 1937 and launched an armed rebellion in 1938. The revolt was limited to
Cedillo's home state of San Luis Potosí and was successfully put down within
a couple of months. Almazán ran for president in 1940 as the candidate of
various conservative parties. He threatened a rebellion if the regime did not
recognize his victory and in fact sought support for his movement in the United
States. Cárdenas had done his work so thoroughly, however, that no serious
threat could be mounted, and Almazán returned to attend Avila Camacho's
inauguration. Lieuwen summed it up this way, "When Cárdenas assumed the
presidency in 1935, he soon ousted the ailing Calles and the conservative
Amaro; Cedillo was goaded into rebellion and destroyed in 1938, and Almazán
was tamed by his electoral defeat in 1940, whereupon Cárdenas himself retired."[60]

Lieuwen may exaggerate the degree to which regional caudillos were eliminated. Even after the above four were neutralized, the central government still
had to contend with Román Yocupicio in Sonora, Miguel Alemán in Veracruz,
the Avila Camacho family in Puebla, and even Cárdenas himself in Michoacán.
However, the power of regional strongmen certainly declined relative to the
central government from 1935 to 1940.

Table 2.1
Military Share of Federal Expenditures, 1921–1952

Years	President	Military Share
1921-24	Obregón	44%
1925-28	Calles	31
1929-30	Portes Gil	34
1930-32	Ortiz Rubio	29
1933-34	Rodríguez	24
1935-40	Cárdenas	18
1941-46	Avila Camacho	17
1947-52	Alemán	10

Source: Dan A. Cothran and Cheryl C. Cothran, "Mexican Presidents and Budgetary Secrecy," *International Journal of Public Administration* 11 (3), 1988, p. 326.

After each rebellion, the army was purged of thousands of rebels. The size of the army was stabilized at about fifty-five thousand regular troops under Cárdenas, and the share of the federal budget devoted to the military, as seen in table 2.1, fell from 44 percent under Obregón to 31 percent under Calles to 18 percent under Cárdenas. The trend continued; since World War II, Mexico has devoted a smaller share of its resources to the military than almost any other Latin American country except Costa Rica.

Another important element in depoliticizing the army was the program of professionalization that began as early as 1917. Whether professionalization generally makes a military more or less likely to intervene in politics is a debatable issue. Some scholars such as Huntington and Lieuwen argue that professionalization usually leads to decreased military intervention in politics. However, the military coups in Latin America in the 1960s and 1970s, after decades of professionalization, brought this thesis seriously into doubt. In modern Mexico, however, rebellions were always led by revolutionary generals and never by professionally trained younger officers.[61] It seems likely, therefore, that increased professionalization did contribute to taking the Mexican military largely out of politics. Under Cárdenas, the army was reduced in size, but pay was increased. Soldiers were given more training and education and more benefits such as hospitals and schools for their children, life insurance, and severance pay. At the same time, Cárdenas tried to give the army a more civilian outlook. Military education and training emphasized its civilian origins and responsibilities, and in numerous speeches to the army, he stressed the importance of respecting civilian authority. The army was also systematically used in civilian public works projects, and a lottery draft was established in 1939 to further break down the caste or hereditary nature of the army.

Finally, Cárdenas incorporated the military into the new corporatist party in 1938. When he was questioned about the wisdom of doing this, he responded that the military was already in politics and he was merely trying to force its activities into the open and subject it to the influence of the other sectors. Some scholars believe that this was a masterstroke in his strategy of removing the military from politics. If nothing else, the necessity of working with civilians in policy formulation and in candidate selection (to the degree that the party actually did these things) helped to impress the military with either a healthy respect or a disdain for politics. The military sector of the party was eliminated in the early 1940s, after which soldiers could participate only as individuals in one of the remaining three sectors.

This is not to say that the military was completely excluded from politics after 1940. It remained one of the pillars of the regime in performing "residual political roles" such as providing coercion when needed, affording an alternative avenue of political communication between peasants and the central government when peasants were dissatisfied with local politicians, and exercising some direct political participation when individual officers filled some posts in the bureaucracy and congress.[62] In addition, a general was usually president of the revolutionary party until 1964.

For various reasons, therefore, the military largely refrained from overt political involvement after 1940. Of course, factors other than Cárdenas's actions were no doubt important. The U.S. government consistently supported the government in Mexico after 1920 and embargoed the sale of arms to rebels. The unreceptiveness of the U.S. administration to rebellion was a major reason that General Almazán decided not to challenge the election results in 1940. In addition, the rapid economic growth, the subordination of unions and peasants, and the rapprochement with the church all helped to reconcile conservatives and business to the regime after 1940. Thus the policies of Cárdenas greatly reduced the likelihood of military intervention by weakening the military, constructing strong civilian institutions, and thereby radically altering the structure of incentives against rebellion.

Building the Presidency

If Cárdenas had only built support for the regime, constructed an institutionalized party, and depoliticized the military, he would have accomplished far more state building than most Latin American political leaders. However, he took the next logical steps beyond these accomplishments: he strengthened the presidency as an institution and, by his example, resolved the important succession question. In fact, establishing a mechanism for presidential succession was perhaps the most long-lasting political reform to come out of the Revolution. What sets Mexico apart from most other Latin American countries, at least until Costa Rica, Colombia, and Venezuela institutionalized and stabilized their political processes in the 1950s, is the institutionalization of the presidency. The major characteristics of this institutionalization are the relative autonomy of the presidency from direct societal pressures and the regularity of succession.

By the early 1930s, politically relevant forces had coalesced into several blocs in Mexico. The regime was dominated by a coalition of Calles and Cárdenas supporters, with Cárdenas and his reform-minded supporters in a decided minority before June 1935. The cabinet, the party, and congress were all dominated by supporters of Calles. Although the conservative Callistas and the reformist Cardenistas were "reigning" together, they actually were far apart on policy issues such as land reform, encouragement of labor, state control of the economy, and foreign investment.

The Callistas probably had the support of a majority of revolutionary generals, many of whom by this time had become wealthy landowners or businessmen and who, therefore, had much to protect from the reformers. The reform coalition consisted of the Cardenistas and their radical supporters in labor and agriculture. According to Wayne Cornelius, the distribution of political resources in the early months of the Cárdenas administration was approximately 65 percent for the conservative coalition and 28 percent for the reform coalition—a remarkable imbalance.[63] That makes Cárdenas's achievement all the more remarkable. How did he do it?

Even before Cárdenas became president, he set about building the personal and institutional power that would allow him to govern effectively. As indicated above, his travels during the 1934 campaign brought him into contact with thousands of people and convinced many of them that he cared about their problems and intended to do something about them. During those same travels he got to know local and regional leaders better and forged alliances with many of them. During the first year in office he encouraged labor to organize and to bargain collectively, and he encouraged peasants to organize themselves into larger groups. Anticipating the challenge from Calles and his followers, he had begun moving military zone commanders immediately after becoming president, putting those he trusted in key posts.

By early 1935 the Calles supporters within the government became increasingly alarmed at the direction of government policies, particularly on labor and land reform. In an article in the newspaper *Excelsior,* Calles strongly criticized the labor unrest and the splitting of Congress into personalistic factions. He also made a veiled threat to Cárdenas by referring to the forced resignation of Ortiz Rubio as president in 1932. According to Nora Hamilton, Calles's statement was supported by "business organizations, senators and deputies, generals and state governors, as well as by CROM and the CGT,'' two major labor confederations.[64] Cárdenas responded the next day in *El Nacional* (June 14, 1935), saying that he had never sought to promote factions and that the labor unrest was understandable, considering the conditions of labor.

But Cárdenas's response went far beyond words. He moved boldly and swiftly to purge the regime of Callistas. On June 15 he called a cabinet meeting and asked for the resignations of all cabinet members who, with the exception of Portes Gil and Francisco Múgica, went straight to Cuernavaca to report to Calles! On June 17 Cárdenas announced a new cabinet and installed his own supporters. Over the next few weeks he purged additional Callistas from all levels of government, bureaucracy, party, and labor and agrarian organizations. He sent aides throughout the country to determine the sentiment of state governors and military zone commanders. Any who hesitated to express their loyalty to Cárdenas were removed or transferred away from key posts. Army units of known loyalty were concentrated around the capital. As Cornelius says, ''The sheer rapidity with which these changes were made caught the Callistas by surprise, and threw them and their allies off balance.''[65]

As a result of his swift and bold actions, Cárdenas and his allies had significantly increased their control of the political system by late June 1935. Cárdenas and his supporters had been strengthened, Calles and his supporters had been considerably weakened, and the revolutionary generals had been effectively neutralized for the time being. The distribution of power after the lightning strokes of June 1935 showed a radical reversal: approximately 40 percent for the Cardenistas and 25 percent for the Callistas. In addition to ''objective'' changes such as the cabinet turnover and the shifting and removal of military commanders, important ''subjective'' changes also occurred as a result of the events of June. Members of the elite throughout the system apparently saw that their interests no longer lay in supporting Calles. The new reality enticed many of them to throw in their lot with Cárdenas. But Calles continued to challenge Cárdenas, and so in April 1936, Calles and three of his closest associates were put on a plane and expelled from the country. By this time, the political power of the Cardenistas and their labor and agrarian supporters had increased to about 60 percent, whereas Calles's resources had tumbled to near zero, with a separate group of revolutionary generals holding at about 30 percent and still quiescent.[66]

Cárdenas was interested not only in enhancing the power of the president within the central government but also in consolidating the power of the central government itself within the larger political system. As Nathaniel Weyl and Sylvia Weyl noted as early as 1939, ''Cárdenas's target was the Mexican *caudillo* tradition.''[67] Just as he tried to establish the formal authority of the presidency, he tried to destroy the arbitrary power of regional strongmen. The destruction of the power of regional strongmen had, in fact, been a major project of central government leaders in Mexico since at least 1919. Regional caudillos were subdued in various ways, including assassination; Zapata was murdered in 1919 and Villa in 1923. By the time Cárdenas became president, most of the major regional leaders of the Revolution had been either co-opted or assassinated. By 1934 only a couple of truly significant caudillos remained—Tomás Garrido Canabál of Tabasco and Saturnino Cedillo of San Luis Potosí. Cárdenas brought Garrido Canabál into his cabinet as minister of agriculture (actually he may have been imposed on Cárdenas by Calles). During the cabinet reshuffle of June 1935, the anti-Catholic Garrido Canabál was replaced by Cedillo. Thus Cárdenas gained at least temporary support from Cedillo and perhaps lessened the government conflict with the church as well. This meant that Cárdenas would have at his disposal Cedillo's private army of twenty thousand in case the conflict with Calles came to violence.

After consolidating his power against Calles, Cárdenas next moved against Cedillo in a manner that demonstrates Cárdenas's political skill. Cedillo was one of Cárdenas's earliest supporters before his nomination for president, but the different policy values of the two put them on a collision course. Cedillo opposed Cárdenas's land distribution to communal *ejidos* and tried to maintain his independence from the central government. He also had close ties to the fascist "Gold Shirts" organization and other radical right-wing groups opposed to Cardenista reforms. Moreover, it appeared that Cedillo was preparing for open rebellion against the government as he stockpiled heavy armaments and acquired airplanes in his San Luis Potosí stronghold. While Cedillo was still in the cabinet in 1935–36, Cárdenas sent agents into San Luis Potosí to spy on the caudillo's activities. Cedillo resigned from the cabinet in protest in August 1937 and returned to San Luis Potosí. Cárdenas then assigned Cedillo as military zone commander in Michoacán, Cárdenas's home state, where he could be kept under close watch by loyal Cardenistas. Then the government liquidated the aviation school that Cedillo had established in San Luis Potosí as a pretext for the purchase of military aircraft and other heavy equipment. Several units of federal troops of doubtful loyalty were removed from the state and replaced by units loyal to Cárdenas. The head of the agrarian department and numerous technical personnel were sent to San Luis Potosí to step up the distribution of land to those peasants who had not benefited from Cedillo's own very particularistic land-distribution program. This created a base of peasant farmers loyal to the Cárdenas government.

In these ways, Cárdenas eroded Cedillo's resource base at the same time that he provoked him into tipping his hand. Finally, when the new government party began organizing in his state in the spring of 1938, Cedillo rebelled. But after the brilliant series of steps Cárdenas and his associates had taken over the previous year, including persuading most revolutionary generals that it was in their interests to remain neutral, the central government had little difficulty in putting down the rebellion in a few weeks.[68] With Calles, Garrido Canabál, and Cedillo, Cárdenas had defeated threats from both the left and the right. But the struggles were not fought merely to increase his personal power. As one observer put it, "Cárdenas destroyed their power because their existence interfered with the nation which he was trying to build.''[69] He wanted a nation with a strong and stable political system dominated by an institutionalized presidency.

Another aspect of building the presidency in order to build the state was settling the question of the succession to the presidency, which is one of the most difficult problems with which any political system must grapple. Jean Blondel has observed that the succession of leaders is one of the most central problems in politics. Regularity of succession is so important because it not only brings present stability but also makes future stability more likely. That is, regularity becomes an independent variable in itself. As Blondel wrote, "In a country in which successions have been regular and governments are recognized to be stable, members of opposition groups will simply rule out the possibility of coming to power in an irregular manner."[70] Thus stability begets more stability.

Continuismo has been perceived by many Latin Americans as a problem, and numerous constitutions forbid a president from remaining in office beyond one term. Latin American countries have tried in various ways to limit the power of the president, including a plural executive (Uruguay) and a semiparliamentary system (Chile, Brazil, Peru), but the most widespread technique has been some sort of limit on presidential terms.[71]

When General Obregón and his supporters overthrew President Carranza in 1920, it was the last successful military revolt in Mexican history. Obregón was elected president in 1920 and Calles in 1924; this was the first time since 1884, under Díaz, that the presidency had changed hands peacefully.[72] After Obregón was reelected in 1928, he was assassinated by a devout Catholic in protest against the regime's antichurch policies and the prospect of their continuation under Obregón. No Mexican president has served more than one term since. Hence the common Latin American problem of presidents staying in office indefinitely was in the process of being resolved by 1928, although it would allegedly reemerge at least twice in the next twenty-four years. In addition, the presidency was still not insulated against "praetorian" pressures from society. After his presidential term ended in 1928 and president-elect Obregón was assassinated, Calles did not remain in the presidency beyond the end of his term, although he retained political power as the *jefe maximo*. Calles had the elected president removed from office in 1932 when the president's actions became unacceptable to him. In addition, the revolutionary generals continued to threaten the stability of the regime. Therefore, only limited progress had been made in stabilizing presidential succession by 1934.

Thus, in the years immediately before Cárdenas became president, that aspect of political stability represented by the succession question was somewhat muddied. A president had been reelected to a second term (Obregón), although he was assassinated before he could take office. Then a former president (Calles) had dominated the sitting presidents from behind the scenes for six years and had actually unseated one of them (Ortiz Rubio). Calles then tried to interfere with Cárdenas and perhaps even intended to remove him in 1935–36. The procedures for succession and incumbency were, therefore, not completely resolved by 1934.

Cárdenas made a number of important contributions to a resolution of the succession question in actions that he took both during and after his presidency. First, he mobilized power to protect his own presidency against Calles's threat to dominate or remove him. That action made it more likely that future presidents would be allowed to serve their full terms without being dismissed, as Ortiz Rubio had been in 1932, because it demonstrated the resources that could be mobilized by the president in the Mexican political system. Because Cárdenas was a popular president with great political skill, his actions in 1935 and 1936 perhaps suggested the extreme rather than the usual, but they did at least demonstrate what was possible. Future would-be caudillos would have to beware of attempting to dominate an incumbent president from behind the throne.

Then, as his own term neared its end, there was much support for the popular Cárdenas to run again. A petition was signed by a majority of state governors, many generals, and the secretary of the labor central, CTM, and presented to Cárdenas asking him to run for reelection. Cárdenas might have chosen to do what so many other Latin American leaders had done, but he firmly refused. Admittedly, Calles did not run for reelection either. But since Cárdenas was extremely popular and was also twelve years further removed from Obregón's assassination and its dampening effect on reelection aspirations, Cárdenas's self-denial is all the more impressive.

Next he selected a moderate to succeed him, rather than the reformer who might have been his first choice. Moreover, he did not select just any moderate, but the minister of defense, the man who could best keep the military in line. Clearly the overriding goals behind his actions at this time were social peace and regime stability. It seems likely that Cárdenas concluded in 1940 that Mexico had bumped up against "the limits of autonomy" in the international capitalist system and that it would therefore be prudent to accommodate the regime more fully to the demands of capitalism.[73] Cárdenas's first choice as president may well have been the popular General Francisco Múgica, a leftist revolutionary who had been one of Cárdenas's chief mentors. Múgica favored continued land reform, generosity to labor, oil expropriation, the admission of Leon Trotsky into Mexico, and other leftist policies.[74] On the right was a popular revolutionary general, Juan Andreu Almazán, who was decidedly more probusiness. Both Múgica and Almazán very much wanted to be president and both sought the PRM nomination. When it became clear that Cárdenas did not intend to choose either one of them, they followed different paths. Múgica chose to stay in the party, whereas Almazán became the candidate of several new conservative parties. In choosing a "moderate" successor who was also a general, Cárdenas confirmed that his primary goal was the stabilization and institutionalization of the regime, even if it meant the sacrifice of some of his substantive policy preferences such as land reform and labor relations. He did not want the turmoil that had characterized Mexico in the past to continue into the future. The leader of the new conservative party, PAN, later said, "If in 1939 there had not been a political solution to the state of anxiety in Mexico, we would have had a tremendous revolution."[75]

Even so, the 1940 election was not without conflict. Election day proved to be "one of the bloodiest" in Mexican history.[76] Perhaps the passions of the times, with many countries deeply divided between left and right, would have produced such turmoil no matter who the government candidate was. (Political systems all over the Western world were being polarized by the extremes of communism and fascism.) Also, Cárdenas had treated many dissidents much more gently than had Calles and Obregón, who allegedly had ordered the murders of numerous political opponents. Therefore, the resurgence of the conservatives in 1940 and the subsequently hard-fought election should be seen not only as a reaction to Cárdenas's leftist economic policies but also as a response to his notable leniency toward dissenters.

One might assume that Cárdenas would have wanted to make the 1940 election the most honest that Mexico had seen, in keeping with his publicly proclaimed values of honesty and probity. In fact, in September 1939 Cárdenas announced his determination to guarantee free and honest elections. However, the 1940 elections appear to have been as rigged as any before or since. Either Cárdenas could not control the electoral process or he chose not to risk an Almazán victory, which might have undone many of the socioeconomic gains of the Revolution such as land reform and oil expropriation. The official results were strikingly skewed in the regime's favor:

Avila Camacho   2,476,641

Almazán   151,010

Sánchez Tapia   9,840

Almazán was highly popular, especially among the middle and upper classes, and almost certainly received many more votes than 150,000. As Frank Brandenburg says: "To this day not a few impartial observers insist that Almazán really won the election."[77] That seems unlikely, considering that most of the population were workers and peasants who had just been favored by Cárdenas, but Almazán surely received more than 6 percent of the vote.[78] Almazán declared himself the winner and left for Cuba to try to persuade the U.S. secretary of state, Cordell Hull, who was attending a conference there, to declare that the United States would at least be neutral in the conflict, and Almazán also approached U.S. businesses for funds with which to buy arms.[79] But the U.S. government apparently gave Almazán no encouragement, and after the Democratic victory in November 1940, the White House announced that Vice President-elect Henry Wallace would attend Avila Camacho's inauguration as President Franklin Roosevelt's representative.[80] A few election-related disturbances occurred in northern Mexico, but Cárdenas ignored them. He said that he did not consider Almazán and his supporters to be in revolt against the government and insisted that they were free to return to Mexico.[81] If Cárdenas had chosen a leftist such as Múgica or a rightist such as Almazán as his successor, it seems probable that the political violence in 1940 would have been far greater than it was. Thus by ensuring the election of a moderate successor and by treating dissenters liberally but firmly, Cárdenas contributed to the largely peaceful resolution of the 1940 election.

The next phase of Cárdenas's political career was in some ways the most interesting of all. Political scientists do not often look closely at what political leaders do after they leave office, yet that phase of their lives can be quite relevant for the political system, especially if they remain popular. Cárdenas retired from the presidency with an enormous reservoir of popular support and elite loyalty. Would he use these resources to perpetuate personal power and to rule behind the throne, as so many leaders including Obregón and Calles had done, or would he lend his prestige to the institutionalization and stabilization of the system? Both Calles and Cárdenas had definite policy preferences after they left office; that is not what distinguishes them from one another. Rather, Cárdenas, unlike Calles, placed a greater value on consolidating institutions than on pushing for particular substantive policies or perpetuating his own personal power.

Cárdenas neither retired completely from politics nor dominated the government after his term. Rather, he attempted to walk a fine line between the two extremes of domination and abnegation. He continued to contribute to the building of the presidency without trying to control it. In fact, he "underplayed his own popularity with the Mexican masses in an effort to strengthen Avila Camacho and *the prestige of the presidency.*"[82] Because so many Mexican peasants and trade unionists looked to him for personal leadership, Cárdenas could not totally abandon the "Revolutionary family," but he was willing, as many others had not been, to participate in leadership rather than to monopolize it.

Unlike Calles, who had stayed in Cuernavaca, fifty miles from the capital, Cárdenas returned to his home state of Michoacán after he left the presidency. When Mexico entered World War II in May 1942, Cárdenas was appointed chief of operations in the Pacific Zone to prepare against a possible Japanese invasion. Then in September 1942 he was appointed minister of defense and served in that capacity for three years, resigning as soon as the war was over.[83] This period too had positive effects on political stability and the institutionalization of the presidency. By serving in the cabinet, Cárdenas lent his great prestige to Avila Camacho and to the regime in general. His service demonstrated to the public that Cárdenas still supported the government even though it had become more conservative than he might have liked. By serving as minister of defense, rather than in some other post, he was also in a position to continue the removal of the military from overt participation in politics.[84]

Another issue that illustrates Cárdenas's commitment to exercising, with restraint, his influence for political stability was the matter of choosing presidential candidates in 1952 and 1958. One version of the story has it that President
Miguel Alemán (1946–52), who turned out to be a very strong president, considered running for reelection in 1952. Martin Needler says that when Cárdenas
was told about Alemán's possible reelection bid, he told Alemán in no uncertain terms that he disapproved of reelection because of its potentially destabilizing effects.[85] Not all observers agree that Alemán actually intended to run for
election,[86] but whatever the facts of the reelection story, once Alemán began
trying to decide who would succeed him, he announced that the "consensus"
of opinion favored Fernando Casas Alemán, who symbolized to some of the
elite many of the worst qualities of the Alemán administration, such as authoritarianism, conservatism, and corruption. Brandenburg notes, "At this point,
Cárdenas and Avila Camacho forcefully stepped back into Revolutionary Family leadership."[87] But in keeping with his past practices, Cárdenas acted with
restraint. Rather than provoking an open break with Alemán, he consulted privately with various political leaders, and a compromise emerged. Alemán
would finish out his term, and all segments of the party would support Adolfo
Ruiz Cortines, a noncontroversial career civil servant noted for his integrity.[88]
Although accepting a moderate, Cárdenas received assurances that the masses
would receive greater attention in the new administration, once again demonstrating that although his top priority was the stability and integrity of the political system, he also pressed for specific substantive policies when doing so was
not disruptive. Cárdenas contributed, therefore, to the legitimacy and stability
of the political system by pushing for a new administration that would be less
dramatically corrupt and less single-mindedly probusiness in its public policies.

He exercised his guiding influence once again in 1957 as the elite considered
a successor to Ruiz Cortines. This time Cárdenas felt the need to become even
more public in his actions than in 1951. The conservative wing of the party,
centered around ex-president Alemán, was lobbying strongly for a conservative
successor. Their position had deteriorated under Ruiz Cortines partly because
of his intolerance of their greater-than-usual corruption. But they were regroup-
ing and were determined to convince Ruiz Cortines of the desirability of a
conservative successor. Cárdenas's supporters convinced Cárdenas that if he
sat quietly by, the right wing would sweep the nomination by convincing Ruiz
Cortines that most of the elite wanted a conservative president in 1958. Therefore, after more than fifteen years of abstention from public campaigning, Cárdenas became active in talking to regional elites and making public speeches
on the necessity of defending the Revolution.[89] Once the left focused around
Cárdenas, Ruiz Cortines had more room for maneuver between the two elite
blocs and selected a moderate leftist, Adolfo López Mateos, to be the next
president.[90] By mobilizing the reformist forces to counterbalance the right
Cárdenas once again contributed to the authority of the incumbent president.
Apparently Cárdenas never tried to impose a particular successor but only fa-

vored some and vetoed the ones he and his supporters found truly objectionable.

Thus Cárdenas contributed to the institutionalization of the presidency in two closely related ways. He contributed to the integrity of the presidency as the central block in the Mexican political structure that could withstand the pressures of factions and of personalist ex-presidents. He also did much to confirm the value and practice of no reelection of the executive. These qualities may seem of limited value to North Americans, who are accustomed to executives acting within the relatively tight constraints of institutions. But for Latin America, with its tradition of personalistic dictatorial rule that often perpetuates itself for long periods of time and often is removable only by violence, they were no mean accomplishment. Giving the president supreme power, but changing presidents every six years, was a way of retaining much of the Mexican tradition of the strong executive yet restraining it from going beyond certain limits. Cárdenas did a great deal to consolidate that pattern. As Tannenbaum wrote in the preface to William Townsend's biography of Cárdenas:

He demonstrated what seemed the impossible: that a president could retire, and refrain from trying to dictate the future politics of the nation. . . . The peaceful transmission of the office of the presidency is the greatest single gift that he has given to Mexico. His mere presence is an assurance that there will be no revolution against the government in power, and no re-election. If that becomes a tradition, Cárdenas will have permanently changed the character of Mexican politics.[91]

Table 2.2 shows some of the salient benchmarks on the road to institutionalization of the Mexican presidency. It illustrates that the evolution of a new political pattern is often a slow and incremental process that may take many years and may occur in numerous small steps. From the beginning of the Revolution in 1910 to the firm consolidation of the pattern in 1952 were forty-two years of turmoil, violence, and consolidation.

CONCLUSION

Although the past is often the best predictor of the future, societies are not required to repeat the patterns of the past; they can develop new habits of behavior, new methods of interaction. Such change is greatly facilitated if leaders have a vision of what the new society can look like, if choices are made that move the society in that direction, and if resources are mobilized skillfully to achieve the goals. Cárdenas was a master at accumulating power and then using it to construct political institutions. Cárdenas built elite and popular support, constructed a political party to channel that support, defeated competing caudillos, co-opted labor and agrarian leaders, and then proceeded to transfer his personal power to other men and institutions and to watch over them until the new pattern was firmly in place. One author aptly describes the Cárdenas years as ''one of the most rapid, massive periods of institutional change that

Table 2.2
The Institutionalization of the Mexican Presidency

Date	Important Events
1920	Last successful military revolt to overthrow president.
1924	First peaceful transfer of presidential power since 1884 (Obregón to Calles).
1928	Presidential term changed from four to six years. Last president to run for a second term (Obregón).
1929	Last major military revolt (unsuccessful).
1934	First presidential election since the Revolution without a military rebellion.
1938	Last minor military revolt.
1940	First president to finish full six-year term (Cárdenas).
1946	Last military man leaves presidency (Avila Camacho). First civilian president to serve full term since Revolution comes into office (Alemán).
1952	Reelection issue laid to rest through struggle between Alemán and Cárdenas.
1994	Tenth president to serve full six-year term leaves office (Carlos Salinas).

has ever taken place in Latin America without a polity exploding into civil war or being cruelly repressed."[92]

The transfer of power in Mexico has, of course, always been within one group. It is still true, at least at the federal level, that "no government in Mexican history has ever surrendered as a result of an electoral defeat."[93] In other words, stability is not democracy. Perhaps Cárdenas built too well; the party and sectors that he constructed were so all-encompassing and the elite defense of them so monopolistic that political pluralism has had a difficult time taking root in Mexico, and that no doubt has had implications for the distribution of economic benefits. Yet it seems that Cárdenas valued democracy, and so a major mystery is why he did not insist on fair elections in 1940. Apparently he simply could not stomach the idea of an antirevolutionary group gaining power after all the bloodshed that was required to dislodge them from power.

In important ways, the political institutions created by Cárdenas and his generation have been remarkably adaptable. They were broad enough to include people from socialists to conservatives and adaptable enough to respond to the dominant pressures of the moment, such as Avila Camacho's move to the right in 1940 and Echeverría's move to the left in 1970. But as of the early 1990s, they had not demonstrated enough flexibility to allow truly fair elections or to contemplate turning national power over to an opposition party. Can the regime that Cárdenas built contemplate the possibility of allowing real political participation and fair elections that might result in the regime's loss of numerous local and state governments, control of the Congress, and even the presidency itself? It remains to be seen whether the Mexican political system will successfully meet the next challenge—the transition to fair elections and multiparty democracy, which a large majority of the population seem to want. Mere institutionalization is not enough. Institutions must be congruent with the values of a people at a particular time. Institutions that were in harmony with these values at one time may be out of tune with that society's values at another time. Regular presidential succession may no longer be enough to satisfy a majority of the population if that succession is always within the same party. Thus Cárdenas's resolution of these problems helps to explain the stability of the political system for several decades, but it is uncertain that these institutional arrangements can continue to satisfy a majority of Mexicans today.

Today Mexico is facing the most severe test of its unique political system since 1940. Parties from both the right and the left are challenging, as never before, the structure that Cárdenas put in place in the 1930s. It is ironic that Cárdenas's son is the major opposition candidate challenging the institutionalized one-party system created by his father, but whatever happens, that system laid the foundation for a remarkably resilient political arrangement. The political system of Mexico has continued from 1920 to the present without a violent change of government; no other Latin American government has approximated that length of time. The institutionalization of certain aspects of the Mexican political system in the 1930s was a major factor contributing to that stability. Cárdenas thus laid the foundations for the "perfect dictatorship," a relatively legitimate "benign authoritarianism" in which the leaders changed regularly and most social forces were incorporated into the regime.[94]

NOTES

1. For Washington, see Glenn Phelps, *George Washington and American Constitutionalism* (Lawrence: University Press of Kansas, 1993). For Atatürk, see Robert Ward

and Dankwart Rustow, eds., *Political Modernization in Japan and Turkey* (Princeton: Princeton University Press, 1964). For Betancourt, see Robert J. Alexander, *The Venezuelan Democratic Revolution: A Profile of the Regime of Rómulo Betancourt* (New Brunswick, N.J.: Rutgers University Press, 1964).

2. Mentioning Castro raises an important point: institutionalization alone is not enough. If a regime is to endure, it must be acceptable to a large part of the population and have the other qualities discussed throughout this book. Communist regimes in Eastern Europe and the Soviet Union were highly institutionalized, but they were toppled as soon as their populations were allowed to do so. The fundamental point is that no single factor explains political stability. Rather, it is the interaction of several factors.

3. I deliberately use the phrase *personal power*, rather than *charismatic power*, because Cárdenas accumulated charismatic as well as other forms of influence. However, charisma was only one component of his personal power. For the original discussion of charismatic and other forms of authority, see Max Weber, *The Theory of Social and Economic Organization*, ed. Talcott Parsons (New York: Free Press, 1964, originally translated in 1947), pp. 328–69.

4. *Institutionalization* could be defined broadly enough to include the regularization of violent conflict as a dominant mode of political interaction. One could then say that the Mexican political system "institutionalized" violence as the primary method of selecting presidents from 1820 to 1876. What I am talking about here is the institutionalization of primarily nonviolent means of decision making. For an argument that Mexican political stability rests not on institutions at all, but on "political discipline and political negotiation," see Susan Kaufman Purcell and John F. H. Purcell, "State and Society in Mexico: Must a Stable Polity Be Institutionalized?" *World Politics* 32 (2), 1980, pp. 194–227.

5. Karl Deutsch, *Politics and Government* (Boston: Houghton Mifflin, 1974), p. 195.

6. For fundamental discussions of institutionalization, I lean on Weber, *Theory of Social and Economic Organization*; George Homans, *Social Behavior* (New York: Harcourt, Brace and World, 1961); Peter Berger and Thomas Luckman, *The Social Construction of Reality: A Treatise in the Sociology of Knowledge* (Garden City, N.Y.: Doubleday and Company, 1966); and Ulrich Witt, "On the Evolution of Economic Institutions" (paper presented to the Public Choice Society, San Francisco, 1988). See Witt for the distinction in the literature between those who believe that institutions emerge mostly spontaneously and unconsciously versus those who believe that institutions are often consciously created and nourished by individual leaders.

7. Some political scientists continued to emphasize the importance of institutions during this time; e.g., see Samuel Huntington, *Political Order in Changing Societies* (New Haven: Yale University Press, 1968).

8. Peter Evans, Dietrich Rueschemeyer, and Theda Skocpol, eds., *Bringing the State Back In* (New York: Cambridge University Press, 1985); Eric Nordlinger, *On the Autonomy of the Democratic State* (Cambridge: Harvard University Press, 1981); and Eric Nordlinger, "Taking the State Seriously," in Myron Weiner and Samuel Huntington, eds., *Understanding Political Development* (Boston: Little, Brown and Company, 1987), pp. 353–90.

9. For example, see James March and Johan Olsen, "The New Institutionalism: Organizational Factors in Political Life," *American Political Science Review* 78 (3), 1984, pp. 734–49, and James March and Johan Olsen, *Rediscovering Institutions: The*

Organizational Bases of Politics (New York: Free Press, 1989). At the same time, other scholars cautioned us not to exaggerate the independence of the state from social forces but to be aware of "the limits to state autonomy" (Nora Hamilton, *The Limits of State Autonomy: Post-Revolutionary Mexico* [Princeton: Princeton University Press, 1982]) and to recognize that many countries might still have "strong societies and weak states" (Joel S. Migdal, "Strong States, Weak States: Power and Accommodation," in Weiner and Huntington, *Understanding Political Development*). Nevertheless, the point had been made: the state and its component institutions might have some independent influence on society and public policy.

10. March and Olsen, *Rediscovering Institutions,* p. 17.

11. Ibid., p. 162.

12. Jon Elster, *Nuts and Bolts for the Social Sciences* (New York: Cambridge University Press, 1989), p. 150. In fact, contrary to March and Olsen, Elster is using the concept of "institution" precisely to mean a structure of incentives, in contrast to social norms and internalized norms.

13. Ibid., p. 158. Or as Lindenberg says, "Most theories in sociology should explain phenomena on the collective level, and these explanations should be grounded in theories on the individual level." Siegwart Lindenberg, "The Method of Decreasing Abstraction," in James Coleman and Thomas Fararo, eds., *Rational Choice Theory: Advocacy and Critique* (Newbury Park, Calif.: Sage Publications, 1992), p. 18.

14. Irving Louis Horowitz, "The Norm of Illegitimacy," in Bogdan Denitch, ed., *Legitimation of Regimes* (Beverly Hills: Sage Publications, 1979), p. 27.

15. James Hanson, "Federal Expenditures and 'Personalism' in the Mexican Institutional Revolution," in James W. Wilkie, ed., *Money and Politics in Latin America,* Statistical Abstract of Latin America Supplement 7 (Los Angeles: UCLA Latin American Center Publications, 1977), p. 1937.

16. For a fascinating account of the explicit efforts of the political leadership to construct a legitimizing myth of the Revolution, see Ilene O'Malley, *The Myth of the Revolution: Hero Cults and the Institutionalization of the Mexican State, 1920–1940* (Westport, Conn.: Greenwood Press, 1986).

17. See Roderic Camp, *The Making of a Government: Political Leaders in Modern Mexico* (Tucson: University of Arizona Press, 1984).

18. Joseph Rothschild, "Political Legitimacy in Contemporary Europe," in Bogdan Denitch, ed., *Legitimation of Regimes* (Beverly Hills: Sage Publications, 1979), pp. 38–39.

19. Michael C. Meyer and William L. Sherman, *The Course of Mexican History,* 2d ed. (New York: Oxford University Press, 1983), p. 324.

20. Martin Needler, *Mexican Politics: The Containment of Conflict,* 2d ed. (New York: Praeger Publishers, 1990), pp. 14–15.

21. Frank Tannenbaum, *Mexico: The Struggle for Peace and Bread* (New York: Alfred A. Knopf, 1956), p. 43.

22. Until 1904, the presidential term was four years. In 1904, it was extended to six years. The Constitution of 1917 reduced it once again to four years; a constitutional amendment extended it once again to six years as of 1928.

23. Lorenzo Meyer, "Historical Roots of the Authoritarian State in Mexico," in José Luis Reyna and Richard S. Weinert, eds., *Authoritarianism in Mexico* (Philadelphia: Institute for the Study of Human Issues, 1977), p. 9.

24. Ibid., p. 8.

25. Theda Skocpol, *States and Social Revolutions: A Comparative Analysis of France, Russia, and China* (New York: Cambridge University Press, 1979).

26. For an emphasis on the state-building activities of Presidents Obregón and Calles from 1920 to 1928, see Richard Tardanico, "Revolutionary Nationalism and State Building in Mexico, 1917–1924," *Politics and Society* 10 (1), 1980, pp. 59–86; and Richard Tardanico, "State, Dependency, and Nationalism: Revolutionary Mexico, 1924–1928," *Comparative Studies in Society and History* 24 (3), 1982, pp. 400–423.

27. Michael Burton and John Higley, "Elite Settlements," *American Sociological Review* 52 (3), 1987, pp. 295–307.

28. Cheryl Lassen, "Political Strategies for Transforming Industrializing Economies: A Populist Approach" (Ph.D. diss., Cornell University, 1982).

29. Joe C. Ashby, "The Dilemma of the Mexican Trade Union Movement," *Mexican Studies* 1 (2), 1985, pp. 278–79.

30. Judith Adler Hellman, *Mexico in Crisis*, 2d ed. (New York: Holmes and Meier, 1983), p. 40.

31. Hamilton, *Limits of State Autonomy*, p. 125.

32. Robert Paul Millon, *Mexican Marxist: Vicente Lombardo Toledano* (Chapel Hill: University of North Carolina Press, 1966), p. 135.

33. Albert Michaels, "Mexican Politics and Nationalism from Calles to Cardenas" (Ph.D. diss., University of Pennsylvania, 1966), p. 92.

34. Alma Maria Garcia Marsh, "Ideology and Power: A Study of the Mexican State under Porfirio Díaz (1876–1911) and Lázaro Cárdenas (1934–1940)" (Ph.D. diss., University of Texas, 1982), p. 181.

35. Michaels, "Mexican Politics," p. 110.

36. Not that land distribution always has the effect of increasing political support by the beneficiaries; see Carlos Salinas de Gortari, *Political Participation, Public Investment, and Support for the System: A Comparative Study of Rural Communities in Mexico*, Research Series No. 35 (La Jolla: Center for U.S.-Mexican Studies, University of California, San Diego, 1982). As Ann Craig points out, this conclusion is particularly interesting considering the later importance of Salinas in the regime. See Ann L. Craig, *The First Agraristas* (Berkeley: University of California Press, 1983), p. 247.

37. Michaels, "Mexican Politics," p. 240, emphasis in original. For a firsthand account of the popular response, see William C. Townsend, *Lázaro Cárdenas: Mexican Democrat*, 2d ed. (Waxhaw, N.C.: International Friendship Publishers, 1979), pp. 257–60.

38. See Ruth Berens Collier and David Collier, *Shaping the Political Arena: Critical Junctures, the Labor Movement, and Regime Dynamics in Latin America* (Princeton: Princeton University Press, 1991).

39. Reading the enormous number of requests from individuals makes it difficult to believe that Mexicans are as fatalistic and passive as they are frequently portrayed. However, the requests do illustrate the highly centralized nature of the Mexican political system. Many Mexicans looked to the central government to solve problems that would have been handled at the local level or privately in most Western countries.

40. Stephen H. Haber, *Industry and Underdevelopment: The Industrialization of Mexico, 1890–1940* (Stanford: Stanford University Press, 1989), p. 188.

41. Hamilton, *Limits of State Autonomy*, p. 235.

42. However, the fact that business did pretty well for most of the Cárdenas years, especially 1935–38, did not necessarily make businessmen like his policies. It merely mitigated dislike of the populist president.

43. Camp, *The Making of a Government*, p. 21.

44. Roderic Camp, *Mexico's Leaders* (Tucson: University of Arizona Press, 1980), p. 19.

45. Jean Meyer, cited in Ernest Duff, *Leader and Party in Latin America* (Boulder, Colo.: Westview Press, 1985), p. 33.

46. Robert Scott, *Mexican Government in Transition* (Urbana: University of Illinois Press, 1964).

47. Duff, *Leader and Party in Latin America*.

48. James W. Wilkie and Edna Monzón de Wilkie, *Mexico visto en el siglo XX: entrevistas de historia oral* (Mexico: Instituto Mexicano de Investigaciones Económicas, 1969), pp. 317–18.

49. See Scott, *Mexican Government*, pp. 134–44; Frank Brandenburg, *The Making of Modern Mexico* (Englewood Cliffs, N.J.: Prentice-Hall, 1964), pp. 90–95. Given his policy preferences, no doubt Cárdenas hoped that the Mexican regime that he was helping to build would pursue populist policies in the future. However, the institutionalized regime would be in a position to pursue whatever policies the leaders of the moment chose, whether populist or not. To say that Cárdenas helped to build a strong regime is not to say that in the future it would always do what he preferred. He did not like many of the conservative policy choices of his successors, and in fact he occasionally took an active part in politics after he left the presidency in an effort to influence the direction of government policy.

50. Clientelism, or patron-client relations, as a basis for political support and appointment to office continued to be important in Mexico, but now they took place within the revolutionary party.

51. According to Juan Linz in his seminal work, ideological flexibility is a common characteristic of authoritarian regimes, as contrasted with the ideological rigidity of totalitarian regimes. See Juan Linz, "An Authoritarian Regime: Spain," in E. Allardt and Y. Littune, eds., *Cleavages, Ideologies, and Party Systems* (Helsinki: Westermarck Society, 1964).

52. Huntington, *Political Order*, p. 79.

53. Ibid., p. 196.

54. Viviane Brachet-Márquez,"Explaining Sociopolitical Change in Latin America: The Case of Mexico," *Latin American Research Review* 27 (3), 1992, pp. 91–122.

55. Edwin Lieuwen, *Arms and Politics in Latin America* (New York: Praeger, 1960), p. 101.

56. Edwin Lieuwen, *Mexican Militarism: The Political Rise and Fall of the Revolutionary Army, 1910–1940* (Albuquerque: University of New Mexico Press, 1968), p. 57.

57. James W. Wilkie, *The Mexican Revolution: Federal Expenditures and Social Change since 1910*, 2d ed. (Berkeley: University of California Press, 1970), p. 102.

58. Lieuwen, *Mexican Militarism*, p. 111.

59. Lieuwen may exaggerate the extent to which this group stood above the rest, since other central government figures and regional strongmen were also important. However, these five were certainly among the most powerful.

60. Edwin Lieuwen, "Depoliticization of the Mexican Revolutionary Army, 1915–1940," in David Ronfeldt, ed., *The Modern Mexican Military: A Reassessment* (La Jolla: Center for U.S.-Mexican Studies, University of California, San Diego, 1984), p. 53.

61. Ibid., p. 54.

62. Interestingly, the proportion of military men among upper-level political elites actually increased slightly under Cárdenas, compared with the Calles years of 1924–34. This may have been a reflection of Cárdenas's need for support for his efforts to seize power from Calles, enact populist policies, and build new institutions. After 1940, the percent generally decreased. See Peter H. Smith, *Labyrinths of Power: Political Recruitment in Twentieth-Century Mexico* (Princeton: Princeton University Press, 1979), pp. 94–95.

63. Wayne Cornelius, "Nation-Building, Participation, and Distribution: Reform under Cárdenas," in Gabriel Almond, Scott Flanagan, and Robert Mundt, *Crisis, Choice, and Change: Historical Studies of Political Development* (Boston: Little, Brown and Company, 1973), p. 441.

64. Hamilton, *Limits of State Autonomy*, p. 124.

65. Cornelius, "Nation Building," p. 441.

66. Ibid., pp. 445–46.

67. Nathaniel Weyl and Sylvia Weyl, *The Reconquest of Mexico: The Years of Lázaro Cárdenas* (New York: Oxford University Press, 1939), p. 166.

68. The most thorough account of the career of Saturnino Cedillo and his relationship with Cárdenas is found in Dudley Ankerson, *Agrarian Warlord: Saturnino Cedillo and the Mexican Revolution in San Luis Potosí* (DeKalb: Northern Illinois University Press, 1984). Also see Lieuwen, *Mexican Militarism,* and Cornelius, "Nation Building."

69. Michaels, "Mexican Politics," p. 198.

70. Jean Blondel, *World Leaders* (Beverly Hills: Sage Publications, 1980), p. 81.

71. Harry Kantor, "Efforts Made by Various Latin American Countries to Limit the Power of the President," in Thomas V. DiBacco, ed., *Presidential Power in Latin American Politics* (New York: Praeger Publishers, 1977), pp. 21–32.

72. A minor exception was in 1911, when Madero peacefully succeeded interim president Francisco de la Barra, who had become president on the resignation of Porfirio Diaz.

73. Albert Michaels, "The Crisis of Cardenismo," *Journal of Latin American Studies* 2 (1), 1970, pp. 51–79; Hamilton, *Limits of State Autonomy*, pp. 254–60; Ariel José Contreras, *México 1940: industrialización y crisis política* (Mexico: Siglo Veintiuno Editores, 1983).

74. Hamilton, *Limits of State Autonomy*, p. 256; Contreras, *México 1940*, p. 14.

75. James W. Wilkie and Albert Michaels, eds., *Revolution in Mexico: Years of Upheaval, 1910–1940* (Tucson: University of Arizona Press, 1984), p. 259.

76. Brandenburg, *Making*, p. 93. For a graphic description of election-day violence in Mexico City, see Betty Kirk, *Covering the Mexican Front: The Battle of Europe versus America* (Norman: University of Oklahoma Press, 1942), pp. 238–43.

77. Brandenburg, *Making*, p. 93.

78. Needler, *Mexican Politics*, p. 28; also Brandenburg, *Making*, p. 93.

79. Luis Medina, *Del cardenismo al avilacamachismo*, vol. 18, *Historia de la Revolución Mexicana* (México, D. F.: El Colégio de Mexico, 1978), p. 125.

80. E. David Cronin, *Josephus Daniels in Mexico* (Madison: University of Wisconsin Press, 1960), p. 257.

81. William Weber Johnson, *Heroic Mexico: The Violent Emergence of a Modern Nation* (Garden City, N.Y.: Doubleday and Company, 1968), p. 421.

82. Brandenburg, *Making*, p. 94, emphasis added.

83. Pere Foix, *Cárdenas*, 3d ed. (México, D. F.: Editorial Trillas, 1971), chapter 17.

84. For his memoirs during this period, see Lázaro Cárdenas, *Obras I: Apuntes, 1941–1956* (México, D. F.: UNAM, 1986, originally 1972). Unfortunately for the scholar, Cárdenas—like most of the few Mexican politicians who have written memoirs—tells us little of policy conflicts within the regime.

85. Martin Needler, "Review Essay: Daniel Cosío Villegas and the Interpretation of the Mexican Political System," *Journal of Interamerican Studies and World Affairs* 18 (2), 1976, p. 250.

86. For example, Scott, *Mexican Government*, p. 212.

87. Brandenburg, *Making*, p. 106.

88. Ibid., p. 107.

89. Scott, *Mexican Government*, p. 208.

90. Brandenburg, *Making*, p. 112.

91. Townsend. *Lázaro Cárdenas*, pp. vii–viii.

92. Lassen, "Political Strategies," p. 99.

93. Lieuwen, *Mexican Militarism*, p. 150.

94. The "perfect dictatorship" is a term used by Mario Vargas Llosa in 1990 *(Proceso*, no. 723, September 10, 1990); "benign authoritarianism" has been used by various writers, including Dale Story in *The Mexican Ruling Party: Stability and Authority* (New York: Praeger, 1986), p. 6. The emphasis on Cárdenas in this chapter is not meant to imply that other presidents contributed nothing to state building. Obregón and Calles were very important in this regard (see Tardanico). As for removing the military from politics, Camp argues that Avila Camacho deserves credit at least equal to Cárdenas, since he eliminated the military sector from the party, retired many revolutionary generals and promoted officers for professional merit, continued to reduce the military share of the budget (even during World War II), created a presidential guard as a counterweight to the army, and selected the first civilian full-term president.

That the military did not "intervene" in the sense of overthrowing governments after the 1920s does not mean that the military was completely out of politics. In fact, one factor that may have contributed to satisfying the political impulses of members of the military was that they could participate in politics in various ways, including running for congress and state governorships and serving in staff positions in the PRI. Military men who became disaffected from the regime could even work in opposition campaigns, although the price could be high. In 1952, a number of high-level officers supported the presidential candidacy of Miguel Henríquez Guzmán, a defection to which President Alemán responded firmly. According to Camp: "Alemán confronted them in an extremely inflexible manner, instructing his defense secretary to grant unlimited leaves— tantamount to discharging them from active duty—rather than the usual limited leave to campaign. It was a very plain message to the officer corps: support the government's candidate or leave the service" (Roderic Camp, *Generals in the Palacio: The Military in Modern Mexico* [New York: Oxford University Press, 1992], p. 26). In this way, Alemán also contributed to depoliticizing the military, at least in the sense of prohibiting it from engaging in *opposition* politics.

3

Economic Growth and
Political Support

LEGITIMACY AND ECONOMIC GROWTH

For a political regime to be legitimate and stable, it must achieve certain goals; one of the most important of these is economic growth. Other things being equal, a government that presides over economic prosperity will be seen as deserving to remain in power, whereas one that presides over economic stagnation will not. In fact, political rulers were held responsible for economic conditions long before they had much knowledge or ability to manage their economies. U.S. presidents such as Martin Van Buren and Grover Cleveland were defeated for reelection largely because of economic recessions over which their governments had little control. Since the Great Depression and the development of theories of macroeconomic policy, governments have been held even more accountable for ensuring economic prosperity.

In a political system with competitive elections, a period of slow economic growth and high unemployment will weaken the electoral strength of the party in power, and a recession will often lead to its defeat at the polls.[1] For example, George Bush's defeat in 1992 probably owed much to slow economic growth. Even in a political system without competitive elections, poor economic growth will tend to weaken the legitimacy and hence the stability of the regime. Of course, the political legitimacy of a regime may be so strong that it can withstand a relatively long period of economic failure, but it is also true that prolonged economic failure will gradually erode the legitimacy of any regime. The collapse of communism in Eastern Europe and the Soviet Union is stark testimony to that fact. Since Communist and other authoritarian regimes are not legitimated on the basis of the will of the people as manifested in elections, but on the basis of what they achieve for their people, they are particularly susceptible to being judged on grounds of social and economic effectiveness.[2] Therefore, a long period of inadequate socioeconomic performance can

erode their authority, as became dramatically evident in the Soviet Union and
Eastern Europe by 1990.

A fundamental basis of legitimacy for any ruling elite is how it came to
power, whether by competitive elections, in the case of the liberal democratic
polities, or revolution, in the case of the former Soviet Union and Mexico. But
legitimacy derived from regime origins can wear thin after many years of poor
economic performance; eventually a ruling elite must deliver the goods or see
its legitimacy eroded.[3] The troubles of regimes that have recently democra-
tized, such as those in Latin America and the former Soviet Union, show that
every type of regime is vulnerable to such demands. Even in relatively stable
systems, political discontent is often a function of the economic performance
of a society. Political unrest tends to recur in "cycles of protest that grow
periodically out of the basic conflicts in capitalist society."[4] This is a valid
generalization, except that it could be broadened to include all societies, even
socialist ones. One could say that political unrest tends to recur in cycles of
protest that grow periodically out of the basic conflicts in the economy. All
economies wax and wane, experience unemployment or inflation, and then see
mounting political discontent as a result. That discontent will manifest itself in
electoral defeat of the government in one regime and perhaps violent overthrow
of the regime in another.

The relationships between economic performance and political stability are
not simple, of course. Is growth in total GNP most important, or GNP per
capita? Is high unemployment more important than inflation in undermining a
regime's legitimacy? A major difficulty is that unemployment and inflation are
often inversely related, so that when a government attacks the one, it is vulnerable to the other.[5] Some have argued that a long period of economic growth
followed by a sharp downturn is likely to produce a violent reaction from the
populace.[6] Others have claimed that what counts is the "relative deprivation"
of a group compared to other groups with whom they compare themselves.[7] Or
is the very process of economic growth and development politically destabilizing, as suggested by numerous writers such as Mancur Olson, Lawrence Stone,
Samuel Huntington, and Eric Wolf?[8] Especially in its early stages, rapid economic growth can destabilize a regime as new social groups, such as the working and middle classes, increase in size and power. They tend to make political
demands for greater participation in government and economic demands for a
larger share of the material riches produced by their society. If the regime is
willing to create new channels of participation for these emerging groups, as
was the British government in the nineteenth century, their integration can be
accomplished with relatively little turmoil. If, however, a regime tries to suppress the new groups and their demands, the result may be social turmoil and
political instability.

There is probably no absolute level of any economic indicator that constitutes
a threshold across which no society can pass with impunity. The United States,
for example, suffered unemployment rates of 25 percent in the early 1930s

without experiencing a revolution, but it did decisively elect a new president. Mexico has often had unemployment rates of 15 percent and underemployment rates of 40 percent without a great deal of social turmoil. Clearly, other factors besides economic performance affect political stability, factors discussed elsewhere in this book. Nevertheless, the greater the economic hardship, the more discontented a population will become with its government. The exact relationship between economic performance and political stability will vary across societies, over time, and among groups within the society. And under certain conditions, economic growth can even contribute to political instability. However, the general relationship in the long run is reasonably clear: slow economic growth, high unemployment, high inflation, and worsening inequalities all contribute to an erosion of regime legitimacy. Conversely, high economic growth, low unemployment, moderate price increases, and moderate inequalities (that at least are not growing rapidly and noticeably) will tend to contribute to legitimacy and thus to the stability of a political regime.

This chapter will examine the economic performance of Mexico from 1940 to 1970, a period of rapid economic growth. It will then look at the public policies that allegedly contributed to such rapid growth. Finally, it will ask what implications the pattern had for political support for the regime.

MEXICAN ECONOMIC GROWTH, 1940–1970

By historical standards, the world economy grew relatively rapidly in the years after World War II. In fact, the 1950s and 1960s were "the most remarkable two decades of economic growth in modern history."[9] The gross domestic product of the industrialized countries grew at about 4 percent per year during the 1950s and 5 percent during the 1960s. Even allowing for population growth, the rise in per capita gross domestic product for the industrialized countries was strong during this time. From 1960 to 1973, the industrial countries grew at a rate of about 3.8 percent a year, before slowing down to less than 2 percent a year for the remainder of the 1970s.[10]

It is not surprising, therefore, that this period was characterized by various "economic miracles." The first was probably the "German miracle" of the 1950s and 1960s, then the Italian miracle, the Brazilian, the Mexican, and of course the most astounding economic transformation of all, the Japanese. Later, the "four little tigers" of Asia—Taiwan, South Korea, Hong Kong, and Singapore—roared onto the world economic scene. In fact, many of the developing countries grew well during this time. For example, the GDP of Latin America grew at an average rate of 5.5 percent during the 1960s.[11] Mexican economic growth must, therefore, be seen in the context of general growth in the world economy. However, the growth of the Mexican economy was also unusual in some ways. The rate of Mexican economic growth was both higher than the world average and relatively stable for a longer period of time. While the industrial economies grew at the rate of 4.5 percent from 1950 to 1970, the

Table 3.1
Percent Growth in Gross Domestic Product and Population

	Years	GDP	Population	Per Capita GDP
Avila Camacho	1941-46	6.2%	2.9%	3.3%
Alemán	1947-52	5.8	2.9	2.9
Ruiz Cortines	1953-58	6.8	3.1	3.7
López Mateos	1959-64	6.7	3.3	3.4
Díaz Ordaz	1965-70	6.8	3.4	3.4

Source: Miguel Ramírez, *Mexico's Economic Crisis* (New York: Praeger, 1989), p. 46.

Mexican economy grew by over 6 percent per year. As one well-known economic historian wrote in 1978, "From 1940, Mexican growth continued for thirty-five years with a stability matched by few, if any, developing nations of the contemporary world."[12] The growth rates for the presidential terms from Avila Camacho to Díaz Ordaz are given in table 3.1.

An even more relevant comparison is with the other countries in the region. From 1935 to 1956, the per capita product of Latin America as a whole grew by about 25 percent, while that of Mexico grew by about 37 percent, or almost 50 percent faster. The contrast was particularly great with Argentina, which grew during this entire period by only 6 percent per capita. This fact may go far toward explaining much of the political volatility of Argentina during this time. While Mexico went smoothly from one civilian president to another from 1940 to 1970, Argentina experienced military coups in 1943, 1955, 1958, 1963, and 1976. During the 1950s and 1960s, Mexico's economy continued to grow well. In fact, it was virtually tied with Brazil for the fastest growing of the large economies of Latin America. (However, the fact that Brazil experienced a military coup in 1964 and then military rule for the next two decades indicates that rapid economic growth alone does not guarantee political stability.) Table 3.2 compares economic growth rates for the region and the larger Latin American countries from 1950 to 1970.

By contrast, the pattern for Argentina was almost tailor-made to contribute to political instability. The Argentine economy was relatively stagnant in general but punctuated by deep recessions followed by bursts of expansion that fueled inflation.[13] Mexico also experienced some variation, but the actual growth rates were always relatively high during the period. Even at their highest, Argentine growth rates did not equal the Mexican average of 6.5 percent for the period.

Mexico's per capita economic growth rates would have been even higher if the population had not grown so rapidly. Because of the rapid decline of the

Table 3.2
Growth Rates of Gross Domestic Product/Capita

Area	1950-60	1960-70	1950-70
Latin America	1.9%	2.9%	2.40%
Argentina	.9	2.6	1.75
Brazil	3.6	3.2	3.40
Chile	1.8	2.0	1.90
Colombia	1.5	2.2	1.85
Mexico	2.5	4.2	3.35
Peru	2.9	1.8	2.35
Uruguay	.8	.7	.75
Venezuela	3.8	2.7	3.25

Source: John Sheahan, *Patterns of Development in Latin America* (Princeton: Princeton University Press, 1987), p. 95.

death rate at the same time that the birthrate remained at a relatively high level, the population grew at a fairly rapid rate. For example, by 1960 the Mexican birth rate was 4.6 percent, whereas the death rate had declined to 1.1 percent, for a net increase in population of 3.5 percent a year. One result of this high population growth was that the increase in per capita GDP was considerably lower than the overall growth in GDP. However, the increase in real per capita GDP was still 3.3 percent for the period from 1945 to 1970, a very healthy figure by international standards. However, if Mexico had had its economic growth rates and Argentina's low population growth rates, its per capita achievements would have been even more impressive than indicated in table 3.2. Considering the Mexican economy as a whole, therefore, we could conclude that the regime performed very well in its task of guiding the society toward economic growth.

How did Mexico achieve consistently high economic growth rates from 1940 to 1970? Did government policies promote this growth? What policies did the Mexican government use to encourage the remarkable economic growth rate of over 6 percent in GDP and more than 3 percent in GDP per capita from 1940 to 1970? What other factors contributed to the growth?

Location

One important factor is not a matter of government policy but of geography and history. The country's proximity to the United States no doubt has played an important role in the recent economic history of Mexico. In terms of economic growth, it is important that Mexico is located next to a country that is the largest market in the world, one of the world's leading sources of investment capital and new technology, and a place to which millions of Mexican laborers could immigrate during these three decades. The U.S. economy has always been a latent factor in Mexican economic development, and sometimes it has played a more obvious role. Along with Britain and France, the United States played an important part in the development of the Mexican economy during the period of Porfirio Díaz's rule from 1876 to 1911. For example, U.S. investment grew by more than five times from 1897 to 1911. The $1.1-billion U.S. investment was almost three times the size of the French investment of $400 million and four times the size of the British investment of $300 million by 1911. Foreign investment greatly expanded the railroad grid as well as certain commodities for export, notably minerals, cattle, and cotton.[14]

Foreign investment plummeted, of course, from 1910 to 1920, then gradually increased again in the 1920s and 1930s. Then the virtual U.S. boycott of the Mexican oil industry after the nationalization in 1938 had a strong negative effect on the Mexican economy and on foreign investment. Gradually after 1938, however, the United States and Mexico reestablished warmer economic relations, and despite the Mexican laws that favored domestic over foreign investment, American firms continued their penetration of the Mexican economy. By 1970, 80 percent of direct foreign investment came from the United States. The bulk was in the modern manufacturing sector, instead of in mining and transportation, as in the earlier period.[15] Whatever the costs in economic independence, it seems clear that in terms of economic growth, Mexico benefited from its location near the United States.[16]

In addition, the United States was consistently the largest market for Mexican exports. Mexican exports grew well during the 1940s, increasing by almost four times during the decade. However, once the war ended, imports grew much faster than exports, which became a major source of weakness of the Mexican economy after 1950. The current dollar volume of exports increased by 66 percent in the 1950s and then rose by 114 percent in the 1960s. Unfortunately, imports increased even faster; the current account deficit (the difference between exports and imports) was a whopping $946 million in 1970. This was partly a result of the fact that as time passed after 1954, the fixed peso became increasingly overvalued relative to the dollar, meaning that imports were artificially cheap and exports artificially expensive. Thus having a huge economy next door was a mixed blessing. Mexico enjoyed a ready market for its goods, but its larger neighbor had an equally easy time supplying the Mexican market with goods. This was despite the fact that the government enacted various policies to encourage exports and discourage imports. This protectionist policy emerged suddenly. "In 1956, 25 percent of the total imports were controlled, but by 1970 almost 80 percent of all imports required a license before they could enter the country." [17]

A second way in which proximity to the United States played an important role in the Mexican economy was emigration. Large-scale emigration began in 1942 with the bracero program, as the United States requested that Mexico help with the Allied war effort by providing labor for U.S. agricultural production, filling in the manpower shortages created by the war. This program lasted until 1965. Since that time, emigration has largely been illegal, or undocumented. Over the entire period from 1942 to the 1970s, hundreds of thousands of Mexicans emigrated to the United States each year in search of work, either legally or illegally, permanently or temporarily, accumulating to several million. Perhaps one-third to one-half stayed in the United States, while the remainder returned to Mexico, usually with considerable earnings. This meant that unemployment and poverty in Mexico were never as bad as they might have been if the safety valve of migration had not been available. Large numbers of workers sent or took huge sums of money back to their hometowns, money that stimulated the Mexican economy. It has been estimated that undocumented Mexicans alone, not to mention documented ones, remitted about $1 billion a year from the United States to Mexico by the 1980s. [18] Emigration to the United States has ebbed and flowed and has been heaviest precisely when the Mexican economy was weakest, as in the 1980s. Such emigration might have sparked political discontent if the huge gap between the wealthier and more democratic United States and the poorer and more authoritarian Mexico had been used by returning Mexican workers to fuel discontent within Mexico. However, the effect of the migration seems to have been almost entirely to pacify the Mexican population, rather than to incite it. The opportunities to the north and the purchasing power that such economic opportunities afforded added to the growth of the Mexican economy and the stability of the Mexican polity.

The magnitude of emigration from Mexico and its connection to economic conditions can be seen in table 3.3, which shows the top five sources of legal immigration into the United States. In the 1950s, Mexico sent approximately 300,000 legal emigrants to the United States, behind Germany and Canada. By the 1980s, a disastrous decade for Mexico economically, Mexico had become the first source of legal immigrants, with almost one million for the decade.

In addition to the legal immigrants, a significant number of illegal immigrants also entered the United States, especially during the 1970s and 1980s. The Immigration Reform and Control Act of 1986 gave amnesty to over three million illegal aliens, 75 percent of whom were estimated to be from Mexico. This may significantly understate the number of illegal immigrants in the United States by the late 1980s, however; the number has been estimated to be between three and ten million. In the single year of 1989, the U.S. Border

Table 3.3
Immigration to the United States: Top Five Source Countries

Rank	1950s Source Country	Size of Flow (in 1000s)	1980s Source Country	Size of Flow (in 1000s)
1	Germany	478	Mexico	976
2	Canada	378	Philippines	478
3	Mexico	300	China	306
4	United Kingdom	203	Korea	303
5	Italy	186	Vietnam	266

Source: George Borjas and Richard Freeman, "Introduction and Summary," in G. Borjas and R. Freeman, eds., *Immigration and the Work Force* (Chicago: University of Chicago Press, 1992), p. 2.

Patrol apprehended 954,000 persons attempting to enter the United States illegally, about the same number as it apprehended in 1982. Many were probably the same individuals entering several times, rather than 954,000 different individuals, but many others were no doubt *not* apprehended, and so that figure might be roughly accurate. If 75 percent were from Mexico, that would be 715,000 illegals added to the almost 100,000 legals for a total from Mexico per year by the 1980s of 815,000.[19]

The importance of proximity was also intensified by the coming of World War II. As the United States shifted to war production, it was unable to produce as many products for export as it had, and so Mexican business stepped in to fill the gaps in the Mexican domestic market. This externally enforced policy of import-substitution industrialization began a pattern that persisted through seven presidential terms, lasting over forty years, during which the economy grew by an average of 6 percent a year.

Policies for Growth

During the war, the Mexican government became fully committed to the goal of industrialization.[20] As an integral part of its strategy of industrialization, the Mexican government enacted various kinds of restrictions on imports to stimulate domestic production. The Avila Camacho administration provided tariff protection for virtually every new industry that appeared in Mexico during the war, and subsequent governments continued that protection. A distinction was made between raw materials and other types of inputs to the industrial process on the one hand and finished consumer products on the other. The result was that import duties on raw materials tended to remain low while tariffs on finished products eventually climbed as high as 100 percent.[21] Even at this level, Mexican tariffs were only about average for Latin America.[22] In addition to tariffs, the government imposed a broad system of import licensing to control the importation of products that the government believed could be produced domestically. By 1970, about 80 percent of imports were subject to licensing requirements. The hope was that domestic producers would gradually be able to compete in the world market and would no longer need such protection, but few products made the transition, a fact that would come back to haunt Mexico by the 1980s.

Another form of protection was provided by the peso devaluations that the government conducted in 1949 and 1954. Between 1947 and 1949, the value of the peso fell from 4.85 pesos to 8.65 pesos per dollar, a fall of almost 80 percent. In April 1954 the peso was devalued by almost 50 percent in one day, from 8.65 to 12.50 pesos to the dollar.[23] Although these devaluations raised the cost of imported inputs for Mexican industry, they also reduced the cost of Mexican exports and thus helped further stimulate Mexican industry. However, the 1954 devaluation also gave rise to major popular protests by middle- and lower-income groups as well as a decline in confidence in the regime by business. Criticism of the government was unusually harsh and outspoken at this time, which helps to explain why the government took such forceful action to pursue price stability.

Tax policy was another device employed by the regime to encourage industrialization. Taxes remained low by international standards during this entire period. In addition to generally low taxes, the Mexican government also used specific tax policies to encourage the industrialization process. In 1941 the Avila Camacho administration exempted new enterprises from most forms of taxation for periods of five to ten years. In addition, new firms—as well as those deemed "essential"—received exemptions from tariffs on imported raw materials and machinery. The government also enacted other subsidies to encourage investment, and it maintained a ceiling on interest rates that made borrowing relatively cheap during the period of high inflation from 1940 to 1955. Later, when the government maintained a stable peso and price stability, borrowing remained relatively cheap for Mexican entrepreneurs because of the ceiling on interest rates and the political stability that made Mexico an attractive place for foreign and domestic capital to invest.

Another condition that contributed to economic growth was that wages increased more slowly than prices. One reason for this pattern was the large-scale migration of labor from rural to urban areas, which provided a large pool of cheap labor for urban industry. Millions of rural campesinos left the countryside and migrated to the cities, especially the capital, greatly increasing the supply of labor and thus depressing wages. In addition, the regime was willing and able to use the political institutions created during the 1930s to restrain the demands of labor. In the 1930s, urban labor had been organized into government-approved unions and then incorporated into the ruling party, where its demands could be monitored and moderated. Although the slow growth in real wages may have been undesirable from the point of view of labor, it allowed business to accumulate capital for further investment. Some research suggests that real wages fell from 1938 to 1955.[24] Yet the real per capita income of Mexico in general rose during this period. The apparent contradiction is resolved by the fact that even though the real wages of a given job may have declined, overall wages rose as employment generally shifted from agriculture to industry and from lower-skilled to higher-skilled jobs.[25] In particular, real wages in manufacturing grew at 3.8 percent a year from 1956 to 1972, about the same rate of growth as GDP per capita during this period. Thus the wages of manufacturing workers rose at the same pace as per capita income in general.

Unfortunately, prices rose rapidly during the first fifteen years of the period. Like many other Latin American governments, from 1940 to 1955 the Mexican government accepted a certain amount of inflation as a price of rapid economic growth. During this fifteen-year period, prices rose an average of 10 percent per year, and after the 1954 devaluation of the peso, prices shot up by 30 percent in twenty months.[26] This sparked protests by middle- and working-class groups and shook business confidence in the regime. This unrest came just two years after the significant challenge to the regime led by the populist General Miguel Henríquez Guzmán. A member of the Cardenista wing of the PRI, Henríquez Guzmán left the party in protest against the conservative pro-business policies of the government, especially the inflation that was eating away at the wages of the working class, and ran for president against the PRI candidate Adolfo Ruiz Cortines in 1952. Therefore, because of pressure from both the left and the right, and because of the economic logic of the situation, the political elite decided that the surest way to ensure economic growth and political stability was to try to eliminate inflation. Thus the government departed from the typical Latin American strategy of high government spending, low taxation, and monetization of the resulting fiscal deficit to a policy that involved more foreign borrowing to finance the deficit. The regime was able to maintain a stable peso for the next twenty-two years, with one of the lowest inflation rates in Latin America. During the 1960s, for example, Mexico had an average annual inflation rate just under 3 percent, compared with 20 percent for Argentina, 29 percent for Chile, and 48 percent for Brazil.[27] Mexico's radical departure from the Latin American model meant that of the four biggest Latin American economies (Brazil, Mexico, Argentina, and Chile), Mexico was the only one that moved from inflation to relative price stability during this period. In addition, its currency remained fixed at 12.50 pesos to the dollar for the entire period from 1954 to 1976.

This single policy decision on inflation illustrates the interaction of the fundamental qualities that account for Mexican political stability. The change of policy demonstrates the adaptability of the Mexican regime in shifting from a policy that it decided was no longer desirable as part of its overall strategy of economic growth to one that it thought would be more conducive to stable growth. The institutionalization of the regime gave it the confidence needed to pursue a policy that would not be popular with all sectors of society. The high degree of elite cohesion allowed the regime to be flexible enough to pursue a new strategy that would contribute to short-term problems, such as higher unemployment, but that would lay the foundation for longer-term economic growth. The ability of the Mexican government to pursue such a strategy stands in stark contrast to the inability of the Argentine government at almost exactly the same time to pursue a similar strategy with enough consistency to do any good. The Argentine government tried to pursue policies of economic stabilization at various times during the 1950s and 1960s, but labor unrest usually impelled the government to retreat from such policies before they could have a positive impact. Thus Argentina was characterized during this period by ''stop-go'' economic policies and by recurrent military coups.

To a certain extent, this policy continuity was a result of the continuity of personnel. The career of Antonio Ortiz Mena is a good example of this continuity, at least during two presidential terms. He served as minister of the treasury (Secretaría de Hacienda y Crédito Público, or SHCP) from 1958 to 1970, under both Adolfo López Mateos and Gustavo Díaz Ordaz. Of course, for one person to continue in the same position for many years can provide continuity, but it can also produce stagnation. Many of the ministers in the government of Porfirio Díaz served for many years and grew old in their jobs. The result in that case was policy stagnation. In the case of modern Mexico, however, it appears that a reasonable balance was struck between continuity and renewal. Ortiz Mena and his associates were able to provide Mexico with a consistent set of macroeconomic policies during this period that contributed to rapid economic growth with low inflation, which in turn contributed to political stability.

Not only was there considerable continuity in personnel and policy, but economic policy was unified in one powerful department, the Treasury (SHCP). As one observer wrote:

In Mexico, the separation between fiscal policy and monetary affairs has traditionally been slight. This is because the secretary of the treasury is charged with overseeing both the fiscal revenues function of the federal government and the financial policy of the Central Bank. Inasmuch as the Banco de Mexico is an agency of the Treasury, the orthodox separation of public finances and monetary policy is absent in Mexico. . . . During the period of Stabilizing Development, the subordinated role of the Central Bank provided an ideal mechanism for a very close coordination of fiscal policies and monetary management; indeed, it is almost impossible to separate monetary policy from fiscal policy during that period, so closely were they synchronized. This was possible because the Ortiz Mena–Rodrigo Gómez team thoroughly dominated Mexico's finances during that period.[28]

(Gómez was head of the Bank of Mexico during much of this time.) Thus economic effectiveness was partly a result of certain policies and the continuity provided by a single regime with a cohesive group of policymakers.

Finally, government spending was used in Mexico to stimulate economic growth and development. It is true that private investment increased more dramatically, from 48 percent of total capital formation from the early 1940s to 70 percent of the total by the early 1960s, while public investment fell from 52 percent of the total to 30 percent in the same period. But on average, during this thirty-year period, the public sector provided 30 percent of all gross fixed capital formation.[29] Although the public share declined, it was nevertheless substantial, especially in the early, crucial, years.

Even more important than the size of the public share of investment capital was how it was used. The share of public investment devoted to agriculture fell from about 20 percent in 1940 to 11 percent in 1960. These funds were used after 1940 not so much for land distribution as for development of the agricultural infrastructure, especially large irrigation projects that disproportionately benefited large holdings. By 1970, Mexico had more land under irrigation than any other country in Latin America.[30] At the same time, agricultural production shifted away from crops for domestic consumption, such as beans and corn, and toward crops for export, such as wheat. Thus not only did the share of public investment going to agriculture decline, but its composition changed from the promotion of small agriculture under Cárdenas to greater attention to infrastructure for large-scale export production.

Meanwhile, the share of public investment directed at industrial projects increased substantially. Avila Camacho doubled the share from 5 percent of total public investment to 11 percent, Alemán doubled it again to 20 percent, and Ruiz Cortines increased it by half again to about 30 percent of total public investment by the end of the 1950s. Large amounts were put into electrification and petroleum production. Policymakers identified bottlenecks in transportation and industry and used government investment to break them. Large government investment in the government-owned railways in the 1940s and 1950s helped to reduce transport inefficiencies that had resulted from the economic growth. Whereas under Cárdenas, public investment in agriculture consumed four times as much of total public investment as did industry, by the 1950s the share for industry was three times that of agriculture.

In addition to the distinction between agriculture and industry, another way to organize data on government expenditures has been offered by James Wilkie. He arranged federal government expenditures into three categories. *Economic* expenditures primarily include infrastructure such as irrigation, communication, and other public works. *Administrative* programs include military, debt, pensions, and general government. *Social* spending consists of education, public health, welfare, and similar programs. Wilkie arrived at the distribution given in table 3.4.

Table 3.4
Mexican Federal Budgetary Expenditure by Type of Emphasis and
Presidential Term

Years	President	Actual Percentage Distribution		
		Economic	Social	Administrative
1935-40	Cárdenas	38	18	44
1941-46	Avila Camacho	39	17	44
1947-52	Alemán	52	13	35
1953-58	Ruiz Cortines	53	14	33
1959-64	López Mateos	39	20	41
1965-70	Díaz Ordaz	41	21	38
1971-76	Echeverría	45	24	31

Sources: James W. Wilkie, *The Mexican Revolution: Federal Expenditures and Social Change since 1910*, 2d ed. (Berkeley: University of California Press, 1970), p. 32 for 1935–58, and James W. Wilkie, *La revolucion Mexicana: Gasto federal y cambio social* (México, D. F.: Fondo de Cultura Económica, 1978), pp. 322, 358 for 1959–76.

From the 1930s until the 1960s, the economic development share of the Mexican budget increased and the social and administrative shares declined. The proportion of federal expenditures devoted to economic development rose from 22 percent in 1933 to an average of 52 percent during the 1950s, before declining in the 1960s. Meanwhile, the share of the federal budget going to social and administrative purposes fell from the 1930s to the 1950s, before climbing once again. An oddity of the Mexican budget was that actual expenditures usually turned out to be much larger than the amounts originally budgeted at the beginning of any fiscal year (in contrast to the situation in most developing countries). As additional money became available during the budget year, most Mexican governments also used the extra money disproportionately for economic development purposes, rather than for social programs, illustrating once again the high priority placed on economic growth.[31]

Meanwhile, some other Latin American countries were devoting their growing revenues to the expansion of government bureaucracies, social security benefits, and public housing.[32] For example, Argentina under Juan Perón from 1945 to 1955 devoted almost 70 percent of all capital formation—both public and private—to housing and other government services, while economic infrastructure was starved for new investment.[33] The industrialization policies of

Mexico differed sharply from those of Argentina in almost every way, and these differences no doubt accounted for much of the gap in economic performance between the two countries.

Not only did the priorities of the Mexican regime differ from those of many other Latin American countries, but the Mexican government also managed to do a lot with a little. It taxed relatively lightly and then concentrated its minimal resources on economic growth. During the 1940s and 1950s, the ratio of taxation to GDP was lower in Mexico than in all other Latin American countries except Guatemala and Honduras. Low taxation is typical of countries in the early stages of industrialization; however, even taking that into account, the tax burden was very light considering what the Mexican government was trying to achieve. Various international studies consistently called on the Mexican government to raise its level of taxation in order to provide more public services and not to rely so heavily on foreign borrowing, but the government increased taxes only very slowly during this period. Government spending increased from only 10 percent of GDP in 1940 to 11 percent in 1950 and 12.4 percent in 1960. Most Latin American governments at this time taxed and spent much larger shares of their national income than did Mexico.

Although the Mexican state grew very large by the mid-1970s, from 1940 to 1970 it still represented a relatively modest part of the economy, and the achievements of the Mexican state in guiding the economy during this time are all the more remarkable when this is taken into account. Public-sector income increased from only 10 percent of the GDP in 1940 to 15 percent in 1964, a large relative rise (50 percent) but not a large absolute one (only 5 percent). Although the Mexican government took only about 12 percent of national income from 1940 to 1960, it managed to devote about 40 percent of that income to public investment. It was able to do this in part because it spent comparatively little on the military. Mexico could afford the luxury of spending little on defense because it had a neighbor to the north against which it could not defend itself, a neighbor to the south against which it did not need to defend itself, and a population that generally accepted the regime for reasons explained throughout this book. Thus the regime did not need a large army. The share of the budget devoted to the military declined steadily from 1920 to 1950. By the 1960s, Mexico spent less than 9 percent of central government expenditures on the military, compared with the Latin American average of just over 12 percent.[34]

Thus it is clear from both budgetary data and economic results that the Mexican political elite followed a strategy of promoting rapid economic growth, even at the cost of perpetuating great inequalities of income and wealth. But it is not only budgetary and economic data that demonstrate the Mexican elite's commitment to rapid economic development; their stated ideological values indicate such a commitment as well. After interviews with many members of the Mexican political elite over a period of several years, Roderic Camp described the ideological foundations of the modern Mexican elite and of Mexican presidents as consisting of several values. Paramount among them were a belief in a large state role in economic development, a preference for pragmatism over divisive ideology, and a strong commitment to peace, order, and political stability.[35]

Thus the Mexican strategy for development that evolved after 1940 and endured until 1970 was based on a number of interrelated policies. A strong and stable government enforced low wage increases on the urban working class while imposing generally low taxes on the population, especially on business and higher-income individuals. This allowed a high savings rate by business and the wealthy for investment in economic growth; the private investment was complemented by government investment aimed at projects that contributed heavily to economic development. The government maintained a stable peso and low inflation to create a climate of predictability that enticed domestic and foreign capital to invest in the economy. To encourage domestic capital to invest in the industrialization of the country, the government maintained restrictions on imports in certain industries through high tariffs and rigorous import-licensing requirements. Exemptions were given for imports that were necessary as inputs for the industrialization process, such as machine tools. Government spending on defense and social programs was kept low so that the available scarce revenues could be aimed at economic development through industrialization and large-scale agriculture.

Thus high economic growth was achieved by a combination of proximity to the United States, worldwide economic growth, and specific public policies that encouraged industrialization. But economic conditions affect not only a society as a whole but also specific individuals and groups. How did Mexican economic growth affect various social groups, and therefore, what implications did the pattern of economic growth have for political support for the regime?

GROWTH FOR WHOM?

For our purposes, the main reason to examine economic growth is to see what it may have contributed to the stability and legitimacy of the Mexican regime. Because GDP is such an aggregated figure that masks many details, it is useful to consider how various groups did during this period of economic boom. Who benefited from the strategy of development pursued by the Mexican regime from 1940 to 1970?

Business

In recent decades, governments of all kinds have discovered the degree to which their political success is dependent on economic prosperity and how heavily economic prosperity depends on the goodwill of business. As long as a large portion of a society's capital and managerial expertise is controlled by those who own or manage large business firms, the performance of those economies will depend on the optimism of private business. Thus business is a group without whose support, or at least acquiescence, the government of any capitalist society would find it difficult to carry on. How, then, did the Mexican regime perform from 1940 to 1970 on the measures that were important to business?

Business wants many things from government. It wants a solid infrastructure of public goods such as national defense, law and order, education, roads, ports, and the like. It often wants a structure of economic regulation that allows it to pursue profits in a relatively secure and predictable way. This may include high tariffs on its own products and low tariffs on the imports of its inputs. It usually wants low taxes, particularly on high income and especially on profits and capital gains. And it wants high economic growth so that there will be growing markets for its products.

Rapid economic growth is important to business, and we saw that the Mexican economy grew relatively rapidly from 1940 to 1970 and beyond. While the Mexican economy in general grew by more than 6 percent a year from 1940 to 1970, the manufacturing sector grew by almost 8 percent. At this same time, the agricultural sector slowed down from a growth rate of 8 percent in the 1940s to a more sluggish 4 percent from 1950 to 1970.[36] Yet even in agriculture, the growth was concentrated in the sector of large commercial farms that produced crops for export rather than smaller farms that produced for the domestic market.

Rapid economic growth contributed to both the ability and the willingness of domestic capital to invest in further growth. Although domestic business had confidence in the Porfirian regime from the 1880s to 1910, only about one-third of all investment came from domestic Mexican sources, whereas two-thirds was from abroad, just as in the United States at the same time, domestic capital simply did not exist in sufficient quantities to finance the industrial development that occurred during this period. By contrast, Mexico's economic growth after World War II generated domestic capital to the extent that almost 90 percent of investment capital came from domestic savings until the late 1960s.[37]

Mexico was not only growing; to a large extent it was also developing. Whereas "growth" is merely an increase in any measure such as total GNP, "development" involves the systematization of growth through an increase in complexity of the economy. Thus an economy might experience a growth in the dollar value of bananas exported, but we would call it "development" only if the economy became more diversified and more capable of sustaining economic growth through a self-perpetuating process of investment. As Roger Hansen noted: "Growth rates measure changes in physical output; economic development measures the institutionalization of the growth process itself. Development entails the better use of natural and human resources, changes in the structure of an economy, and the enhanced capacity to increase production through the savings-investment process."[38] Thus two fundamental characteris-

Table 3.5
Distribution of the Economically Active Population by Type of Activity,
1940–1970

Year	Agriculture	Industry	Services
1940	65%	13%	22%
1950	58	16	26
1960	54	19	27
1970	39	23	32

Sources: Roger Hansen, *The Politics of Mexican Development,* 2d ed. (Baltimore: Johns Hopkins University Press, 1973), p. 43 for 1940–60; Nora Lustig, *Mexico: The Remaking of an Economy* (Washington, D.C.: Brookings Institution, 1992), p. 17 for 1970. Lustig leaves 6 percent "unspecified."

Table 3.6
Structure of Production (Percent of Gross Domestic Product)

Category	1940	1950	1960	1970
Agriculture	23	21	16	12
Manufacturing	18	21	24	26

Source: Hansen, *Politics,* p. 43 for 1940–50, and Lustig, *Mexico,* p. 16 for 1960–70.

tics of economic development are diversification and the sustainability of growth. Up to a point, Mexico was moderately successful in both of these areas.

From 1940 to 1970, the Mexican economy became decreasingly agricultural and increasingly industrial, as reflected in the significant changes in the occupational structure during this period. In 1940, 65 percent of the economically active population worked in agriculture and only 35 percent in industry and services. By 1970, that ratio had been almost reversed, with 55 percent in industry and services and less than 40 percent in agriculture (see table 3.5). Thus the Mexican economy, as indicated by employment, came to be dominated less by agriculture and characterized more by a balance of economic activities.

Not only did the structure of occupations change, but of course the structure of production changed as well. As shown in table 3.6, the share of the gross domestic product produced by agriculture dropped from 23 percent in 1940 to

12 percent in 1970 while the share produced by manufacturing climbed from 18 percent to 26 percent.

The PRI is composed of three major sectors for small farmers or peasants, urban workers, and the middle class. Big business as such is not represented within the governing party. It was excluded in the original design of the corporatist party in 1938 under Lázaro Cárdenas, and it was never brought in, even by such a probusiness president as Miguel Alemán (1946–52). This does not mean, however, that business had no voice in the regime. Business had created peak associations by the early years of the twentieth century, at about the same time that they were being created in the United States, and these associations kept up a constant dialogue with government. In addition, the larger firms approached executive departments directly when they wanted special treatment.

When Cárdenas created the sectoral organization of the PRM, he encouraged business to organize itself for a dialogue with the government, even though that dialogue would not take place through the party.[39] It seems likely that Cárdenas excluded big business for two reasons. First, he recognized that business had the resources to give it great power relative to labor, without any help from government, and he apparently believed that one function of government was to try to correct some of the "natural" imbalance in the relationship between capital and labor. Second, he and his successors wanted the regime to be imbued with a legitimacy derived from the Revolution. For that to be the case, the regime must be seen to represent primarily workers and peasants, not big business—the disadvantaged, not the advantaged. Thus Cárdenas created an incomplete corporatism in the party, in that a major social force was excluded. He was willing to do this because he was not only creating a mechanism for representation and policy consultation but more fundamentally a device that would legitimize the regime in the eyes of the popular classes. He had no doubt that business would be well-represented in policy councils even without formal representation in the party.

At first, of course, business was ill at ease with the regime reconstructed by Cárdenas. Just when business thought revolutionary fervor had settled down in the 1920s and early 1930s under Obregón and Calles, the Cárdenas administration embarked on a whirlwind of economic reforms that ranged from encouraging strikes to expropriating land and oil. As a result, capital flight and inflation increased during the Cárdenas years, as business felt itself under siege. It is no accident that the main conservative party had its origin during Cárdenas's term as president. The Partido de Acción Nacional (PAN) was created in 1939 largely in response to the leftist policies of Cárdenas.

The end of Cardenista reforms came, however, even before the end of his term. His reformist policies had alienated business and perhaps contributed to a new recession by 1938 (although the more important cause of the 1938 Mexican recession may have been the U.S. recession of 1937–38). Thus in his last year or two in office, Cárdenas himself set the "counterrevolution" in motion, or at least acceded to it. He discouraged labor from further strikes, expropriated virtually no more property other than some agricultural land, and generally tried to assure business that the regime was not anticapitalist.[40] Finally, he selected the moderate General Manuel Avila Camacho as his successor.

Avila Camacho made it clear that he intended to behave in a way that was congenial to business (and to that other bulwark of conservatism, the church). As part of the new conciliatory posture toward business, his administration enacted a new Law of Chambers of Commerce and Industry, which allowed the creation of separate organizations for the two economic sectors. For the manufacturing sector, this led to the creation of the Confederación Nacional de Cámaras Industriales (National Confederation of Chambers of Industry, or CONCAMIN), which included the Cámara Nacional de la Industria de la Transformación (National Chamber of Transformation Industry, or CANAC-INTRA). On the commerce side (mainly retailing), the Confederación Nacional de Cámaras de Comercio, or CONCANACO, was also organized in 1941. A major goal of these organizations was to provide a forum in which industrialists could try to educate politicians and the public in the desirability of industrial growth.

Business did not like the leftward tilt of labor under Cárdenas, and it especially did not like the Marxist leader Vicente Lombardo Toledano. Thus, despite being his boyhood friend, Avila Camacho replaced Lombardo Toledano with Fidel Velázquez as head of the large labor confederation, the CTM. Velázquez rooted out what he considered the Communist domination of the CTM that had developed under Lombardo Toledano. Velázquez began what would be a half-century domination of the labor central, extending into the administration of Carlos Salinas. Although small wage increases were granted to urban labor, they did not keep up with the rapid inflation of the war years, as prices in Mexico City more than doubled from 1940 to 1945. The government enacted measures making strikes more difficult, and so labor was inhibited from using that weapon to push for higher wages. Labor became a bit less enamored of the regime during this time, but business prospered.

As in many countries, the distinction between the left and the right in Mexico concerns not so much whether government plays an active role in society and economy but what sort of active role. Both the left and the right saw the need for the state to take a role as a guide or "rector" of the economy, and even under the moderate Avila Camacho, the number of state-owned firms increased. However, President Avila Camacho put business representatives on the boards of many of the state enterprises, and his administration forged a labor-management social pact that virtually eliminated strikes during World War II.[41] His administration strengthened the Nacional Financiera, a government-owned bank for providing loans to industry and to oversee the industrial process. Meanwhile, the government helped Mexicans take advantage of the shortages created by U.S. attention to the war. Nacional Financiera made loans to encourage industrialization while the government enacted tax exemptions and tariff protection and allowed foreign participation in industrialization under the condition that Mexicans own a controlling share of each firm.

The Alemán administration (1946–52) is widely regarded as being perhaps the most single-mindedly probusiness administration in Mexican revolutionary history. Yet this administration also increased investment in public enterprises, with the addition of forty-one new state firms. The end of World War II brought a slump in manufacturing exports, as the United States and other countries converted to peacetime production. The regime sought to fill some of the gap through the encouragement of agriculture. Large-scale agriculture was especially enhanced through the development of rural infrastructure, and it responded by strongly increasing its share of exports. Mining and agricultural exports grew from 61 percent of the total in 1945 to 89 percent of the total in 1950.[42] To stimulate industrial production, the Alemán administration relaxed controls on the import of capital goods and tightened them on consumer goods. This contributed to a large inflow of machinery and equipment from abroad which in turn facilitated the growth of domestic production. This model of import substitution was strongly supported by business. The Alemán government also constructed a huge new campus for the National University of Mexico, which contributed significantly to the expansion of higher education opportunities for the middle class.

Alemán also demonstrated that he meant to restrain labor so that its demands would remain within what economic growth could afford, leaving business with ample profits to invest in further growth. Soon after taking office, he used the army to crush a strike of the oilworkers union and then imposed a tough settlement on the union. Two years later, he intervened in a factional dispute within the railroad workers union and imposed a tame labor leader on that union, a leader whose nickname (''El Charro'') gave rise to a new word, *charrismo,* to describe a labor leader who was subordinated to the government as opposed to one who looked out for the interests of the workers. Alemán also engaged in large-scale public works to improve the transportation network. His government modernized the railway system and completed Mexico's segment of the Pan-American Highway and the Isthmus Highway. It also built a four-lane highway from Mexico City to Acapulco and began to develop that little town into a major tourist destination.

Soon after Adolfo Ruiz Cortines became president (1952–58), Mexico went into recession. The new president pursued policies, such as price controls, to control inflation; business did not like some of the policies, and capital flight increased. Ruiz Cortines initially engaged in economic austerity, trying to reduce the government deficit in order to reduce dependence on foreign borrowing. But he maintained Alemán's emphasis on development of the economic infrastructure and streamlined the government bureaucracy a bit. When labor began to protest the government's neglect of its interests, the Ruiz Cortines administration increased social spending somewhat. However, inflation continued, and in April 1954 the government announced a devaluation of the peso, a major turning point in Mexican economic policy. During the Ruiz Cortines years, prices increased an average of 7.3 percent a year while wages rose 5 percent a year. This allowed greater profits for business, and kept inflation to a moderate level by Latin American standards, a fact that pleased both business and the middle classes to some extent.

Ruiz Cortines's secretary of labor, Adolfo López Mateos, dealt skillfully with labor unrest—repressing some, negotiating with others, but in one way or another resolving all of the disputes. Largely for that reason, he was selected to be the next president for the period from 1958 to 1964. At first, President López Mateos pursued policies favorable to labor, making concessions in social security, profit sharing, and other areas; but in return he demanded labor discipline. Moreover, most of his economic concessions were aimed at the demands of the middle sectors of society, including business. As his administration wore on, he tilted more definitely toward business in order to placate that sector after his early prolabor policies. However, he decreased the share of the budget going to economic development and increased the share for social programs, from 14 to 20 percent of the total.

The Díaz Ordaz administration was unabashedly probusiness, and virtually all of its policies were intended to strengthen private investment. Yet like other administrations, his saw a constant increase in the size of the public sector. Protected markets allowed prices of Mexican products to rise above world levels, and wage increases were greater than the increase in productivity.[43] Díaz Ordaz accepted the model that agricultural exports would finance industrial development, but unfortunately, agricultural exports began to decline after 1965. He tried to broaden the internal market through public investment in rural areas and fostered foreign investment.

Middle and Working Classes

In addition to business, and to some degree overlapping with it, another sector that benefited from the economic growth policies of the period 1940–70 was the urban middle class. In fact, one of the principal results of the economic development of this period was a significant increase in the size of the middle class. The class and occupational structure of the economy changed fundamentally from 1940 to 1960. As shown in table 3.7, the proportion of the population defined as lower class fell from 83 percent to 60 percent while the middle class expanded from 16 percent to 34 percent of the population.

By another indicator, the proportion of the population that was poor had declined steadily since 1910, if not before. James Wilkie combined such characteristics as illiteracy, speaking only an Indian dialect, customarily going barefoot, and other hallmarks of poverty in Mexico into a single poverty index. By that measure, and specifying 1940 as the base of 100, "poverty" declined, as shown in table 3.8.

Table 3.7
Class Structure of the Mexican Population

	1940	1960
Upper	1.0	6.5
Middle	16.0	34.0
Lower	83.0	60.0

Source: Hansen, Politics, p. 39.

Table 3.8
Poverty Index for Mexico, 1910–1960

1910	124
1921	115
1930	109
1940	100
1950	86
1960	72

Source: Wilkie, The Mexican Revolution, chapter 9.

However, other data suggest that simply possessing the trappings of modernity did little to help the poor during this period. One study suggests that the real wages of workers in the federal district fell from an index of 100 in 1938 to 50 in 1952, or almost one-half from the late 1930s to the early 1950s. They rose slowly over the next twenty years, but did not reach the 1938 level again until 1971.[44] Presumably this sluggish rise in workers' income was a result of wage increases that lagged behind the rate of inflation. During the early part of this period, inflation in Mexico was somewhat similar to that in most of Latin America. However, inflation subsided in the following years, averaging only about 2.5 percent a year during the 1960s, as shown in table 3.9.

Therefore, even though wage increases may not have kept pace with inflation, neither did Mexico experience the rampant inflation of some Latin American countries, inflation that eroded support for their regimes. For example,

Table 3.9
Price Index for Mexico City, 1941–1970

Presidential Term	Price Index
1941-46	14.4
1947-52	9.9
1953-58	5.7
1959-64	2.3
1965-70	2.8

Source: Ramírez, *Mexico's Economic Crisis*, p. 46.

inflation in Argentina was generally over 20 percent a year during the 1950s and 1960s. Thus the modest inflation rates in Mexico, especially after 1955, meant that even small increases in wages would not entirely be eaten up by price increases, as happened in so many other Latin American countries.

Some studies suggest that workers' real wages declined for over a decade after 1938 before beginning to rise slowly again in the early 1950s. This may have undermined support for the PRI among the urban working class. However, because of the changing composition of the work force, many individuals moved up to higher-paying jobs. Thus Mexican workers benefited more from "a shift in the occupational structure toward higher-paying jobs than from increases in real wages in given occupations."[45] The share of the labor factor in GDP rose from about 25 percent in 1950 to 35 percent by 1970. Meanwhile, the share of GDP accounted for by capital fell correspondingly from 67 percent to 53 percent.[46] This may have mitigated some of the loss of support that might otherwise have resulted from the decline in real wages for given jobs.

The Poor

However, despite the changing occupational structure and declining inflation, the share of national income going to the poorest groups apparently declined after 1960. A major problem with data on income distribution in Latin America is that it is almost impossible to find two sources that agree. Not only do studies differ on the magnitudes; they also often disagree even on the direction of change. One study may show an increase in inequality while another study shows a decrease for the same period. Nonetheless, a preponderance of studies

Table 3.10
Income Distribution by Quintile

Group of Families	1963	1968
I	4.6	3.5
II	7.1	7.3
III	11.9	11.5
IV	22.2	19.7
V	54.2	58.0

Source: Ramírez, *Mexico's Economic Crisis,* p. 73.

suggests that income inequality in Mexico increased from the 1950s to the 1970s, before a turnaround in the late 1970s. Table 3.10 shows the percent of national income going to each 20 percent, or quintile, of the population for 1963 and 1968.

The bottom group's share of total income suffered the sharpest fall, declining from about 4.6 percent in 1963 to about 3.5 percent in 1968, while other groups just about remained the same or improved. The most dramatic shift (in absolute terms) was in the income share collected by the upper quintile; their share rose from 54 percent to 58 percent in the mid-1960s. The pattern seems to be that middle- and higher-income people did well while lower-income people did not. However, data on income distribution vary a great deal from study to study, and caution must be used in interpreting such figures. Nonetheless, the general pattern seems to be that "stabilizing development was a model that fulfilled the economic hopes and ambitions of Mexico's modern classes, but not of those that still subsisted in—or close to—the traditional sectors."[47]

This applies especially to peasant farmers, who did not fare well during this period, partly because of large population increases and small government investment in infrastructure and credit that would have benefited them. Nevertheless, they remained the group that most predictably voted for the PRI. This, however, was probably due more to the ease of controlling their vote than to any material benefits they received from the regime.

One of the most thorough studies of the Mexican economy during this period concluded that although reliable data on income distribution are notoriously difficult to obtain, the available data suggest that by international standards, income was distributed quite unequally in Mexico and perhaps became more unequal in the 1950s. For example, the poorest 60 percent of the population

Table 3.11
Population of Mexico, 1910–1960

	Population (thousands)	Birth Rate (per 1,000)	Death Rate (per 1,000)	Rate of Natural Increase of Population (per 1,000)
1910	15,160	46	33	13
1921	14,800	45	28	17
1930	16,553	44	27	17
1940	20,143	44	24	20
1950	26,433	45	18	27
1960	36,003	46	13	33

Source: Clark Reynolds, *The Mexican Economy* (New Haven: Yale University Press, 1970), p. 18.

received just under 25 percent of the income by 1960. During roughly the same period, the poorest 60 percent of the population received 36 percent in the United Kingdom, 34 percent in the United States, 30 percent in Ceylon, and 28 percent in India.[48]

Of course, Kuznets pointed out in 1955 that economic growth was typically accompanied first by a trend toward greater income inequality, then a stabilizing of shares, and then finally a decline in inequality.[49] This pattern is largely a result of several accompanying variables: (1) an acceleration and then deceleration in the rate of population growth, first through a fall in the death rate and then through a fall in the birthrate (the first stage means that even an increasing family income must be divided among a larger family, thus producing a fall in per capita income); (2) increasing differences in productivity between rural and urban sectors; (3) larger increases in returns from profits and rental income than for wages; (4) the greater ability of upper-income people to save and thus to reap the benefits of profits and rental income; and (5) a swing in incidence of taxation that is at first regressive, especially on trade, and then progressive, especially on income.[50]

The growth of the Mexican population has been dramatic in the twentieth century. The rate of population growth rose from 1.3 percent a year in 1910 to 2 percent in 1940 and to 3.3 percent by 1960. This was largely a result of a drop in the death rate, rather than an increase in the birthrate, as shown in table 3.11.

This high rate of population growth continued until the mid-1970s, when it began to decline. The rapid population increase was largely a result of characteristics that accompany the modernization process, such as public health measures and improvement in nutrition. Thus more babies survived, and older people lived longer, producing a nearly two-thirds drop in the death rate from 1910 to 1960, even as birthrates remained stable. The result was a population explosion that eroded, on a per capita basis, many of the overall gains that lower-income people were reaping from the process of economic growth.

CONCLUSION

The segments that benefited disproportionately from the economic growth of 1940 to 1970 were large and mid-size business, urban labor, and the urban middle classes. Business benefited from the policies of import-substitution industrialization whereby Mexican firms and their workers were protected from international competition. Although troubles were building up for the future, by and large the Mexican economy did very well during this period of three decades. Millions moved from the poorer classes into the working and middle classes, and thousands moved from the middle classes into the ranks of the rich.

The effectiveness of the Mexican regime was, therefore, relatively high, at least as measured by the criterion of economic growth. The government fostered economic growth largely through policies designed to favor business (what might in the United States be called "trickle-down economics"). It generally avoided populist policies, which would have satisfied workers more, but which would probably have alienated the business support on which the regime depended. Capital flowed into Mexico during this time, industry flourished, and employment grew. A highly institutionalized government with a unified political elite was able to keep business contented with tax, subsidy, and tariff policies that made it easier for Mexican business to make a predictable profit. Thus one of the most important elites—business—upon which the success of political regimes depend in capitalist societies had good reason to be relatively content.

At the same time, organized urban labor did relatively well as the economy became more industrialized and workers moved into higher-paying jobs. One study suggests that, after falling by one-half from 1938 to 1952, workers' real wages in Mexico City slowly climbed to the 1938 level again by 1971. Thus organized labor made real gains during this period, although apparently only after initial setbacks. If the demands of labor went beyond what the regime was willing to allow, the government used the set of control methods available to it, including the imposition of *charro* labor leaders who generally cooperated with the government in holding down wage demands, the settlement of strikes on terms favorable to business, and repression when other methods failed to achieve the desired results. Although the level of control—especially repression—waxed and waned during the thirty-year period, it remained intense enough at all times to maintain a high degree of labor discipline, a strategy not unlike that used by other authoritarian political systems such as South Korea and Taiwan during this time.

A common phenomenon in the early stages of industrialization is a rapid increase in the rate of population growth. For several decades, birthrates remain high—typical of an agrarian society—while death rates plummet as a result of better public health and nutrition. Consequently Mexico, like many developing countries, experienced a population explosion during the period examined in this chapter. That fact helps to explain why per capita income and income distribution among the poorer groups did not improve faster than it did. Nonetheless, the Mexican economy developed strongly during these three decades, and Mexican society became increasingly middle class. For this and other reasons discussed throughout this book, the regime was able to maintain enough support to remain in power with virtually no serious challenges to its authority.

This chapter has argued that one factor making for regime legitimacy and hence political stability was the effectiveness of the regime in fostering economic growth from 1940 to 1970 (and in fact until 1982). But if economic growth is a factor contributing to political legitimacy and hence stability, why did Mexico remain politically stable in the 1980s, when economic growth came to a crashing halt? This shows the importance of the other factors for political stability—institutionalization, adaptability, elite cohesion, and coercion. While discontent grew in the 1980s largely as a result of the economic crisis, the elite remained relatively unified on the surface, even though some cracks began to appear in the ruling party. A group on the left wing of the PRI called the Democratic Current organized to press for changes both in socioeconomic policies and in the internal workings of the party, including the way the PRI's presidential nominee was selected. Eventually many of this group broke away from the PRI in 1987–88 and offered Lázaro Cárdenas's son as their candidate for president. In addition, the conservative PAN was able to win a number of local elections in the early 1980s, partly because of the economic crisis and partly as a result of the regime's willingness to experiment with greater democracy in an effort to defuse the discontent. Therefore, a lack of economic growth did produce discontent and some loss of support for the PRI in the 1980s. Nevertheless, the regime remained unified enough, and it was willing to use fraudulent elections and physical repression in its determination to remain in power.

Conversely, economic growth by itself is not enough to produce political stability. Mexico enjoyed high growth under Alemán, and yet in 1952 the regime faced its greatest political challenge in many years because of corruption, the decline of populist policies, and other issues. Despite the economic accomplishments of the regime after World War II, inflation, corruption, and declining real wages for some working-class groups did significantly damage its legitimacy. However, that is where the other factors came into play. After a new administration came into office in 1952 and paid more attention to the concerns of those who were disenchanted by developments over the previous few years, the discontent declined. Time after time, the Mexican regime has demonstrated this ability to adapt to the pressures that were uppermost at any particular time, in conjunction with coercion in case adaptability and the other factors were not adequate to the task.

However, although the economic model of "stabilizing development" that prevailed from at least 1955 to 1970 brought a number of economic benefits to Mexico, it also planted the seeds for future problems. Unlike several Asian countries during this same period, Mexico over-protected its manufactures and thus failed to develop an efficient manufacturing sector that could compete in the growing world market. It is true that the state has played an important role in guiding the economies of most late-developing countries, but the precise role has varied from one country to another. The government in Taiwan, for example, was able to pursue a coherent development strategy that emphasized exports.[51] Argentina, on the other hand, was so deeply divided between those economic interests that were export-oriented and those that were domestic-oriented (in addition to the intense hostility between capital and labor) that the government could never consistently achieve a coherent strategy of economic development.[52] Mexico at least achieved a coherent economic strategy for much of the postwar period, even if it was not necessarily the most effective for economic growth. The country probably would have been better off to pursue an export strategy more single-mindedly than it did and not preoccupy itself so much with efforts to protect its domestic industry. Whereas Mexico's economic growth averaged a very respectable 6 percent from 1945 to 1980, Taiwan and South Korea achieved growth rates of almost 8 percent during this period.[53] It seems likely, therefore, that the Mexican economy and others in Latin America could have grown even faster and in a more sustained way if they had relied less on inward-looking development and more on an export-led strategy.[54] For example, exports as a share of GDP fell from about 10 percent in 1950 to 4.3 percent in 1970, before recovering to 9 percent by1980.[55]

Largely because of the limitations of the Mexican development model, therefore, certain segments of the population became increasingly discontented in the 1960s. The major complaint, however, was not the overall rate of growth but the distribution of the benefits of growth (although if the growth rate had been higher, there would have been more to distribute). Those who favored greater equality of wealth and income, including some intellectuals, students, and members of the disadvantaged classes, thought that the regime had not done nearly enough to pursue social justice. Thus despite the economic growth since 1940, the growing inequalities, the alleged inattention to education, and also the demand for political liberalization all became the basis for a protest movement that was determined by the late 1960s to force the regime to change course. How the regime responded to those demands is the subject of the next chapter.

NOTES

1. For example, see Edward Tufte, *Political Control of the Economy* (Princeton: Princeton University Press, 1978), and Douglas Hibbs, *The Political Economy of Industrial Democracies* (Cambridge: Harvard University Press, 1987).

2. Stephen White, "Economic Performance and Communist Legitimacy," *World Politics* 38 (3), 1986, pp. 462–82.

3. For example, see Gabriel Almond and G. Bingham Powell, Jr., *Comparative Politics*, 2d ed. (Boston: Little, Brown and Company, 1978), pp. 30–34.

4. Sidney Tarrow, *Democracy and Disorder: Protest and Politics in Italy, 1965–75* (Oxford: Clarendon Press, 1989), p. 3.

5. This trade-off is shown in the "Phillips Curve." See Bruno Frey, *Modern Political Economy* (New York: John Wiley and Sons, 1978), p. 127.

6. James C. Davies, "Toward a Theory of Revolution," *American Sociological Review* 27, 1962, pp. 5–19.

7. Ted Robert Gurr, *Why Men Rebel* (Princeton: Princeton University Press, 1970).

8. Mancur Olson, "Rapid Economic Growth as a Destabilizing Force," *Journal of Economic History* 23, 1963, pp. 529–52; Lawrence Stone, "Theories of Revolution," *World Politics* 18, 1966, pp. 159–76; Samuel Huntington, *Political Order in Changing Societies* (New Haven: Yale University Press, 1968); and Eric Wolf, *Peasant Wars in the Twentieth Century* (New York: Harper and Row, 1969). For a summary of these and other arguments about the causes of political unrest and revolution, see Thomas Greene, *Comparative Revolutionary Movements*, 3d ed. (Englewood Cliffs, N.J.: Prentice-Hall, 1990).

9. Walt W. Rostow, *The World Economy: History and Prospect* (Austin: University of Texas Press, 1978), p. 247.

10. Arnold Heidenheimer et al., *Comparative Public Policy*, 3d ed. (New York: St. Martin's Press, 1990), p. 133.

11. Rostow, *World Economy*, pp. 284, 346.

12. Ibid., p. 492.

13. See Carlos Waisman, *Reversal of Development in Argentina* (Princeton: Princeton University Press, 1987).

14. Raymond Vernon, *The Dilemma of Mexico's Development: The Roles of the Private and Public Sectors* (Cambridge: Harvard University Press, 1963), pp. 42–43.

15. Peter Smith, *Labyrinths of Power: Political Recruitment in Twentieth-Century Mexico* (Princeton: Princeton University Press, 1979), p. 41.

16. Not everyone agrees that Mexico's location next to the United States has been an advantage. For a contrary view, see David Barkin, "Mexico's Albatross: The United States Economy," *Latin American Perspectives* 2 (2), 1975, and David Barkin, *Distorted Development: Mexico in the World Economy* (Boulder, Colo.: Westview Press, 1990).

17. Rene Villarreal, "The Policy of Import-Substituting Industrialization," in José Luis Reyna and Richard S. Weinert, eds., *Authoritarianism in Mexico* (Philadelphia: Institute for the Study of Human Issues, 1977), p. 73.

18. Alan Riding, *Distant Neighbors: A Portrait of the Mexicans* (New York: Vintage Books, 1984), p. 480.

19. George J. Borjas and Richard B. Freeman, *Immigration and the Workforce* (Chicago: University of Chicago Press, 1992), p. 3.

20. The following discussion of economic policies, unless otherwise indicated, relies on Sanford Mosk, *The Industrial Revolution in Mexico* (Berkeley: University of California Press, 1950); Clark Reynolds, *The Mexican Economy* (New Haven: Yale University Press, 1970); Vernon, *Dilemma of Mexico's Development;* Roger Hansen, *The Politics of Mexican Development,* 2d ed. (Baltimore: Johns Hopkins University Press, 1973); Roberto Newell and Luis Rubio, *Mexico's Dilemma: The Political Origins of Economic Crisis* (Boulder, Colo.: Westview Press, 1984); and Miguel D. Ramírez, *Mexico's Economic Crisis: Its Origins and Consequences* (New York: Praeger Publishers, 1989).

21. Mosk, *Industrial Revolution,* pp. 67–83.

22. John Sheahan, *Patterns of Development in Latin America* (Princeton: Princeton University Press, 1987), p. 87.

23. Ramírez, *Mexico's Economic Crisis,* pp. 68–69.

24. Ifigenia Martínez de Navarrete, *La distribución del ingreso y el desarrollo económico de México* (México, D.F.: Instituto de Investigaciones Económicas, 1960), and Jeffrey Bortz, "Wages and Economic Crisis in Mexico," in Barry Carr and Ricardo Anzaldua Montoya, eds., *The Mexican Left, the Popular Movements, and the Politics of Austerity* (San Diego: Center for U.S.-Mexican Studies, University of California, 1986), pp. 33–46.

25. Hansen, *Politics,* p. 50.

26. Ibid., p. 49.

27. Sheahan, *Patterns,* p. 102.

28. Newell and Rubio, *Mexico's Dilemma,* p. 141.

29. Hansen, *Politics,* p. 43.

30. Ibid., p. 45.

31. Dan A. Cothran and Cheryl C. Cothran, "Mexican Presidents and Budgetary Secrecy," *International Journal of Public Administration* 11 (3), 1988, pp. 311–40. Also see Dan A. Cothran, "Budgetary Secrecy and Policy Strategy: Mexico under Cárdenas," *Mexican Studies* 2 (1), 1986, pp. 35–58.

32. Tom Davis, "Introduction" to Tom Davis, ed., *Mexico's Recent Economic Growth* (Austin: University of Texas Press, 1967), pp. 8–9.

33. Carlos F. Díaz-Alejandro, "An Interpretation of Argentine Economic Growth since 1930," Part One, *Journal of Development Studies* 3, 1966.

34. Hansen, *Politics,* p. 69.

35. Roderic Camp, *The Making of a Government: Political Leaders in Modern Mexico* (Tucson: University of Arizona Press, 1984), pp. 130–40.

36. Hansen, *Politics,* p. 42.

37. Ibid.

38. Ibid., p. 43.

39. Roderic Camp, *Entrepreneurs and Politics in Twentieth-Century Mexico* (New York: Oxford University Press, 1989), p. 20.

40. Albert Michaels, "The Crisis of Cardenismo," *Journal of Latin American Studies* 2 (l), 1970, pp. 51–79.

41. Newell and Rubio, *Mexico's Dilemma,* p. 84.

42. Ibid., p. 88.

43. Ibid., p. 109.

44. Bortz, "Wages and Economic Crisis," p. 45.

45. Newell and Rubio, *Mexico's Dilemma,* p. 80.

46. Ibid., p. 160.

47. Ibid., p. 110.

48. Reynolds, *Mexican Economy,* p. 75.

49. Simon Kuznets, "Economic Growth and Income Inequality," *American Economic Review: Papers and Proceedings,* May 1955, cited in Reynolds, *Mexican Economy,* p. 75.

50. Reynolds, *Mexican Economy,* p. 82.

51. Alice Amsden, "Taiwan's Economic History: A Case of *Etatism* and a Challenge to Dependency Theory," in Robert Bates, ed., *Toward a Political Economy of Development: A Rational Choice Perspective* (Berkeley: University of California Press, 1988), pp. 142–75.

52. Guillermo O'Donnell, "State and Alliances in Argentina, 1956–1976," in Bates, *Toward a Political Economy,* pp. 176–205.

53. Nigel Harris, *The End of the Third World: Newly Industrializing Countries and the Decline of an Ideology* (New York: Viking Penguin, 1986).

54. Nora Lustig, *Mexico: The Remaking of an Economy* (Washington, D.C.: Brookings Institution, 1992). Also see Enrique Iglesias, *Reflections on Economic Development: Toward a New Latin American Consensus* (Washington, D.C.: Inter-American Development Bank, 1992).

55. Miguel Ramírez, "Stabilization and Trade Reform in Mexico: 1983–1989," *Journal of Developing Areas* 27 (2), 1993, pp. 173–90. Also see Nora Hamilton and Eun Mee Kim, "Economic and Political Liberalisation in Mexico and South Korea," *Third World Quarterly* 14 (1), 1993, pp. 109–36, and John Weiss, "Trade Policy Reform and Performance in Manufacturing: Mexico 1975–88," *Journal of Development Studies* 29 (1), 1992, pp. 1–23.

4

Adaptability and the Crises of 1968–1978

POLITICAL ADAPTABILITY AND POLITICAL STABILITY

We have seen that institutionalization and economic growth can promote the stability of a political regime. Yet those two qualities alone are not enough to ensure a regime's endurance. Many highly institutionalized regimes have collapsed partly as a result of their own rigidity, the Communist regimes being the prime examples in recent years.[1] Likewise, economic growth can certainly contribute to regime legitimacy and stability, but it can also create conditions for greater instability. Growth is not neutral; it almost always favors some groups over others, at least in the "short run" of a generation or so. For these reasons, a regime that wants to remain in power, if its rule is to be based on anything other than coercion, must be flexible enough to adjust to emerging social demands. It must address the sources of social frustration that can lead to efforts to replace the regime. Hence adaptability is another characteristic that can help a regime to survive.

Regime adaptability has been explored by numerous scholars. Chalmers Johnson has noted that adaptable political elites can avert revolution through "conservative change." The case studies in Gabriel Almond, Scott Flanagan, and Robert Mundt's book emphasized how explicit choices by elites for moderate change in response to the dominant pressures of their eras helped regimes maintain political stability even in difficult times. By contrast, the "breakdown of democratic regimes" has sometimes occurred in Latin America because of the rigidity of elites and their unwillingness to respond to growing pressures for change.[2] John Sloan's study of public policy in Latin America convinced him that "a nation must develop the capacity to shift gears in policy emphasis every five to ten years."[3]

The Mexican regime has often been willing to respond to increasing pressures for change by selecting leaders and pursuing policies to defuse dissent.

After the assassination of the revolutionary hero and former president Alvaro Obregón in 1928, President Plutarco Calles persuaded Congress to select an Obregón supporter as the interim president in order to dissipate suspicion that Calles was behind the assassination. When the depression led to a buildup of pressures for populist policies by 1933, Calles selected someone supported by the populist-agrarian wing of the party as the next president (Lázaro Cárdenas). When his populist policies—such as land distribution, increases in workers' wages, and oil expropriation—exacerbated the economic difficulties and alienated big business and the wealthy, Cárdenas chose a moderate to succeed him in 1940. Then in 1946 the probusiness Miguel Alemán was selected to continue the policies of industrialization that seemed to be working well. However, when the corruption of the Alemán administration became the salient political issue in 1952, the upright Adolfo Ruiz Cortines was chosen as successor. Adolfo López Mateos was chosen in 1958 in part because of his success in dealing with labor unrest. The selection of Gustavo Díaz Ordaz in 1964 could, in retrospect, be seen as the exception to the rule. It could be argued that the political elite failed to assess accurately the public mood in selecting him as nominee, although the youth rebellion had not yet manifested itself enough in 1963 for the elite to take it into account as a criterion in presidential selection. Thus the Mexican regime generally used the regularized succession to respond to the pressures that were impinging on the system at a given time.

The regime's flexibility has been displayed not only in who was selected but also in the policies that each new administration pursued: Cárdenas, populist redistributive policies; Manuel Avila Camacho and Alemán, economic growth through industrialization; Ruiz Cortines, an anticorruption program as well as continued economic growth; López Mateos, policies to mollify labor after several years of labor unrest; and Díaz Ordaz, order in a disorderly time. Apparently the political elite decided in 1968 that the primary need was maintenance of public order for the upcoming Olympic Games, and so the government ruthlessly cracked down on dissent and put a virtual stop to public demonstrations for many months. But this repression created a crisis of legitimacy for the political system, prompting many to wonder whether this regime deserved to be in power.

By the late 1960s, several factors came together to create an explosive situation in Mexico, producing the greatest threat to the regime in several decades. First of all, the Mexican model of economic development was beginning to show strains. It is true that the pace of economic growth continued unabated during the presidential term of Díaz Ordaz (1964–70), but the social imbalances created by that growth contributed to political tensions at a time when students and other activists were influenced by a worldwide climate of dissent. The initial challenge to the authority of the Mexican regime during this period came from the left as middle-class students protested the great inequalities that had accompanied the Mexican model of economic development. Students were eventually joined by middle-class office workers, urban labor, and peasants in protesting the trickle-down, probusiness policies of the regime. Those two stresses were then joined by a third—the government's commitment to host the 1968 Olympic Games—bringing the tensions to a crashing climax in late 1968.

Luis Echeverría's government (1970–76) responded to the dissent with a mixture of populist economic policies, greater cooptation of university graduates into positions in government and party, and eventually the repression of those who continued to protest the government's policies. The number of state firms increased tenfold as the government sought to use such firms to deal with social problems. Although the leftward movement of the regime satisfied some critics, it elicited the predictable response from business and conservatives, who vehemently opposed the government's populist measures. The reaction of business then led to the second crisis of this period.

Such conflict might have toppled many other Latin American regimes, but the fundamental strengths of the Mexican system once again manifested themselves. Mexico's institutionalized succession meant that those who opposed Echeverría's policies could look forward to a new administration, unlike in many other Latin American countries, where personalistic dictators' indefinite hold on power offered little hope of a change in public policy. Sure enough, the new president—José López Portillo—began his term in 1976 by adapting to the emerging pressures and reassuring business that his administration would be more congenial to their interests than the Echeverría administration had been.

At this time political stability was put under heavier stress than at any other time between 1935 and 1988, yet the system survived. While Echeverría was president of Mexico, many of the twenty Latin American republics experienced either an ongoing personalist dictatorship or a military coup. By contrast, the Mexican regime successfully made a peaceful transition from one president to another. Thus the Echeverría years dramatically illustrate the flexibility of the Mexican regime in adapting to the demands of the time. This chapter examines Mexican politics from 1968 to 1978, a time when the regime adapted by first moving sharply to the left from 1971 to 1976 under Echeverría. Then when the leftward movement itself created new tensions, the regime responded once again by moving to the right under López Portillo in 1976. Thus within a few years, the Mexican regime twice demonstrated in dramatic fashion one of its cardinal qualities—the ability and willingness to adjust its policies in ways calculated to deal with the most urgent pressures on it.

THE FIRST CRISIS

In recent years, it has been common for *crisis* and similar terms to be used to characterize Mexico. Thus we see accounts such as *Mexico's Economic Crisis,* "The Crisis of Presidentialism," and even *Mexico: Chaos on Our Doorstep.*[4] However, this sense of crisis is not new but had its genesis in the early 1970s. From 1940 to 1968, Mexican politics were relatively calm, although this period was punctuated by some turmoil, such as serious electoral challenge in 1952 and major labor unrest in 1959. However, these were relatively mild challenges compared with what was to come. From the mid-1960s to the mid-1970s, Mexico experienced political turmoil the like of which the country had not seen since the 1930s. Just after the presidency of Echeverría, books began to appear with such titles as *The Future of Mexico, Authoritarianism in Mexico,* and *Mexico in Crisis.*[5]

The late 1960s and early 1970s were years of political unrest throughout much of the world. Young people demonstrated in country after country as a contagion of political dissent swept through the industrialized world. Governments in many countries overreacted, although the degree of overreaction was generally in keeping with the political traditions of the particular country. In France, massive demonstrations and other forms of popular mobilization eventually led to the resignation of President Charles de Gaulle in 1969. In the United States, massive antiwar protests, the "police riot" outside the Democratic National Convention in 1968, and the shooting of students by the National Guard at Kent State in 1970 were signs of the times. In Germany and Italy, political violence escalated from 1966 to 1972, with levels of political terrorism that shocked Europe. Therefore, this was a time of intense political conflict in many countries, including even the "developed" ones. The events in one country undoubtedly had a demonstration effect on events in other countries. This is not to deny that indigenous issues existed in every country, but the spirit of the times, characterized especially by the mobilization of the young and of university students in particular, was infectious. The politically aware in Mexico knew of these events in other countries and were to some degree affected by them.

Díaz Ordaz, president from 1964 to 1970, was widely regarded as conservative and unsympathetic to the concerns of the student movement. Moreover, he was determined to maintain order for the Olympic Games, to be held in Mexico City in October 1968. This was the first time that a Third World country had hosted the Games, and the Mexican government did not want disruptions to mar the image of Mexico as a modernizing nation. As in many other countries in the late 1960s, however, students in Mexico had mobilized to protest various issues. Political discontent exploded on campus after campus throughout the country, and especially in Mexico City, from 1966 to 1968. A massive strike at the national university in 1966 led to the resignation of the rector, and federal troops had to be used to restore order on campuses in Sonora and Michoacán.

The major issue in the 1968 confrontation was government repression and the lack of civil liberties. The demands of the major student organization, the National Strike Council, called for a dismantling of repressive organizations employed by the government to beat and otherwise intimidate critics. According to Judith Hellman, "The student movement was essentially calling for the recognition of constitutional guarantees and the protection of civil liberties provided by the constitution."[6] But gradually the complaints expanded to include a criticism of the regime's record on social justice. The students were incensed at a government that would spend millions of dollars on the Olympic Games while millions of Mexicans lived in extreme poverty. Many young people were also upset at a political system that forced them to compromise their integrity by accepting a corrupt regime if they hoped to get a government job.

The dissident movement of the 1960s was broader than previous ones, which usually were limited to one group, such as urban labor. Its breadth and the fact that it included so many middle-class, educated young people made it fundamentally more threatening than previous ones because of the fear that the dissenters could mobilize a larger following to challenge the regime. Moreover, it came at a particularly embarrassing time for the regime. The government wanted Mexico to make a good impression on the world as host of the Olympics. Capable of mobilizing more than five hundred thousand people for a demonstration in the Zócalo, the dissidents tried to take tactical advantage of the government's sensitivity at this time. Unfortunately, they miscalculated the seriousness of the government's commitment to maintaining control. On October 2, 1968, just ten days before the Olympic Games were scheduled to open, a large crowd of students and others gathered in the Plaza of Three Cultures in the Tlatelolco district of Mexico City. Apparently without warning, army troops suddenly appeared and opened fire on the demonstrators, killing three to four hundred and injuring many more. At least two thousand were arrested.[7] The regime had obviously made a calculated decision to put an end to the student unrest in one bold move. This was an unbelievable slaughter in a country that was widely viewed in Latin America as a model regime.

In addition to the student unrest of this period, there were other signs of discontent with the regime. One was the declining share of the vote for the official party. In 1958 the PRI had received 90 percent of the presidential vote. By 1964 that had declined to 83 percent. Although this may not seem to be a large drop, in a political system with managed elections, even a small decline may be an indicator of serious difficulties. It is possible, of course, that the drop in support for the PRI may also have been a sign of the greater openness of the system, rather than only a measure of dissatisfaction with the PRI. For example, the electoral law of 1963 had provided for some proportional representation through awarding "party deputy" seats in the Chamber of Deputies to parties that won at least 2.5 percent of the popular vote for the Chamber. This had little impact on the vote for president, but it affected the composition of the Chamber of Deputies. The opposition share of deputy seats increased from 3 percent in 1961 to 17 percent by 1964.[8] Yet, as often happens when a relatively authoritarian regime takes small steps toward liberalizing political participation in an effort to satisfy the opposition, this move may have whetted the opposition appetite for more.

Another indicator of popular disenchantment with the regime was the increased level of voter abstention. The rate of abstention by eligible voters increased from 29 percent in 1958 to 35 percent in 1970.[9] Abstentionism is not easy to interpret, but it seems likely that it is more often a result of dissatisfaction than of satisfaction. Another indicator of popular discontent with the regime was the growing level of disrespect for the executive. López Mateos (1958–64) was the last president able to attend public functions without eliciting jeers.[10] For example, a large student demonstration of August 27, 1968, was punctuated by cries of "Death to the Monkey Díaz Ordaz." Public vilification of the president was a new phenomenon in Mexican history and may have been partly responsible for the vehemence of the regime's response to mass demonstrations in 1968.

By 1970, therefore, popular support for the Mexican regime had weakened considerably. Why did this occur? One of the major values that a government is expected to pursue is a growing economy with reasonably equitable distribution of the benefits of that growth. In chapter 3 we examined the "Mexican economic miracle," by which the real gross domestic product grew by an average of over 6 percent a year from 1940 to 1970, one of the highest growth rates in the world. Moreover, the growth rate of the Mexican economy did not slow down in the 1960s; during Díaz Ordaz's term (1964–70), it reached 6.8 percent, the same as in the previous two presidential administrations. Per capita real GDP also grew as fast during this period as it had previously (3.4 percent). Was there, then, an economic basis for the discontent?

Although there was no slowdown in total or per capita GDP during the Díaz Ordaz years, certain imbalances were notable. First, agricultural output consistently lagged behind industrial output from 1941 to 1964, but from 1965 to 1970 the gap grew particularly large (8.7 percent growth in industrial output versus 3.3 percent annual growth in agricultural output). This was partly a result of the huge gap between public investment in industry and in agriculture, which grew ever larger from 1953 to 1970. By the Díaz Ordaz years, the government spent 40 percent of its total investment on industrial development and only 11 percent on agricultural development.[11] Although Mexico had become increasingly urban, 40 percent of the population was still rural in 1970. Yet agriculture produced only 12 percent of GDP by that date.[12] There was a growing public awareness that economic growth had been accomplished at the expense of Mexico's poorest citizens, the rural peasants, one of the main groups that the revolutionary party had promised to help.

Not only did the rural population reap the benefits of economic growth less than did the urban population, but as typically occurs in the early stages of industrialization, income and wealth in general became more unequal after the 1930s. One study reported the Gini Coefficient (a measure of income inequality) for Mexican household income as follows (the larger the coefficient, the more unequal the distribution of income):[13]

1950   .526

1957   .551

1963   .555

1968   .577

1975   .579

Although data on income distribution must be viewed with caution, it appears that income inequality grew worse in the three decades after World War II. In addition, the percentage of disposable income received by the poorest 40 percent of the Mexican population dropped from 14 percent of the total in 1950 to only 8 percent by 1975.[14] Not only were Mexico's poorest becoming worse off relative to other social classes, but the poorest twenty percent of the population apparently also became worse off in absolute terms between 1950 and 1968. Some data suggest that their real income declined by 12 percent during this period and continued that decline into the 1970s.[15]

A previous period of unrest, in the late 1950s, had involved mainly the urban labor movement. In a wave of unauthorized strikes, workers had tried to regain some of the economic ground they had lost in purchasing power since 1945. However, the government responded to the strikes with severe repression in 1958–59, jailing some of the labor leaders for years. Thus the labor movement was largely cowed for a time after 1959. Because economic conditions continued to worsen for the urban and rural poor, these groups were also involved in the unrest of the late 1960s. Peasants especially were involved in considerable conflict over land and other issues. However, as often occurs, intellectuals and other educated groups spoke for the poor in criticizing the inequities of the Mexican economy and the apparent abandonment of the social goals of the Revolution.

The 1968 movement was, therefore, led mainly by representatives of the middle class, urban students, and intellectuals who objected to a model of economic development that emphasized growth so notably over distribution. They demanded more economic opportunities not only for themselves but also for those who had benefited least from the economic growth of the previous thirty years. As indicated before, the demonstrators were also influenced by the worldwide climate of political mobilization and dissent. Once the demonstrations began, however, and the government reacted roughly, the issue of government repression itself became paramount. One of the largest demonstrations occurred when the rector of the National University and a group of well-known professors led some eighty thousand students and teachers through the university and downtown Mexico City in what was to be the first of several very well organized mass demonstrations. As the march continued, shop employees, small merchants, professionals, and other middle-class people left their offices and stores to cheer the demonstrators, and some even fell in behind them.

The regime responded brutally to the student movement for two reasons. The government wanted order for the Olympic Games, which were to begin in a few days. Perhaps more important in the long run, however, was the government's apprehension that the student movement, if allowed to continue, would attract ever-larger numbers of supporters, including workers and peasants. The president apparently decided that the outcome of all this mobilization was too unpredictable to tolerate. Thus the regime reacted in 1968 with shocking repression, which thoroughly intimidated the dissenters. The man to whom the regime turned in 1970 to restore its legitimacy and stability was ironically the minister of the interior who had presided over the massacre at Tlatelolco, Luis Echeverría.

THE REGIME'S RESPONSE

Institutionalization and Adaptability

Popular discontent and mobilization resulted in military coups against numerous Latin American governments during this period. As elites became apprehensive about the level of popular unrest and populist policies, the military toppled the governments of Brazil in 1964, Argentina in 1966, Peru in 1968, and even two of the most stable systems in Latin America—Chile in 1973 and Uruguay in 1974. Many of these military regimes remained in power for years, giving rise to a new term in Latin American politics—the "bureaucratic-authoritarian" regime.[16] Although Mexico may have had some qualities in common with such regimes, it did not fall under the control of a harsh military dictatorship. Seen in a broader perspective, therefore, events in Mexico do not seem so extreme. For example, it has been estimated that up to four hundred people were murdered in Mexico for political reasons from 1970 to 1982. Contrast that with the seven hundred estimated political deaths in Chile from 1973 to 1986, almost twice as many deaths in a country with only one-seventh the population. Or more starkly, contrast it with Argentina, a country with one-third the population of Mexico, that suffered 20,000 political deaths in the "dirty war" of the late 1970s. Even one political death is too many, but all things considered, Mexico handled the turmoil with far less repression than did some other Latin American countries. Thus Mexico experienced dissent, and the government did react with repression during this period, but the regime did not fall. Why did Mexico not succumb to this common Latin American pattern?

First, the level of dissent in Mexico must not be exaggerated. Active public mobilization against certain government policies was probably greater than at any other time in decades, but it remained limited in scope. Although the mobilization was relatively broad compared with past unrest, it involved mainly students and other young people rather than huge numbers of peasants, workers, or the middle class. And most notably, it did not involve the economic elite, who were relatively content with the economic policies pursued by the regime from 1940 to 1970. Nonetheless, the level of mass dissent that occurred in Mexico between 1966 and 1968 might have brought down many a Latin American government. Yet the Mexican regime was not even close to collapse.

One major reason was the degree of institutionalization of the political system, especially the presidential succession. People at all levels, from peasants to university students to army generals and businessmen, could be confident that a new president and administration would take office as scheduled on December 1, 1970, and there was the possibility that matters might improve. For the president and most top officials to change every few years in regular rotation provided at least some basis for hope and patience. As noted previously, there were remarkable similarities between the present regime and the prerevolutionary regime of Porfirio Díaz. Both were highly centralized, relatively authoritarian, and characterized by the use of corruption as a motivational device and the ritual use of elections to renew loyalty to the regime rather than to select leaders. But the most important way in which the Mexican regime in 1970 differed from the Porfirian regime was in its degree of institutionalization, especially in the depersonalization of power and in the rotation in office of government officials, particularly the president.

Institutionalization can contribute to stability in many ways, but one important way is through the circulation of elites. It was true that the new Mexican president always came from within the existing political elite; indeed even the identity of the next PRI candidate became relatively predictable. From 1946 to 1970, four of the five presidents were secretary of *gobernación* (interior) at the time of their selection as the presidential nominee. Yet it is never completely certain who will be selected as the next president, and the top members of the political elite can maintain their hope that they will flourish in the next administration. Also, new presidents often brought new policy emphases, as policy centers of gravity shifted from left to center to right, and back again, across presidential terms.

Many officeholders in the new administration were holdovers from the previous one, and the same basic regime continued. However, the degree of continuity of personnel should not be overstated. Although numerous people made an entire career of appointive and elective government office, a close student of Mexican political recruitment wrote at the end of the Echeverría years: "A person who has reached national office under one president has about a 1 in 3 chance of holding a comparable position under another president. A large-scale change in personnel has thus taken place with every sexennial change in the presidency, and those who disappear from the national scene rarely return."[17]

The change of personnel that comes with each new administration was of a greater magnitude under Echeverría than under most other Mexican presidents, and since the most vociferous attacks came from the left, the administration adapted first in that direction by trying to appease its critics. Echeverría made a special effort to appeal to two groups who seemed most disaffected by the course of Mexican development up to that time—educated young people and intellectuals. He brought more young people into his administration than any previous president, lowered the voting age to eighteen, reduced the age for holding a senate seat to thirty and a chamber of deputies seat to twenty-one. A related move was the creation of a new university, the Autonomous Metropolitan University of Mexico City. This made higher education available to a larger segment of the young and added another source of employment for young professors. Furthermore, the government bureaucracy in general was greatly expanded under Echeverría, particularly in the parastatal agencies, providing jobs for additional university graduates.

Much more than in the United States, Mexican intellectuals have tried to involve themselves in politics and government. It appears that in Latin America, social prestige is achieved more by public influence than by accumulated wealth, as in the United States. By Roderic Camp's calculation, "The majority of Mexico's prominent intellectuals have held posts in the government (53 percent)."[18] Although I am not aware of comparable data for the United States, the figure is almost certainly much lower. Moreover, revolutions are often sparked by the discontent of intellectuals and other members of the "subelite"—those just below the top who are excluded from full enjoyment of the economic, social, or political benefits of the existing system. Thus what intellectuals think about a political regime has important implications for stability. Mexican intellectuals, in comparison with those in the United States, appear to be overwhelmingly leftist. That is, they especially supported the revolutionary tenets that called for policies of nationalism and social justice. Echeverría's move to the left, therefore, was designed as much as anything to attract many of the opinion leaders who had become disaffected by 1970. For example, numerous university professors had been involved in violence against the government during the second half of the 1960s. The regime had always tried to co-opt intellectuals and others whose support was necessary for political stability. Camp notes, "But as opposition to serving the government among certain educated groups and among intellectuals themselves increased in the 1960s, joining the government became an obvious sellout of their ideas and the organizations they represented."[19] Thus Echeverría tried to attract such people back into the fold by reinvigorating the revolutionary credentials of the regime.

The famous sociologist Pablo Gonzáles Casanova was appointed rector of the national university; the novelist Carlos Fuentes acted as a link between Echeverría and liberal U.S. intellectuals and was subsequently appointed ambassador to France. Some leaders of the leftist Movement for National Liberation (MLN) were given important positions, including Victor Flores Olea, who became ambassador to the Soviet Union. Moreover, some leaders of the 1968 student movement even entered the government.[20] Two of the most notable examples of the co-optation of leftists were Jesus Reyes Heroles, a writer and former UNAM professor, who was named president of PRI, and Enrique Gonzáles Pedrero, former director of the faculty of political and social sciences at the national university (and MLN activist), who was appointed secretary general of PRI and director of the government's television station. As Yoram Shapira says, these appointments "infused new blood into the party's leadership and were indicative of the government's intention to improve communication with intellectuals."[21]

Thus many intellectuals did serve in the government, whether for prestige, economic security, or in the belief that they could influence government policy. The Echeverría government took a number of other actions designed at least in part to appeal to intellectuals. It freed numerous political prisoners, increased the university budget, allowed greater university autonomy, tolerated significant criticism in the press, and generally cultivated intellectuals through personal contacts, offers of employment, and other means.[22] Hence the new administration appeared to be adapting to demands for change, at least as far as new personnel were concerned.

Equally as important as the hope of change, real change may accompany the circulation of elites. To solidify their position, the new elites may respond effectively to the main sources of discontent in the previous administration. Thus the various characteristics of the Mexican regime are linked. The institutionalized circulation of elites means that many new people come into office every six years. Although they are from the same political party as those who are leaving office and are closely associated with them, the mere fact that they are different individuals presents at least the possibility that they will see things in a different light and will be open to new policies. Those who move from the middle to the top in the new administration tend to be aware of the problems that need to be addressed and to be familiar enough with the political system to be able to address those problems. That potentially endows the regime with greater flexibility to respond to the accumulated political pressures than regimes with less circulation of elites. Hence the turnover of personnel may focus governmental attention on problems largely ignored by the previous administration and allow the new government to be more effective in dealing with certain problems than was the previous government. Thus the institutionalization, adaptability, and effectiveness of the regime all reinforce each other.

It should be noted that the argument that new leaders make a difference in policy is not universally accepted. For example, much of the research on policy-making in advanced industrial societies suggests that broad structural factors such as the wealth of the country, the pluralist-corporatist style of decision making typical of the late twentieth century, the demands of a capitalist economy, and the bureaucratization of policy implementation virtually dictate how a given regime will respond to particular social problems. In such a structured environment, it would seem that a change of leaders can make little difference. Thus, for example, whereas economic conditions can certainly affect the fortunes of individual political leaders, there is some reason to believe that those leaders and their policies can seldom influence broad economic conditions.[23] If we are inclined to believe that personalistic leaders in less-developed countries hold greater sway over their societies than do leaders in industrial societies, dependency theory reminds us that less-developed countries are even more powerfully constrained by the international economic system than are the industrial countries.

Yet other research suggests that "new leaders do make a difference." One study examined leadership changeover in socialist and Western democratic nations and concluded that new leaders do matter. Especially in their first couple of years, new leaders bring with them changes in budgetary priorities and in the thrust of social and economic policies. This study concluded: "In both socialist and bourgeois democratic states, succession . . . affects the nature of the policy process and hence the amount of change in priorities that occur. In the absence of succession, policy change is generally small and consistent; in its presence, innovation (but circumscribed, it must be emphasized), not incrementalism, is the more pronounced tendency." [24]

Various studies of Mexican policy and budgeting have reached a similar conclusion that change of administration brings changes in policy. It is true that in his 1963 book, *The Dilemma of Mexico's Development,* Raymond Vernon argued that Mexican presidents were increasingly constrained by the institutionalization of power in the Mexican political system. [25] Hence, in terms used in this book, one of the characteristics of the Mexican political system (institutionalization) weakened, rather than strengthened, another characteristic (adaptability). In Vernon's view, therefore, public policy choices emerged as a result of the conflicting interests within the official party, rather than as the preferences of individual presidents. In his 1967 book, however, James Wilkie sought to demonstrate that considerable differences existed in the budgetary priorities of the various presidents, despite the institutionalization of the regime. A summary of those differences can be seen in table 3.4.

Then, using Wilkie's data, James Hanson tested the apparent contradiction between the institutionalization of political power within the regime and the persisting personal power of individual presidents in resource allocation decisions. He compared a "personalistic" explanation of expenditure decisions with an "institutionalized" one in an effort to determine whether presidential preferences or wider institutional forces best account for expenditure patterns. Hanson found significant differences in the pattern of budgetary allocations between presidential administrations. For almost every president, the budgetary figures show a reality that is more complex than the image. López Mateos's image as a president concerned with social programs is upheld both by the budgetary data and by specific programs that his administration enacted, such as land distribution, profit sharing, and other labor and agrarian policies. But Díaz Ordaz's image as a conservative hard-liner is complicated by the budgetary data. Díaz Ordaz continued the balanced pattern of expenditures begun by López Mateos as the share of the budget going to social spending rose to over 20 percent while the share for administration went down. One part of administrative spending is particularly interesting, given Díaz Ordaz's reputation after the violent government response to demonstrations in 1968: the projected share of the budget going to the military held steady during his term, but the actual share declined. On the other hand, Echeverría was known as a populist president, yet he allocated a larger share of the budget to economic programs than was indicated by his projected budget. This is quite surprising, given his anti-business rhetoric. Nonetheless, Echeverría did manage to achieve the highest share for social expenditures in Mexican history, almost 24 percent of actual expenditures, which is consistent with his image. According to Wilkie, the percent of the budget devoted to social programs by presidents from Cárdenas to Echeverría was as follows: Cárdenas, 18; Avila Camacho, 17; Alemán, 13; Ruiz Cortines, 14; López Mateos, 20; Díaz Ordaz, 21; and Echeverría, 24.[26] Thus it can be seen that Mexican presidents sometimes dramatically changed the priorities of public policy. Alemán abruptly dropped the social share of the budget by one-fourth, López Mateos strongly increased it by a third, and Echeverría pushed it to new heights. Thus budgetary data offer some support for the influence of individual leaders, or at least leadership succession, on public policies. As in Valerie Bunce's study, the largest shifts in policy came during the "honeymoon" period of each executive.

The Political Initiatives

When Echeverría was given the presidential nomination of the official party in 1969, he was fully aware that the Mexican political system was in a state of crisis.[27] Mexico had experienced episodes of unrest in the previous three decades, but they paled by comparison. Incidents of unrest since 1940 had been localized and involved specific demands, whereas the unrest after 1966 was much more widespread and involved more fundamental demands for societal change rather than simply specific benefits for particular groups. The demands of the student demonstrators of the late 1960s were far more comprehensive and complex: a more responsive and participatory political system, greater social justice, and a more equitable distribution of income and opportunity.[28] Mexico had become a far more urban and industrial society in the forty years since the creation of the ruling party. The urban middle class seemed to believe that it was not allowed to participate fully enough in politics. In particular, many university students and recent graduates were disenchanted with the political system. They not only demanded different substantive policies to combat what they saw as the serious problems of society but also sought procedural changes that would allow more democratic participation in politics.

When Echeverría received the presidential nomination, he apparently believed that the fundamental problem was the loss of legitimacy that the regime had suffered in recent years. Several basic strategies are available to any political leader facing a crisis of legitimacy, with its frequently accompanying crisis of public order. Politically, a leader can expand participation, either symbolic or real, or he can increase the use of repression to put down challenges to the regime. Economically, a leader also has two basic choices—growth or distribution. He can attempt to stimulate economic growth and hope that the expanded economy will satisfy most people, or he can try to redistribute existing resources. Echeverría tried all four of these approaches, either simultaneously or sequentially, but eventually he came down most forcefully for redistribution and repression.

The specific policy choices that political leaders make are partly a function of their definition of the problems that they face. Since at least 1876, the Mexican regime has tended to define its central political problem as the need for political order. This is not unusual, since virtually all governments define their fundamental political problem in that way. Where regimes or administrations differ is in the strategies that they use and the constraints that they put on themselves as they pursue the essential goal of political order. The Porfirian regime from 1876 to 1911 pursued political order with a minimum of political participation by society. The postrevolutionary regime since 1920 has pursued political order with a modicum of highly structured political participation. The revolutionary regime has always structured political participation very tightly within one party, with its constituent organizations closely controlled by the government. The last thing that it wanted, especially at this time, was a large amount of uncontrolled political activity that could get out of hand. The absolute constraint within which each Mexican president since 1920 has worked is that the ruling group would retain the presidency and virtually all other political offices. That meant, therefore, that the regime could not look to a turnover of power to an opposition party for solutions to the key problems of political order and regime legitimacy. Allowing an opposition party to come to power was not seriously considered. Instead, the expansion of participation was limited to minor changes and symbolic gestures. Beyond that, most of the burden of adapting to social pressures and maintaining regime legitimacy came to rest on the presidential succession within the revolutionary party.

The political strategy of allowing greater political participation took various forms. In 1963 the government had tried to reduce discontent by making it easier for opposition parties to gain official registration and to win seats in the Chamber of Deputies. But the continued monolithic control of power by the PRI had so demoralized opposition groups that two of the older opposition parties (the PPS and the PARM) failed to gain even the minimum 2.5 percent of the national vote in the 1964, 1967, and 1970 congressional elections. Nevertheless, the government awarded them some proportional representation seats in the Chamber. (The PAN did win a number of proportional representation seats by achieving the threshold 2.5 percent of the vote.) Then, in a further effort to build up a credible but nonthreatening opposition, in 1972 the government once again reduced the threshold for gaining proportional representation seats in the Deputies from 2.5 percent to 1.5 percent of the popular vote. This led to the creation of at least eight new parties during the Echeverría sexenio alone. Seven of the eight were generally leftist; only one (the Mexican Democratic Party, or PDM) was conservative.[29]

The 1972 law was typical of the way the Mexican regime tried to use mild electoral reform as a means of recognizing the opposition and incorporating it into the political system. Yet the regime continued to win—through fair means or foul—virtually all federal, state, and local offices other than the proportional representation seats that it assigned to the opposition in the Chamber of Deputies. Thus as in 1963 and later in 1977, 1986, and 1990, the electoral reforms were not allowed to go so far as to threaten the hegemony of the PRI, and yet they bought time for the regime by giving the opposition some hope that future elections would be more competitive.

"Symbolic politics" is another form of participation and is a significant way in which governments maintain their legitimacy and popularity. Methods can range from a flag and a national anthem to the use of war as a device for whipping up patriotism. Policies may be both substantive and symbolic, and in fact most policies have both qualities. That is, they may be intended to have actual effects on "objective" conditions such as income distribution or environmental pollution, but most governments also engage in activities that have mainly symbolic implications. The Mexican regime has put a lot of effort into symbolic politics, and it has become one of the world's leaders in attempting to manipulate symbols to maintain legitimacy and order. The most obvious example of its symbolic politics, of course, is the continuing claim to being a "revolutionary" regime. This claim has included many elements, such as the identification of the party with the government, but it has taken many more specific forms.

After his nomination, Echeverría began an active presidential campaign designed to convince dissidents that peaceful change was possible within the existing system. He conducted the most active and populist presidential election campaign since Cárdenas in 1934. In fact, Echeverría may have envisioned himself as heir to the Cárdenas mantle of populist leadership (Cárdenas died in October 1970, two months before Echeverría took office). Echeverría dressed more casually, especially in the *guayabera* shirt. After his election, he took frequent weekend trips to remote regions of the country. He drew even closer to Fidel Castro than had most other Mexican presidents. He referred to his wife as *la compañera*, or the comrade, in an effort to give a leftist tone to his administration. In all, he tried to endow his administration with the aura of revolution in order to tap into the latent attachment of most Mexicans to that central event of their modern history.

Another policy that was intended to have symbolic effects on people's perceptions of the government was Echeverría's Third World initiative. One of the enduring values of the postrevolutionary Mexican government has been anti-imperialism. Whatever the actual effects on other values, such as economic development, anti-imperialism is a policy objective that many Latin American governments feel compelled to pursue, at least periodically. Thus the Echeverría government tightened restrictions on foreign investment, issued the "Echeverría Letter" on the desirability for the Third World to be economically independent of the leading capitalist countries, and cast an "anti-Zionist" vote at the United Nations, equating Zionism with imperialism and racism. These all had predictable effects on public opinion in the advanced countries, and Echeverría was eventually forced to backtrack on most of them. American Jewish groups launched a tourist boycott that cost Mexico millions of dollars of foreign exchange. The United States retaliated with stepped-up repatriation of illegal Mexican immigrants, imposed a 10-percent surtax on imports, and restricted the exporting of natural gas to Mexico and the importation of meat from Mexico. In 1974 a U.S. trade law eliminated preferential treatment for Mexican goods. The Echeverría government tried to undo the damage of the tourist boycott and foreign investment controls, but the result of his anticapitalist stance was that the Mexican economy suffered at a time when it could ill afford it.[30]

Another aspect of Echeverría's Third World strategy was to establish embassies in dozens of smaller countries with which Mexico supposedly had business to conduct. For example, Mexico opened an embassy in Albania to seek contacts there and to answer inquiries about Mexico. During the Echeverría administration, however, this embassy issued only about one visa per month for Albanians to visit Mexico.[31] In other words, the policy accomplished little more than symbolic gestures of solidarity with other Third World nations. This and other symbolic components of Echeverría's Third World strategy were designed to impress leftist opinion within Mexico rather than to have any significant effect on real foreign policy interests. That is, they were planned to enhance the image of the president and the revolutionary credentials of the regime in general. Such measures were calculated to increase Mexicans' identification with the government, that is, to increase their "symbolic participation."

In addition to increasing participation, the regime also pursued the second type of "political" strategy for maintaining authority, the use of repression. At first, Echeverría appeared determined to reduce the level of repression and to depend more on co-optation to defuse the discontent. He tried to reduce the level of official violence in an effort "to rid himself of the stigma of Tlatelolco," which had dogged him since his participation as secretary of *gobernación* in the slaughter of 1968.[32] Thus, early in 1971 he ordered a general amnesty of imprisoned leaders of the 1968 movement and declared a "democratic opening" *(apertura democrática)* that was supposed to make the government more responsive to criticism and participation, especially from those on the left. However, some serious repression occurred even as early as 1971, the most notable being the "Corpus Christi massacre" on June 10. On this occasion about ten thousand students marching through downtown Mexico City were attacked by "falcons," or paramilitary shock troops, apparently hired by conservative businessmen and dispatched with the approval of the Mexico City government. Echeverría had planned to address the marchers, but his right-wing opponents seized the opportunity to embarrass and weaken the government.[33] Although this instance of repression may not have been instigated by

Echeverría or his close associates, government repression during his administration did increase in response to criticism and violence from the left.

A guerrilla movement had begun in Mexico in the mid-1960s, as in many other countries of the world, including the United States. In 1966, when Echeverría was secretary of *gobernación,* an attack had been made on a military base in Chihuahua by a group of youths in an effort to obtain weapons. Then the "Spartacist" movement, inspired by José Revueltas, began in 1967, and another guerrilla movement, encouraged by Professor Genaro Vásquez Rojas, emerged in Guerrero. The guerrilla movement carried over into Echeverría's term and was generally divided into rural and urban wings, apparently with little coordination between them.

One of the best-known rural guerrilla groups was the National Revolutionary Civic Association (ACNR), which declared in 1971 that it would struggle for the "overthrow of the oligarchy of large capitalists, large landowners, and governing pro-imperialists."[34] The leader of the ACNR was Vásquez Rojas, who was killed during a massive assault by twelve thousand soldiers in February 1972. He was soon replaced, however, by Lucio Cabañas, who renamed the organization the Party of the Poor. Cabañas became perhaps the most famous guerrilla leader in Mexico since the Revolution. According to Samuel Schmidt: "The army initiated a policy of terror to weaken the guerrillas' bases of support. In April 1973 it executed six peasants in Peloncillo, Guerrero, who were accused of sending food to Cabañas. This action started the general repression of the peasants, and the army put down marches and removed land squatters."[35] Soon afterward, Cabañas himself was killed, and the rural guerrilla movement died down considerably by the end of Echeverría's term.

A considerable amount of urban guerrilla activity took place during the first two years of the Echeverría presidency, especially after the student killings on Corpus Christi Day in 1971. Many who favored significant change in Mexico came to the conclusion that it would not happen inside the existing political system. Numerous bombings, bank robberies, and kidnappings occurred, including the kidnappings of the American consul in Guadalajara and of Echeverría's father-in-law, José Guadalupe Zuno. The most notorious was the kidnapping and killing of Eugenio Garza Sada, a very important businessman and leader of the powerful Monterey group. Schmidt lists eighteen "important" guerrilla groups during this period whose activities began to give the impression that the government was losing control of public order. The government reacted with toughness and even brutality. It tortured and killed numerous people suspected of involvement in or knowledge of guerrilla activities.

The same vacillating pattern of liberalization and then restriction can be seen in Echeverría's policies toward the press. At first he invited criticism and a public dialogue, but by 1974, lest the momentum go too far, he moved to impose greater restrictions on the press generally. He placed new government controls on television and had the critical weekly newsmagazine *Por Qué* closed down. In his final months in office, he engineered the ouster of editor

Julio Scherer García and his colleagues at the independent and well-regarded newspaper *Excélsior*.[36] Thus ultimately his policies toward human rights were no more liberal where the press was concerned than in other areas.

The Economic Initiatives

As indicated above, a government can pursue mainly a political or an economic strategy in its efforts to establish and maintain order and legitimacy. Perhaps because the Mexican regime has been unwilling to go very far toward either political participation or repression, it has depended much more heavily on an economic strategy to maintain its legitimacy and stability. That is, the government has not been willing to liberalize and democratize enough to legitimize itself in that way, nor has it employed repression systematically enough to subdue the population and maintain order through sheer force. Therefore, because the Mexican regime has not been willing or able to pursue order and legitimacy through political democracy or repression, it has been forced to pursue legitimacy mostly through an economic strategy. Most Mexican presidents since 1876 have pursued political legitimacy largely through economic growth. In other words, the government has generally tried to solve its political problems through economic means—sometimes through distribution (Cárdenas, Echeverría) and sometimes through growth (the others).

In fact, the economic strategy tended almost entirely in the direction of growth. The regime pursued economic growth almost to the exclusion of any other values up to 1970. Moreover, it pursued growth of a particular kind. Typical of developing countries that sought to catch up quickly with industrial societies, the Mexican regime used a great deal of state intervention in the economy as a means to pursue growth. It is often assumed that there is a harsh trade-off between efficiency and equity, or growth and distribution, at least in the short run, although some observers have questioned whether the trade-off is so inexorable.[37] Echeverría's major concern as president was political stability, and like previous Mexican presidents, he looked to the economy for the solution to that problem. However, unlike the previous five presidents since 1940, he came to believe that the prevailing policies must be changed. He and his advisors believed that no matter how successful prior policies may have been in terms of overall growth, their continuation would result in political disaster. Despite the high rate of economic change, by the late 1960s, Mexicans were debating whether this had been ''development'' or merely growth. For example, the capital-intensity of import-substituting industrialization had contributed to very high unemployment.

At first the Echeverría government followed relatively orthodox economic policies, but the U.S. recession of 1970–71 hit Mexico particularly hard and prompted Echeverría to stimulate the economy, a course that was consistent with his overall goals anyway. Thus for fiscal 1972, Echeverría proposed a large increase in spending and an increase in taxes to pay for it. But because

business so vehemently opposed the bulk of the tax increase, the president
backed down. He got only a small tax increase, but he nevertheless increased
spending greatly, with a resulting large budget deficit. (This was the mirror
image of what happened to Ronald Reagan in the 1980s, who lowered taxes
and called for a decrease in spending. When he got the former but not the
latter, the result was burgeoning budget deficits.)

The economic problem faced by governments is more complex than a choice
between growth and distribution. Even if a government decides to pursue
growth, it still must decide what sort of growth to pursue. From 1940 to 1970,
the Mexican government generally favored industry over agriculture. During
that time, the increase in manufacturing production far surpassed the increase
in agricultural production. Whereas agricultural and industrial production had
grown at the same rate during the 1940s (8 percent), industrial output continued
to grow at about that same rate for the next two decades while the growth rate
of agricultural production declined steadily, to 4.3 percent for the 1950s and
3.6 percent for the 1960s. In fact, during the half decade from 1965 to 1970,
just before Echeverría became president, the annual growth of agricultural output had fallen to 2.2 percent while manufacturing production had climbed to 9
percent. That imbalance alone might have prompted any Mexican president in
1970 to devote more resources to the agricultural sector, but "Echeverría was
also sensitive to the problems of rural areas because of the potential for political
unrest engendered by inequities in the distribution of wealth in the country."[38]
Although the share of the population that lived in rural areas had shrunk since
1940, a significant portion (40 percent) still lived there, and they provided the
PRI with its most solid electoral support. This strong support may have resulted
as much from the ease of controlling elections in the countryside as from rural
contentment with the regime. Nonetheless, solid majorities in the countryside
were necessary for the continued PRI dominance of Mexican politics.

Like most Mexican presidents, Echeverría tended to pursue policies that responded most directly to problems currently threatening the regime. Thus, the
Echeverría administration consciously tried to reorient Mexican development
away from industry and back toward agriculture. The federal investment in
agriculture was increased from 15 percent of the total budget in 1971 to 20
percent in 1976. Within this general shift from industry to agriculture, the administration pursued an even finer distinction. It paid more attention to peasant
farmers and to the production of basic foodstuffs than to large commercial
farmers, as in previous administrations.[39]

One reason that the Echeverría government wanted to divert more resources
to agriculture was to bring down the rural birthrate. Despite the decades-long
rise in average per capita income in Mexico, the rural peasants had seen little
socioeconomic improvement, and thus they continued to procreate as if they
lived in a very poor country.[40] The population continued to grow at a net
annual rate of almost 3.5 percent, and in the 1960s and 1970s, families in
Mexico were over twice as large as those in the West and Japan at a compara-

ble level of economic development.[41] As part of his general Third World approach to problems in the 1970 election campaign, Echeverría at first encouraged Mexican women to bear more children. However, he soon realized that the high Mexican birthrate was a major part of the socioeconomic problem, and so the government began to encourage family planning soon after Echeverría became president. Whether as a result of government efforts or of socioeconomic development, the population growth rate started to fall steadily in the 1970s. After reaching a peak of 3.5 percent for the 1965–70 period, net population growth slowed to 2.8 percent a year by 1982.[42]

To a large extent, the population problem faced by Mexico is endemic to the process of industrialization and modernization, and it has occurred in most of the recently developing countries. The improvement of health programs, sanitary measures, and preventive medicine produce a drop in mortality rates, without an equivalent drop in natality. Thus, Mexico's population was exploding, largely as a result of past social and economic progress. According to Roberto Newell and Luis Rubio: "This posed a structural dilemma of a daunting size and nature. The speed at which capital accumulation had to take place was simply impossible to achieve. Only the long-term effects of educational advancement and of urban conditions on family-size choices could change the nature of Mexico's demographic growth. As to the growing gap between social groups, this too had its roots in structural problems (educational levels, employment, health and social opportunities, and so on) that simply did not yield easily."[43] The early-developing countries, such as Britain and the United States, had a much easier time accommodating the demographic effects of modernization because their death rates dropped more slowly over a period of decades instead of suddenly in just a few years, as in Mexico. Hence the early-developing countries did not experience a population explosion, as did the later-developing countries.

In addition to overly rapid population growth, another hindrance to economic development was the limited size of the domestic market resulting from the poverty of large parts of the population. By greater attention to peasant agriculture, higher public spending, especially for social development programs such as education, and a more labor-intensive approach to industrialization, Echeverría hoped to bring marginal groups into the modern economy and society and to expand the domestic market at the same time.

A major policy of the Echeverría administration was to expand the operations of CONASUPO, the National Staple Products Corporation. This was a marketing board for basic foodstuffs, both for export and import. It bought agricultural products, especially from small peasant farmers, at guaranteed prices and then marketed these products both inside and outside the country. CONASUPO also established retail stores that sold goods to the working classes at subsidized prices. Increasingly under Echeverría, the second function was emphasized as the government opened hundreds of new stores between 1971 and 1976. This policy did contribute to raising the purchasing power of the poorer groups to some extent. However, the massive subsidies also represented a significant drain on government finances.

In addition to shifting emphasis away from industry to agriculture, the Echeverría government also sought to restructure the economy in other ways. It encouraged firms to locate in underindustrialized areas and tried to reform the tax system to capture a larger share of the national income for public spending. The government also attempted to reduce the presence of foreign firms in the Mexican economy by stiffening the requirement for majority Mexican ownership of businesses. The government exposed Mexican *prestanombres*, who lent their names as putative "owners" of foreign firms, encouraged more production for export, placed stricter controls on imports, and sought to strengthen trade relations with nations other than the United States.

An inconsistency in Echeverría's economic strategy was that the president wanted both to force Mexican business to become more productive *and* to protect it even further from foreign competition. The two goals of economic efficiency and economic nationalism are not necessarily incompatible, as Japan and other Asian countries have demonstrated. However, to pursue the two goals simultaneously is difficult and requires a concerted effort by the government to entice firms to become more productive behind the protective walls, as Japan did after 1960. Regarding the first goal, Hellman wrote: "He asserted that the industrial bourgeoisie was going to have to change its notion that the best way to conduct business was by turning quick, high profits from overpriced, poor-quality goods produced for a limited market behind high protectionist walls. The age of 'import substitution' and protectionist policy was over." [44] Thus the government would reduce tariffs to force Mexican firms to compete more energetically against foreign goods and would reduce government subsidies and tax waivers on which Mexican business had come to depend. At the same time, however, the goal of economic nationalism was pursued by tightening the controls on foreign investors. Thus a 1973 Law to Regulate Foreign Investment codified previous controls, mandated that all new companies must have majority Mexican ownership, and established a National Commission on Foreign Investment to review all new foreign investment proposals. Preference would be given to businesses that would produce goods for export. [45]

Although Echeverría was the most reformist president since the 1930s, his policies were generally an intensification of past practices, rather than new departures. He increased the number of firms with government participation from 84 in 1970 to 845 in 1976 and doubled the number of government employees to more than 1 million. Public-sector income as a share of gross domestic product increased from 19 percent in 1970 to 27 percent in 1976 while public expenditures grew from 24 to 34 percent during the same period, with the deficit as a share of gross domestic product growing accordingly. This growth of the public sector provided many more employment opportunities but also required financing the deficit through greatly increased foreign borrowing and a rapidly increasing money supply.

Thus Echeverría's strategy was to pursue growth and distribution simultaneously. The appeal of this strategy was that it could overcome the threat to political stability resulting from a development model that had enriched some but had excluded so many others from the benefits of the "Mexican miracle." For Echeverría, growth and distribution were the twin means of pursuing the ultimate goal of political stability. He hoped to achieve both growth and redistribution, but if growth had to be sacrificed for distribution as a tactic for increasing legitimacy and political stability, that would be his choice. As Laurence Whitehead wrote, "His principle objective was to prevent the danger that he already perceived in connection with political stability, even if that meant paying the price of an economic reversal."[46]

In fact, however, the economy grew almost as rapidly under Echeverría as during previous presidential terms. After a slow start, due partly to the U.S. recession, the Mexican economy picked up speed and grew at an average annual rate of 6.2 percent during his six-year term. The annual real growth rates in GDP were as follows:[47]

1971	4.2
1972	8.5
1973	8.4
1974	6.1
1975	5.6
1976	4.2

OPPOSITION TO GOVERNMENT POLICIES

Populist governments in capitalist countries face a difficult dilemma. They may believe that redistributive policies are desirable, both for political stability and for economic equity. However, they face a business class that is generally opposed to such policies because of ideology and self-interest, a class that has powerful weapons for sabotaging policies that it opposes. In writing of the Cárdenas years, Nora Hamilton called this problem "the limits of state autonomy."[48] The degree of state autonomy has become one of the leading questions in political science today. How independent are governments from social groups, especially business? The Mexican state dominates society more than does the state in many countries, including the United States. Regarding the Mexican state in the economy, Roderic Camp says, "Compared to its northern neighbor, its role is all-encompassing."[49] Mexico has a mixed economy characterized by a combination of private and public enterprise. Fundamentally, however, the Mexican regime has been committed to economic development through capitalism, with the state playing a guiding role. Although the Mexican government is committed to capitalist development, it does not appear to be dominated by the capitalist class, although that class has considerable influence as long as it is serving state ends.[50]

Governments that pursue redistribution in any capitalist system will encounter resistance, but some resistance is stronger than others. Both domestic and foreign business have obvious means at their disposal to prevent governments from seriously threatening their interests. Some observers argued that, as in the Cárdenas years, the Echeverría experience demonstrated the limits of reform. It indicated the difficulty of carrying out a basic reorientation of Mexican development in the direction of greater equality of distribution because of the resistance of business interests.[51]

Almost immediately, the business class disliked virtually everything about Echeverría, his policy proposals as well as his political style. Although Echeverría thought he was consulting business adequately, entrepreneurs soon began complaining. As early as December 15, 1970, only two weeks after Echeverría took office, "the president of the Confederation of Employers of the Mexican Republic (COPARMEX) complained that the government was not consulting with business on new economic policies. He said that, whereas in the past, the government had generally shown business leaders drafts of proposed legislation that would affect business, the new administration was not doing so. Echeverría responded by saying that business should, instead, 'watch over the national interest that each Mexican firm represents.' "[52] This was the opening shot in what would become a war of words between Echeverría and Mexican business.

In addition to his actual policies, which were problematic enough, Echeverría's rhetoric was inflammatory. In part, he was trying to garner support from the left by savaging business, but it turned out not to be a very good bargain. His policies and his rhetoric probably did solidify the left wing of the regime, but that support was bought at a relatively high price.

Whether the "bourgeoisie" were behaving selfishly and unreasonably, as some writers argue,[53] or were merely responding rationally to the incentives that they faced, they responded with the usual set of actions employed by business in such a situation. Fearful that the economic climate was becoming increasingly negative, business and the middle class slowed their investment in Mexico and sent much of their money abroad. The combination of underinvestment and capital flight contributed to a decline in the economic growth rate from 8 percent to about 4 percent a year by the end of Echeverría's term. Regarding Echeverría's reforms, Hellman says, "The reforms did not work because they could not work, given the structure of power, the impotence of peasants and workers' organizations, the intransigence of the conservative bourgeoisie, the opposition of foreign capital, and the general alignment of political forces in Mexico."[54]

For the distributive policies of Echeverría to work, it was necessary to raise additional revenues; thus a central part of the government's strategy was to reform the tax structure in order to broaden the tax base and to increase rates. One would assume that such a strong state, and a "revolutionary" regime with a unified leadership, would be able to enact such a policy with little difficulty. There is disagreement among scholars over how much reform of the tax structure occurred under Echeverría. E.V.K. Fitzgerald argues that little additional progressivity was achieved. However, John Evans believes that Fitzgerald and others understate the degree to which the Mexican tax system was reformed between 1970 and 1982. Evans concedes that no large rapid change occurred, such as Echeverría was attempting, but that incremental changes did take place whose cumulative effects were significant. There were increases in the total tax burden and in receipts from oil and continued efforts to centralize and achieve greater uniformity in tax administration. Evans argues that by 1982, taxes on business in Mexico were actually quite high. However, most of the major changes that he cites took place under López Portillo, not under Echeverría. Moreover, whatever one may think of the burden of Mexican taxes by 1976, the fact is that Echeverría was unable to get business to accept anything approaching the kind of tax reform that he wanted.[55]

It was not only business that opposed Echeverría's policies. His efforts at a political opening would have allowed alternative groups to organize and opposition parties to win more seats in Congress. Yet that would have threatened the many safe seats that had traditionally been reserved for labor representatives. For that and other reasons, the Echeverría administration tried to weaken or unseat the *charro* leadership of the CTM, especially Fidel Velázquez, who had been in office since 1941. Press attacks on the leadership of the unions affiliated with the CTM increased noticeably. But Velázquez and his associates counterattacked with demands for wage increases, a forty-hour workweek, national unemployment insurance, and other measures. They used pressure tactics such as mass demonstrations and threats of a general strike. By 1975, the Echeverría government backed away from its confrontational approach with organized labor in order to gain CTM support for the selection of a presidential successor. Although Echeverría achieved some progress in his efforts to transform politics and the economy, he was partly stalemated by business and labor, both of which felt threatened by the government's proposed policies. The Mexican political system is often called authoritarian, but it is usually flexible in its response to group interests, especially business and, to a lesser extent, labor.

Thus a central quality of the presidency of Luis Echeverría was adaptability, especially to the left, which made the strongest demands at the time. After decades of a single-minded strategy of economic growth, the country was probably ready for some attention to questions of distribution by 1970. The problem was that his administration tried to redistribute more than was sustainable by the revenues available and by the proclivity of capital to take flight. Echeverría's model, on the other hand, sought rapid economic growth in a somewhat different way. Mexico had long been somewhat protectionist in its foreign trade and investment policies, but this aspect of the strategy would receive enhanced

Table 4.1
Some Economic Indicators, 1971–1976

	1971	1972	1973	1974	1975	1976
Public Sector Deficit (% of GDP)	2.5	3.8	5.1	5.5	8.5	9.9
Money Supply (M1) Growth Rates	8.4	21.0	24.0	22.0	21.0	30.0
Inflation Rate	4.4	5.5	12.0	24.0	17.0	20.0
Real Interest Rate (Long Term Bonds)	4.6	3.5	-2.7	-14.0	-6.4	-10.0
Long Term Foreign Debt (% of GDP)	4.2	4.8	6.0	8.0	12.0	16.0

Source: Miguel D. Ramírez, *Mexico's Economic Crisis* (New York: Praeger Publishers, 1989), p. 83.

attention under Echeverría. The country would try to break its dependence on foreign investment and markets and become more independent of the world economy.

Ironically, Echeverría's policies had the opposite effect; they led to huge deficits, increased foreign borrowing, debt, and inflation. Inflation, which had not been a problem for Mexico since the 1950s, suddenly reemerged, largely as a result of growing government deficits and major increases in the money supply as a way to finance the deficits. For the Echeverría years, table 4.1 shows public-sector deficits as a percent of GDP, growth in the money supply, inflation rates, real interest rates, and long-term foreign debt as a percent of GDP.

Because of the huge increase in spending relative to government revenues, the deficit quadrupled as a share of GDP. The increase in the money supply was greatly stepped up to finance the deficit in the absence of significant tax increases (note the huge jump in the money supply from 8 percent in 1971 to 21 percent in 1972). This caused prices to increase rapidly. Of course, some of Mexico's inflation in the 1970s was imported from the world economy in the form of higher-priced imports (including oil and capital), but much was due to government policies. Inflation in turn meant a sharp drop in real interest rates (nominal interest rates minus the inflation rate). That led simultaneously to capital flight and greater government difficulty in borrowing to finance its deficits, which pushed interest rates even higher, contributing to an even higher budget deficit. The government found it increasingly necessary to borrow abroad to finance its budget and trade deficits. This was the beginning of the huge foreign debt that became such a problem for Mexico in the 1980s, although from the vantage point of the 1980s, these figures would look modest.

Echeverría's redistributive goals were understandable, given both the degree of inequality and the severity of political crisis in the country. His goal of rapid economic growth with some degree of redistribution of income departed in only one way from the goal of "stabilizing development" of 1958–70. The goal of economic management policies during this earlier period was economic growth with a minimum of inflation. However, this one difference led to several important policy differences. It implied restraining government spending, the wage demands of labor, and the money supply—all in order to hold down inflation.

During the 1960s, the money supply grew at rates that paralleled those of the economy. For instance, during 1965–70, the real GDP grew by 6.8 percent while the money supply grew by 10 percent, a gap of just over 3 percentage points. Real interest rates averaged 6.5 percent during these years. This provided a strong stimulus for savings and capital formation. From 1965 to 1970, financial savings as a share of GDP increased from 25 percent to 36 percent. By contrast, "under the accumulated pressures of Echeverría's populism, M1 exploded in growth, fueling inflation and making the financial system more unstable overall. . . . The average growth of M1 was almost four times that of the GDP between 1971 and 1976. With this much liquidity in the hands of the public, inflation was unavoidable."[56] Under Echeverría, the GDP grew 6.2 percent while the money supply raced ahead at 21.3 percent, a gap of 15 percentage points. The results were predictable. Largely because inflation exceeded nominal interest rates so greatly under Echeverría, real interests rates were negative, and hence financial savings fell from 38 percent to 32 percent of GDP.[57]

The whole process became a vicious circle in which the government spent more money on more programs, crowding out private investment and frightening private investors about the future, prompting them to cut back their investment even more. This led to more strident rhetoric on the part of a frustrated president and other administration officials about the socially irresponsible nature of business and to even more government spending and investment to make up for what business was not doing. Private investment fell, government spending soared, inflation raged, and the relations between Echeverría and business became worse and worse. By 1976, the atmosphere in Mexico was tense.

One manifestation of the strained relations between the president and some sectors of society was the degree to which rumors and jokes ran rampant throughout Mexican society during this time. Although to my knowledge this has not been studied systematically, societies with less press freedom probably are characterized by more rumors than societies with greater press freedom. The Echeverría years saw a mounting number of rumors as his term wore on. When the government began to espouse the virtues of birth control, the rumor

began that doctors were going through schools giving shots to pupils in order
to sterilize them. As a result of the fear engendered by this rumor, it was said
that one hundred thousand children were not vaccinated against polio. Throughout his term, rumors spread: that a strangler was at large; that basic foodstuffs
would be rationed, which led to panic buying; that bank accounts would be
frozen; and that gasoline was becoming scarce. In Echeverría's final turbulent
year, Mexican society was subjected to a riot of rumors. The following were
heard in various parts of the country, according to Schmidt:

A great deal of property was going to be nationalized, including the banks;
Echeverría was a Communist;
Echeverría had become one of the richest men in the world;
Echeverría, his wife, and their children had all been murdered;
A coup was being organized, sometimes from the left and sometimes from the right; and
Echeverría planned to lead a coup and install a dictatorship.

The rumors became so widespread—and in the opinion of some government
officials so debilitating—that the Chamber of Deputies announced in November
1976 that it would investigate the sources of the rumors. It was widely assumed
within the regime that many of the rumors were started by the "bourgeoisie"
in an effort to weaken Echeverría's hold on power. The rumors found such a
receptive audience perhaps in part because of the tradition of media control and
corruption in a society in which major decisions were made in secret. In addition, many aspects of Mexican life were unsettled during this time. The government was even more interventionist than usual, and political turbulence was
more widespread, with both government and various guerrilla groups practicing
violence on a larger scale than had been common in Mexico. Moreover, it is
possible that the rumors "demonstrated the peculiar social cohesion that exists
in Mexico. People tend to believe their relatives and friends and what they hear
in the cafe, the bar, or at a shoe-shine stand more than they believe the mass
media, which merely repeats the government's version of events." [58]

Mexicans have long been devoted to political humor, and if such expression
could not always find its outlet in public forums such as the mass media, then
it was transmitted informally through word-of-mouth and mimeograph. One
expert on political humor believes that jokes about the president reached epi-
demic proportions under Echeverría. In a political system in which citizens
could not criticize the president very publicly through letters to the editor, talk
shows, and the like or through their votes in competitive elections, they attacked the president through jokes. Many of the rumors originated with the
middle and business classes, who were frustrated with Echeverría's populist
policies. Most of the jokes attacked Echeverría's intelligence and manliness
(machismo). A common joke claimed that his wife ordered him around and
made a cuckold of him.

Echeverría asks Henry Kissinger how he has such success with women.

Kissinger responds: "I go to their house, pound on the door, kick the furniture, and show them that I'm the boss."

Echeverría arrives at his house, pounds on the door, destroys the furniture, and just about finishes off the presidential mansion. A voice from the other room asks: "Is that you, Henry?"

Another joke poked fun at his supposed stupidity.

Echeverría was searching for a diving suit in a sailor's cabin. The sailor comes in and asks, "Mr. President, what are you doing here?"

"Looking for a diving suit."

"Why?"

"Because the captain told me that *down deep* I'm not such an idiot." [59]

The magnitude of the campaign of rumor and humor do not necessarily tell as much about the president as about his critics. Business and the upper middle classes felt threatened by this populist president, and such private criticism was one way to attack the president in a semiauthoritarian political system.

In reality, Echeverría was a flexible president who tried to achieve some degree of social justice in a country where inequality had reached massive proportions. He and his advisors tried to adjust the system in the direction they thought necessary to maintain political stability. In the process, however, they alienated many on whom stability also depended, especially business. The next president adapted in the opposite direction.

LÓPEZ PORTILLO: OIL WEALTH AND LIBERALIZATION

Mexico breathed a collective sigh of relief on December 1, 1976, when Echeverría turned the presidency over to his former minister of finance, Jose López Portillo. The peso had been devalued in 1976 for the first time in almost twenty-five years; Echeverría had approved land seizures by peasants; the country had become deeply indebted to foreign bankers in order to pay the huge costs of social and economic programs; inflation was 20 percent in 1976, and economic growth was a relatively slow 4 percent.

In most other times in Mexican revolutionary history, López Portillo would have been considered a pragmatic progressive like López Mateos, but coming after the strident leftism of Echeverría, he seemed a political moderate. He recognized that his primary task was to restore the legitimacy of the regime that had been tarnished by Echeverría. In 1976, relations between government and business in Mexico were at their worst since the 1930s. Thus one of López Portillo's first priorities was to restore business confidence in the regime. He praised business in his inaugural address; he soon met, dined, and was photographed with various business leaders, including the Monterey Group, and in various ways he tried to reassure business that his government would be different from that of his predecessor.[60] That positive relationship lasted for about two years, until 1979.[61]

The López Portillo government recognized that the protectionist model of economic development had just about reached its limits, and so in 1980 it applied for membership in the General Agreement on Tariffs and Trade (GATT) as a first step toward more liberal and open international trade. However, the government changed its mind in the face of protests from segments of the business community that did not want to give up the benefits of protectionism and face the rigors of international competition.

Regarding the illegal land seizures approved by Echeverría near the end of his term, López Portillo honored the court decision that the seizures were illegal and forced the squatting peasants off the land, but with a minimal amount of force. Then, under the terms of the land reform law, he began proceedings to expropriate the land and to distribute it to the peasants legally. Later, López Portillo declared that although past presidential orders would be implemented, no more land would be expropriated.[62] Thus López Portillo seemed to seek the political approval of peasants for promising to continue distribution of land already expropriated and the approval of business and large landowners by committing the regime to end any further expropriations. The latter would give owners a degree of predictability and therefore willingness to invest in greater productivity. Peasants were legally allowed to lease their land to other landowners in order to create larger parcels.[63] The production of foodstuffs did increase, although much of the rise might well have been due to the heavy rains of 1981.[64]

The López Portillo government tried to address the growing problem of Mexico's inability to feed itself. Although Mexico is a large exporter of agricultural products, it also was importing increasing amounts of agricultural commodities. For example, in 1980 Mexico imported ten million tons of corn, beans, wheat, and other basic foodstuffs worth U.S. $1.5 billion. To address this problem, the López Portillo government took two major actions. First, it declared that no more land would be expropriated, and then in 1980 the government created the Mexican Food System (Sistema Alimentario Mexicano, or SAM) to guide and encourage the production of corn, beans, and other basic commodities. The government provided the peasants with fertilizers, seeds, and other inputs at subsidized prices, promised to buy their products at set prices, and guaranteed them a minimum income in case of natural disaster.

At first, López Portillo demonstrated his prudence in another way as well. Near the end of Echeverría's term, PEMEX (Petróleos Mexicanos) had discovered huge new reserves of oil. However, perhaps out of concern over the increasingly erratic nature of Echeverría's decisions, PEMEX officials apparently did not inform the president of the full extent of the discovery but instead waited for the new administration to take office. Although PEMEX officials then recommended that exploitation should occur at almost the maximum extent that was technically feasible, López Portillo directed that pumping should proceed at a high rate but short of the maximum possible.[65] Both the currency devaluation and oil announcement illustrate a technique that the regime sometimes uses to enhance the significance of the transition to a new president and the adaptability that it often produces. Bad news is often given out while the old president is still in office, whereas good news is held over for the new president.

Thus an oil-driven economic boom guided by the government was part of López Portillo's effort to solve the problem of regime unity and stability. Camp says, "His initial success, combined with the extraordinary increase in oil revenues, revived internal unity within the Mexican state."[66] Another part of his strategy was to sponsor a degree of political liberalization. During the early 1970s, much dissent had taken place outside the official political system. The regime's brutal suppression of the student movement in 1968 and the violent attacks by paramilitary groups on demonstrators in June 1971 provoked the formation of numerous guerrilla movements by convincing many leftist groups that efforts at peaceful reform were futile.[67] Echeverría opened the political system in an effort to reduce discontent, but he also used considerable coercion to repress violent dissent. López Portillo sought to extend the liberalization process by signing, in December 1977, a new electoral law that made it easier for opposition parties to organize and campaign for office.

The reform measure liberalized procedures for party recognition by lowering the percent of the national vote that a party must receive from 2.5 to 1.5 percent. The law increased the size of the Chamber of Deputies from three hundred to four hundred seats, reserving the extra one hundred for proportional representation of minority parties. Political parties also were eligible for some financial support for their campaign expenses as well as greater access to mass media, including television, radio, postal, and telegraph facilities. Several new parties gained official recognition on the basis of their performance in the 1979 and 1982 elections, including the Mexican Communist Party (PCM), the Socialist Workers' Party (PST), and the Mexican Democratic Party (PDM), and of course opposition parties, especially the PAN, were represented in greater numbers in the Chamber than before.[68] The response to the reforms may have been greater than López Portillo and his advisors expected, since the PRI's candidate received only 70 percent of the popular vote in 1982, the lowest share since the creation of the revolutionary party in 1929. The left and the right received the remaining 30 percent in about equal numbers.

Thus López Portillo sought to restore the tarnished legitimacy of the regime by a combination of economic and political strategies. He tried to reestablish good relations with the private sector, relations that had been damaged by the strident populism of Echeverría, and tried to put the economy back on a growth path. López Portillo also sought to open the political system enough that dissidents would not feel that violence was the only form of participation left to them. Once again, the regime demonstrated its proclivity for adapting, at least to some degree, to the dominant demands of the moment.

Table 4.2
Some Economic Indicators, 1977–1982

	1977	1978	1979	1980	1981	1982
Real GDP	3.4	8.2	9.2	8.3	7.9	-0.5
Population	3.2	3.1	3.0	3.0	2.9	2.8
Per Capita GDP	0.2	5.1	6.2	5.3	5.0	-3.3
Inflation	30.0	17.0	20.0	29.0	27.0	98.0

Source: Ramírez, *Mexico's Economic Crisis,* p. 86.

However, the ability and willingness of the regime to adapt has always been limited by certain parameters. For one thing, the regime never seriously considered opening the political system so much that its dominance would actually be threatened. Hence, from the point of view of the opposition, political liberalization never went very far. In addition, the economic strategy of the regime was always constrained by economic and political realities. Adaptability to the left was constrained by the economic resources available; in the long run, a political system can distribute only what its economic system can produce. Adaptability to the right—for example, economic liberalization—was constrained by revolutionary nationalism and business desire for protection. It appeared, however, that in the late 1970s, Mexico would be less bound by these constraints than previously because of the vast wealth available from its oil.

Mexico was both helped and hurt by the oil discoveries. The country had been a net importer of oil in 1973 and thus was hit hard by the huge oil price increases of the early 1970s. With the price increases providing the motivation and the huge new discoveries the possibility, PEMEX stepped up production from .9 million barrels per day in 1977 to 2.25 million in 1980, half of it for export. After two years of sluggish growth, the country achieved economic growth rates for the next four years that were unusual even for Mexico, as seen in table 4.2. But the oil boom came to a screeching halt in 1982 because of stagnant oil prices, overproduction, inflation, and the world recession of 1981–82.

In defense of López Portillo and the Mexican government, Mexico was not alone in mistakenly forecasting higher oil prices. For example, the 1980 *World Development Report* predicted that the price of oil in current dollars would be seventy-eight dollars per barrel by 1990, double the actual price. If the price of oil had risen according to such predictions, Mexico would probably not have experienced the 1982 crisis.[69] However, whatever the price, Mexico was becoming extremely dependent on oil revenues; oil as a share of total exports soared from 10 percent in 1976 to 75 percent in 1982.[70]

López Portillo's election had given hope to those who had been alienated by the policies of Echeverría, especially business and the middle classes. For several years, things seemed to be going well. The vast oil wealth made it appear that at last Mexico could have it all, both rapid economic growth and generous social programs as well. Economic growth rates were high from 1978 through 1981, but inflation was a problem throughout his term. Then in 1982 it all came crashing down, as growth plunged below zero while inflation soared to almost 100 percent.

López Portillo left his successor not only an economic problem but a problem of morale as well. As if the economic crisis with its attendant inflation was not demoralizing enough, the Mexican people were shocked by the magnitude of corruption during the López Portillo years. The president and several of his associates had suddenly acquired enough wealth to build huge and ostentatious mansions in Mexico City and elsewhere. Although Mexicans were accustomed to political corruption, the grand scale on which venality was conducted under López Portillo astonished even a nation inured to such vice. The massive oil wealth, of course, made this level of corruption possible. After López Portillo left office, opposition members of the Chamber of Deputies began calling for an investigation of the former president and others. In addition, noted scholars and journalists also came forth with books with such titles as *Esto Nos Dió López Portillo* (This is What López Portillo Gave Us) and *Los Presidentes*, a critical look at Díaz Ordaz, Echeverría, López Portillo, and de la Madrid. The latter was written by one of the best-known journalists in Mexico, Julio Scherer García, whose independence Echeverría had tried to crush in 1976.[71]

Thus once again a Mexican president left a crisis for his successor to deal with, and once again the new president had to adapt to the pressures produced by the crisis. President Miguel de la Madrid came into office facing rampant inflation, huge budget deficits, massive foreign debt, collapsing oil prices, an economy that was shrinking in size, and a business community that once again had lost much of its confidence in government. He promised that Mexico would meet its international debt obligations, imposed austerity on public spending, sold off hundreds of state firms, and generally tried to deal with the political and economic crisis that he had inherited. He responded by moving vigorously against the blatant corruption of the López Portillo years, a common practice in the first year of a new Mexican administration. Stephen Morris says: "The anticorruption campaign is the institutionalized vehicle for disassociating one administration from another. . . . Typically, the campaign stresses the view that the 'bad apples' of the prior period have been rooted out and that, contrary to the past, the current administration is (finally) serious in pursuing much-needed reforms."[72] In addition, de la Madrid liberalized the political system, at least for a while, signed a new electoral law, and tried to turn the government over to his successor in as good a shape as possible. But his successor, Carlos Salinas would also have a difficult job, as we shall see later. Thus the institutionalized succession provides the country with a new president who can use the old themes to adapt to whichever pressures have built up the most, and the response tends to be proportional to the magnitude of the problem and to the pressures.

CONCLUSION

Some observers believe that the Mexican regime was very seriously weakened by the end of Echeverría's term.[73] When Echeverría left office, he was extremely unpopular and was widely regarded as a failure, at least among the middle and upper classes. It is true that in trying to satisfy certain groups in the system, Echeverría had alienated others. Likewise there was more talk of a coup d'état at the end of Echeverría's term than during any other recent presidency.

Were the failures and the conflict of the Echeverría years due to the shortcomings of this individual president or did they result from the logic of the system? Did Echeverría's populist style alienate business to a greater degree than would have occurred with a more subdued presidential manner? Inflammatory words by the president can contribute to capital flight and noninvestment even if actual goverment policy toward business does not change. The words themselves can persuade business that unacceptable measures may soon be forthcoming. Conversely, it is possible that a political leader can accomplish considerable real reform behind the facade of gentle words and incremental actions. Echeverría alienated business by his strong rhetoric while perhaps not accomplishing as much in the way of increased popular support as he had hoped. Thus to a degree, the president's style, both in actions and in words, contributed to the failures of his term.

No doubt the Mexican political system has not been as responsive to certain demands as various groups might have wanted, but there has been a general tendency for the regime to respond to frustrated forces and to the accumulation of problems. In 1940 the regime moved sharply away from Cárdenas's populist policies, which had begun to produce certain economic problems and social tensions. In 1952 Alemán's authoritarianism, corruption, and extreme probusiness policies sparked a breakaway faction of the PRI to offer Henríquez Guzmán as an alternative candidate. To minimize the damage, the regime nominated a relatively neutral candidate of noted integrity, Ruiz Cortines, instead of Alemán's favorite, who might have continued Alemán's policies, which many objected to. The administration of López Mateos (1958–64) went even further toward placating labor and the peasantry. The goverment of Díaz Ordaz (1964–70) could be seen as rigid and therefore as violating the regime's principle of adaptability. However, even its repressive policies can be seen as an adaptation to the dominant pressures of the time, as he apparently decided that maintaining order was the most important value of the moment. Then Echeverría took the regime to the left and tried to address some of the demands of groups that had not done so well during the previous few years. In reaction to the problems created by Echeverría's populist policies, López Portillo (at first) pursued an approach more congenial to business. However, when oil revenues and high government spending in their turn led to new problems, the next two presidents began to move the Mexican political economy in a new direction, trying to respond to demands for both political and economic change. Thus in terms of economic policy, the Mexican regime has been almost as flexible as many two-party regimes.

But there have been limits to the adaptability. The Mexican regime operated within a particular band. The regime was mostly probusiness, with occasional spurts of populist gestures. For example, Ruiz Cortines increased social spending after labor protests in early 1950s, but he prevented large wage increases, devalued the peso, and did not allow labor to make up its lost purchasing power. He reassured business but controlled labor. Even when the government seemed to be responding strongly to labor demands, it did so selectively and did not hesitate to use repression when demands went beyond what it was willing to allow. For example, in the late 1950s, the regime negotiated with teachers, who were urban and middle class, but at about the same time it repressed the striking railroad workers. Despite these limitations, however, the Mexican regime was relatively adaptable, compared with other authoritarian regimes in the less-developed world.

The institutionalized nature of the regime meant that no matter how much certain groups might dislike this particular president and his policies, they could be confident that he would soon be gone and a new president would replace him. Thus, unlike in many Latin American countries over the past half century, in Mexico the disaffected groups could believe that a little patience (and pressure) on their part could bring in a new executive who might be more amenable to their views. They could, in other words, hope that the regime would once again adapt to their demands. Thus while populist regimes were being overthrown all over Latin America between 1964 and 1976, the Mexican regime once again made peaceful transitions from one president to another.

Yet the Echeverría administration did not resolve Mexico's economic and political problems. To be fair, one should put Echeverría and Mexico into a larger world context. The causes of Mexico's economic problems are, of course, found partly in its position as a relatively poor country that is highly dependent on world capital and markets. That same position also constrains the Mexican government in the policies it can pursue in trying to achieve growth and distribution. Just as Canada will lose physicians to the United States if doctors' salaries are not reasonably close to those prevailing in the United States, Mexico will lose domestic capital and not acquire the necessary foreign capital if the goverment too vigorously pursues policies that alarm those with capital to invest. Because Mexico is dependent on capital that can easily find outlets elsewhere, the least movement by the goverment toward positions that are unacceptable to domestic and international capital can lead to a sudden loss of needed investment. Thus it could be said that even if Echeverría's redistributive policies were not undesirable in themselves, capital in Mexico is so volatile that any Mexican government must be careful about frightening capitalists.

The world context contributed in another way to the problem faced by Echeverría. The late 1960s and early 1970s were a time of political turmoil throughout the world, during which criticism of regimes reached levels not seen since the 1930s. In many countries, this turmoil reflected deep political divisions and often resulted in violence. In July 1968, just three months before the October tragedy at Tlatelolco, the Chicago city goverment engaged in what would subsequently be called a "police riot" outside the Democratic Party National Convention. After Richard Nixon became president in 1969, his administration carried out a whole range of nefarious activities, icluding the one that would eventually be its undoing, the burglary and attempted wiretapping of the office of the Democratic National Committee. Thus the political bitterness in Mexico during the Echeverría years must be seen in this larger context, in which politics had become more intense throughout the world.

This is not to ignore the contribution that his strident personal style might have made to the problem. It probably exacerbated the tensions between government and business. Yet his individual behavior seems to pale as an explanation for the outcomes of his presidency when compared with the effects of the system within which it took place. Although a less combative president might have evoked slightly less resistance than did Echeverría, it seems likely that just about any president who attempted the reforms that he did would have encountered serious opposition. His efforts at tax reform, land distribution, social welfare policies, and the like threatened the economic interests of business and the wealthy too much to go unchallenged. It is notable that a supposedly authoritarian regime such as Mexico's would have had such difficulty in carrying out reforms that more democratic governments enact routinely. Government and business in capitalist societies are caught in an existential relationship in which a certain amount of conflict between them is inevitable. Business seeks to maximize its profits, often through the pursuit of special privileges from the government, privileges that allow unusually high profits. Business often insists on public policies that favor itself while opposing policies that favor others. On its side, government tries to take advantage of the productive virtues of capitalism to achieve economic growth while mitigating the worst excesses of private enterprise. Thus conflict between the two occurs in every capitalist society. But in Mexico the potential conflict is particularly intense. Both business and labor in Mexico are so intent on achieving and maintaining their special privileges that they make government's task very difficult. The conflict is inherent in the political economy of the capitalist state, but it is more intense in Mexico than in some other countries. Like Cárdenas in the 1930s, Echeverría was caught between populist demands and business resistance. The volatility of capital was a major source of this difficulty.

In terms of his "political" strategy, Echeverría used both repression and participation. The amount of repression used by a regime to maintain itself is often inversely linked to the degree of participation that it allows. Other things being equal, the less a regime is willing to allow real participation in politics, the more it will probably resort to repression to subdue the inevitable dissent in order to maintain itself in power. Although the Mexican regime used less violent repression than did several other large Latin American countries at about the same time, it still used a considerable amount, and that amount was a direct result of its unwillingness to expand political participation in any meaningful way, such as allowing free elections. As it turned out, the trend in Latin America (and the world) would be in the direction of more liberal, democratic political systems over the next twenty years. Echeverría was well poised to be a leader in that trend, but he chose not to be. He expanded participation of young people in the bureaucracies of government and party, but he did not come to grips with the fundamental political problem of the Mexican regime— that it is a one-party, semiauthoritarian regime in a world and in a country in which that type of regime is becoming increasingly anachronistic. His political reforms were extremely limited and did not move Mexico toward a resolution of its basic political problem. His electoral reforms were designed merely to give the opposition guaranteed minority representation in the Chamber of Deputies; they were not intended to challege the domination of one party. His encouragement of a short list of PRI presidential contenders in 1975–76 was mere symbolism; there is no evidence that it was intended to allow a broader "electorate" (even within the regime) to choose the future president. As usual the president, acting as "grand elector," chose his own successor. Thus Echeverría's "political" policies do not appear particularly effective in solving the basic political problem of the Mexican regime: how to maintain or restore its legitimacy, its right to rule, in the eyes of most Mexicans. However, his political reforms did buy some time for the regime by guaranteeing the opposition greater representation in Congress.

Political legitimacy is strongly affected, of course, by a regime's effectiveness in managing the economy. However much participation or repression a regime practices, its legitimacy will be greater the more prosperous the society is and the more just the economic distribution is seen to be. With regard to the available economic strategies, Echeverría pursued distribution in hopes that it would lead to growth and to enhanced political legitimacy. Some reasonable degree of distribution of the existing economic wealth is necessary and desirable, and the experience of numerous countries suggests that distribution can contribute to growth. However, for several decades some countries such as Uruguay and Argentina tried to distribute more than they had, in the sense that their governments spent more than they taxed and their societies consumed more than they produced (not unlike the United States in the 1980s). The inevitable result is ballooning government deficits and national trade deficits. Mexico had already started down this road before Echeverría, but the trend gathered powerful momentum during his term. In his desire to distribute in order to enhance social justice and therefore regime legitimacy, he took Mexico down a path from which it is still trying to escape.

Another aspect of Echeverría's economic policies was equally damaging to the welfare of the country in the long run. Protectionism can be a rational long-term strategy for a nation that uses the time well. Behind the protective walls provided by government, a country can build up its domestic industry so that eventually it can enter the world market and compete in at least a few goods. Numerous countries have effectively used such a strategy, not least the United States and Japan. But Mexico seems not to have used the four decades of protection to prepare itself to compete in the world market. Its business became comfortable with the guaranteed profits provided by a captive market, high subsidies, and low taxes. Echeverría made the situation worse by frightening domestic capital and discouraging foreign investment. The president tried to correct some of the negative effects of the Mexican economic model, such as highly unequal income, but he made others worse, such as capital flight.

Echeverría's term was highly conflictual, and he alienated certain groups— most notably business. However, his populist and nationalist policies, though not always carried out well, acted as a corrective to a political strategy that had emphasized economic growth over distribution for thirty years. His strategy brought many intellectuals and young people back into the regime because of its ideological tilt as well as its employment opportunities. Under Echeverría, labor and peasants could believe that the government had not completely for-gotten them. Therefore, the adaptation of his administration seems to have re-stored some of the legitimacy of the regime to those on the left while it cost the regime some credibility on the right. Yet as divisive as his administration was, his successor took office on schedule. In this regard, it is revealing that in the United States, Nixon was driven from office, over thirty of his advisors and aides eventually went to jail, and his party was defeated by the voters at the next election. In Mexico, by contrast, Echeverría finished his term, selected his successor, and was appointed ambassador to France. His choice of López Portillo seemed reasonable, and the presidential succession in 1976 was wel-comed by most Mexicans. Relations between government and business im-proved immediately and dramatically under the new president, suggesting that Echeverría had not done any irreparable damage to the political system.

But by greatly increasing the size and presence of government in the econ-omy, Echeverría made Mexico's fundamental economic flaw even worse and set the country up for the fall that would come in the 1980s. In fairness to Echeverría, an equally serious economic error was López Portillo's mismanage-ment of the oil wealth over the next six years, although perhaps no president could have withstood the pressure to use the oil wealth for immediate benefits. In fact, like many countries in the past twenty years, Mexico has been over-whelmed by the impact of a changing world economy characterized by in-creased competition, volatility of energy prices, huge debt, and slow economic growth. The Mexican government did things that made the problems worse, but to a large extent the world economy imposed harsh conditions on Mexico, and perhaps no president could have done much better than did Echeverría and López Portillo during this time.

At a minimum, Echeverría's lurch to the left allowed the regime to hold onto its left wing for another decade or so. Without this adaptation, it is possible that the defections that occurred in 1988 would have occurred in the early 1970s. In fact, some of the defectors, such as Cuauhtémoc Cárdenas and Porfirio Muñoz Ledo, had served under Echeverría. Therefore, although Echeverría's term was certainly replete with conflict, it may have contributed in a significant way to the continuation of the regime. In any case, the fact that López Portillo found it so easy to reestablish good relations with Echeverría's main critic, big business, suggests that Echeverría had done no lasting damage to that base of the regime's support and had strengthened its ties to other groups.

Thus the Echeverría and López Portillo years demonstrate the ability and willingness of the Mexican regime to adapt, at least to some extent, to the dominant pressures that have built up in society.[74] It is true that the adaptation is within a narrow band (although not much narrower than the range of policy in many two-party systems). It is also true that the regime is, ultimately, much more responsive to the concerns of business than of the popular classes. That is not, however, a result of the *political* power of business as much as a result of its economic power in a capitalist system that depends so much on the will- ingness of business to invest and produce. Moreover, the porous nature of the economic system in small, developing nations means that their governments must be very careful about frightening business and the wealthy, lest they send their capital out of the country or otherwise refuse to invest in economic growth. Despite these limitations, the Mexican regime has shown a significant willigness to adapt its policies periodically to the demands of the popular classes. This helps the regime to retain, at least to some extent, the loyalty of these groups as well as that of their spokespeople, the leftist intellectuals.

The crisis of 1988 shows what can happen when the regime consistently alienates these groups for many years. The political elite can split apart, threat- ening the stability of the regime itself. The next chapter examines this very important variable of elite unity.

NOTES

1. Poor economic performance also contributed to their demise. Moreover, some regimes that may have appeared to be highly institutionalized were, in fact, quite per- sonalistic. Notable examples include the Communist regimes of Stalin, Ceausescu, and Castro.

2. Chalmers Johnson, *Revolutionary Change,* 2d ed. (Stanford: Stanford University Press, 1982); Gabriel Almond, Scott Flanagan, and Robert Mundt. *Crisis, Choice, and Change: Historical Studies of Political Development* (Boston: Little, Brown and Com- pany, 1973); and Juan J. Linz and Alfred Stepan, eds., *The Breakdown of Democratic Regimes: Latin America* (Baltimore: Johns Hopkins University Press, 1978).

3. John W. Sloan, *Public Policy in Latin America: A Comparative Survey* (Pittsburgh: University of Pittsburgh Press, 1984), p. 249.

4. Miguel D. Ramírez, *Mexico's Economic Crisis: Its Origins and Consequences* (New York: Praeger Publishers, 1989); Luis Javier Garrido, "The Crisis of Presidentialism," in Wayne Cornelius, Judith Gentleman, and Peter Smith, eds., *Mexico's Alternative Political Futures* (La Jolla: Center for U.S.-Mexican Studies, University of California, San Diego, 1989), pp. 417–34; Sol Sanders, *Mexico: Chaos on Our Doorstep* (Lanham, Md.: Madison Books, 1986).

5. Lawrence Koslow, ed., *The Future of Mexico* (Tempe: Center for Latin American Studies, Arizona State University, 1977); José Luis Reyna and Richard S. Weinert, eds., *Authoritarianism in Mexico* (Philadelphia: Institute for the Study of Human Issues, 1977); Judith Adler Hellman, *Mexico in Crisis* (New York: Holmes and Meier, 1978).

6. Hellman, *Mexico,* p. 180.

7. The story of the political unrest has been told many times. For a brief account, see Michael Meyer and William Sherman, *The Course of Mexican History,* 2d ed. (New York: Oxford University Press, 1983), pp. 665–71. For more extended accounts, see Hellman, *Mexico,* pp. 173–86, and Samuel Schmidt, *The Deterioration of the Mexican Presidency: The Years of Luis Echeverría* (Tucson: University of Arizona Press, 1991).

8. Dale Story, *The Mexican Ruling Party: Stability and Authority* (New York: Praeger Publishers, 1986), calculated from data on p. 53.

9. Ibid., p. 65.

10. Garrido, "Crisis."

11. Ramírez, *Mexico's Economic Crisis,* p. 48.

12. Nora Lustig, *Mexico: The Remaking of a Economy* (Washington, D.C.: Brookings Institution, 1992), pp. 16–17.

13. David Felix, "Income Distribution Trends in Mexico and the Kuznets Curves," in Sylvia Ann Hewlett and Richard S. Weinert, eds., *Brazil and Mexico: Patterns in Late Development* (Philadelphia: Institute for the Study of Human Issues, 1982), p. 267.

14. Ibid.; Ramírez, *Mexico's Economic Crisis,* p. 73, makes the same general point, although the numbers are somewhat different.

15. Felix, "Income Distribution," p. 269.

16. Guillermo O'Donnell, *Modernization and Bureaucratic-Authoritarianism: Studies in South American Politics* (Berkeley: Institute of International Studies, University of California, 1973). Also see Linz and Stepan, *Breakdown.*

17. Peter Smith, "Does Mexico Have a Power Elite?" in Reyna and Weinert, *Authoritarianism,* p. 139.

18. Roderic Camp, *Intellectuals and the State in Twentieth-Century Mexico* (Austin: University of Texas Press, 1985), p. 23.

19. Ibid., p. 16.

20. Schmidt, *Deterioration,* p. 89.

21. Yoram Shapira, "Mexico: The Impact of the 1968 Student Protest on Echeverria's Reformism," *Journal of Interamerican Studies and World Affairs* 19 (4), 1977, p. 569.

22. Camp, *Intellectuals,* p. 210.

23. For some of the works that raise this issue, see the bibliography in Valerie Bunce, *Do New Leaders Make A Differece? Executive Succession and Public Policy under Capitalism and Socialism* (Princeton: Princeton University Press, 1981).

24. Ibid., pp. 228–29.

25. Raymond Vernon, *The Dilemma of Mexico's Development: The Roles of the Private and Public Sectors* (Cambridge: Harvard University Press, 1963).

26. James W. Wilkie, *The Mexican Revolution: Federal Expeditures and Social Change since 1910,* 2d ed. (Berkeley: University of Califoria Press, 1970), p. 32; and James W. Wilkie, *La revolucion Mexicana: gasto federal y cambio social* (México, D. F.: Fondo de Cultura Económica, 1978), pp. 322, 358.

27. Hellman, *Mexico,* p. 187.

28. Shapira, "Mexico," p. 561.

29. Kevin Middlebrook, *Political Liberalization in an Authoritarian Regime: The Case of Mexico* (La Jolla: Center for U.S.-Mexican Studies, University of California, San Diego, 1985).

30. For a detailed account of Echeverría's Third World policies and their consequences, see Schmidt, *Deterioration,* chapter 5.

31. Keith Roseblum, *Arizona Daily Star,* Dec. 30, 1989.

32. Shapira, "Mexico," p. 567.

33. Hellman, *Mexico,* p. 203.

34. Schmidt, *Deterioration,* p. 84.

35. Ibid.

36. Daniel Levy and Gabriel Székely, *Mexico: Paradoxes of Stability and Change,* 2d ed. (Boulder, Colo.: Westview Press, 1987), pp. 100–104.

37. Robert Kuttner, *The Economic Illusion* (Boston: Houghton Mifflin, 1984).

38. Merilee S. Grindle, "Policy Change in an Authoritarian Regime," *Journal of Interamerican Studies and World Affairs* 19 (4), 1977, p. 531.

39. Ibid., p. 523.

40. Kenneth Godwin, "Mexican Population Policy," in Lawrence Koslow, ed., *The Future of Mexico* (Tempe: Center for Latin American Studies, Arizona State University, 1977), pp. 145–68.

41. Peter K. Hall, "Mexico's Economic Crisis and Need for a New Development Strategy," *Australian Outlook* 38 (1), 1984, pp. 26–32.

42. Ramírez, *Mexico's Ecoomic Crisis,* pp. 46, 86.

43. Roberto Newell and Luis Rubio, *Mexico's Dilemma: The Political Origins of Economic Crisis* (Boulder, Colo.: Westview Press, 1984), p. 131.

44. Hellman, *Mexico,* p. 193.

45. Ibid., p. 194. Also see Richard S. Weinert, "The State and Foreign Capital," in Reyna and Weinert, *Authoritarianism,* pp. 120–22.

46. Laurence Whitehead, "La política económica del sexenio de Echeverría: que salió mal y por qué? *Foro Iternacional,* January 1980, p. 513.

47. Ramírez, *Mexico's Economic Crisis,* p. 83.

48. Nora Hamilton, *The Limits of State Autonomy: Post-Revolutionary Mexico* (Princeton: Princeton University Press, 1982).

49. Roderic Camp, *Entrepreneurs and Politics in Twentieth-Century Mexico* (New York: Oxford University Press, 1989), p. 7.

50. As the collapse of communism demonstrated, governments in socialist countries face the same dilemma, except that the inexorable logic of economics confronts them directly, without a business class interposed between the government and economic reality to confuse the issue.

51. Hellman, *Mexico,* pp. 227–28.

52. Newell and Rubio, *Mexico's Dilemma,* p. 127.

53. For example, Hellman, *Mexico,* and Schmidt, *Deterioration.*

54. Hellman, *Mexico,* p. 214.

55. E.V.K. Fitzgerald, "The State and Capital Accumulation in Mexico," *Latin American Studies* 10 (2), 1978, pp. 263–82, and John S. Evans, "The Evolution of the Mexican Tax System since 1970," *Technical Papers Series,* no. 34. (Austin: Office for Public Sector Studies, Institute of Latin American Studies, University of Texas, 1982).

56. Newell and Rubio, *Mexico's Dilemma,* p. 143.

57. Ibid., pp. 178–83.

58. Schmidt, *Deterioration,* p. 112. The rumors are from p. 111.

59. Ibid., pp. 179–80. In Spanish: "En el fondo, no soy tan pendejo."

60. Levy and Székely, *Mexico,* p. 116.

61. Camp, *Entrepreneurs,* p. 29.

62. Levy and Székely, *Mexico,* p. 60.

63. Ibid., p. 159.

64. Ramírez, *Mexico's Economic Crisis,* p. 87.

65. Martin Needler, *Mexican Politics: The Containment of Conflict,* 2d ed. (New York: Praeger Publishers, 1990), pp. 36–37.

66. Camp, *Entrepreneurs,* p. 28.

67. Middlebrook, *Political Liberalization,* p. 6.

68. Ibid.

69. Lustig, *Mexico,* p. 21.

70. Alan Riding, *Distant Neighbors* (New York: Vintage Books, 1986), p. 213.

71. Juan Miguel de Mora, *Esto nos Dió López Portillo* (México, D. F.: Anaya Editores, 1982), and Julio Scherer García, *Los presidentes.* México, D.F.: Editorial Grijalbo, 1986).

72. Stephen D. Morris, *Corruption and Politics in Contemporary Mexico* (Tuscaloosa, AL: University of Alabama Press, 1991), p. 76.

73. For example, see Schmidt, *Deterioration.*

74. This chapter is not meant to imply a rigid "pendulum" theory of Mexican politics, in which policy swings back and forth from left to right in a predictable way from one presidential term to another. However, numerous observers have noted that different presidential administrations have sought to address pressures that have built up in previous administrations; moreover, changes in emphasis may occur *within* a presidential term, as with López Portillo. See Wilkie, *The Mexican Revolution*; Martin Needler, *Politics and Society in Mexico* (Albuquerque: University of New Mexico Press, 1971); Steven Sanderson, "Presidential Succession and Political Rationality in Mexico," *World Politics* 35 (3), 1983, pp. 315–34; and Dale Story, "Policy Cycles in Mexican Politics," *Latin American Research Review* 20 (3), 1985, pp. 139–62.

5

Elite Unity and Political Stability

To this point we have used several important factors to explain political stability, or a regime's ability to endure. Regimes that are institutionalized, effective, adaptable, that use coercion judiciously, and that exist in a congenial international environment tend to be more stable than regimes without these qualities. This chapter will examine another factor that helps to determine whether a particular regime will persist—elite unity. Over the decades since the Revolution, the Mexican political elite has experienced defections, but the ruling party has remained in power. One reason is that despite the defections, the political elite has stayed relatively united. This chapter will look first at the components of elite unity. Next it will examine the specific methods the Mexican elite has used to ensure unity: common class and educational backgrounds, official corruption and coercion, and the taming of the Mexican military so that it would support the regime rather than oppose it. Finally, the chapter will describe the serious defections that have occurred since 1940, ending with the most recent and serious challenge to elite unity, the election of 1988. Even in this instance, however, the Mexican political elite remained relatively unified behind the regime, in marked contrast to the enormous conflict among elites in some other Latin American countries, most notably Argentina, during much of this period.[1]

THE IMPORTANCE OF ELITE UNITY

The elite of any society is defined as simply *those who have a disproportionate share of resources*. Various types of resources are valued in a society at a given time—money, knowledge, political power—and each type of resource tends to give rise to a particular social group that specializes in that resource— the rich, the experts, the rulers. Thus an elite is the small group at the top of each of these social pyramids, a group that has, per person, a large share of these valued resources. The classic statement of the thesis that elites are important to political outcomes is found in the early-twentieth-century works of the European scholars Gaetano Mosca, Vilfredo Pareto, and Robert Michels. They argued that all societies were characterized by inequality, with a small group at the top virtually monopolizing resources, especially political power.[2] The elite in each area had a disproportionate share of resources, which in various ways translated into power, defined as the probability of influencing others. Some elite theories are empirical, or descriptive; that is, they merely seek to understand the role of elites without necessarily arguing that it is desirable for societies to be governed by elites. Much of the early elite theory, especially that of Mosca and Pareto, was also normatively or ideologically elitist. It argued that elite rule was often good for society.

I agree with Peter Smith, who wrote, "What I take from elite theory is not its unnecessary trappings, and certainly not its ideological propensities, but simply its most elementary insight: that power is distributed unequally, that those who possess it can be identified as an elite, and that the characteristics of the elite offer considerable insight into the operation of society."[3] Perhaps the most important idea to come out of elite theory is, therefore, the simple notion that power is not shared equally; the elite in every society possess an inordinate share, and the way they use it is crucial.

One of the most important ways in which political elites can contribute to political order and regime stability is to agree on the rules of the game for political interaction. One of the most critical issues is to agree on how to decide who will occupy the top positions of power. Elite "settlements" or accommodations can be crucial in moving societies from political instability and violence to peaceful stability. In several cases—such as England in 1688–89 and Sweden in 1809—leaders representing factions of previously disunified elites negotiated arrangements that "eliminated mutual distrust and produced elite consensus and unity."[4] G. Lowell Field and John Higley contend that such elite settlements are rare because the conditions favoring them are relatively rare. A salient condition that favors elite consensus on the rules of the game is that the negotiated settlement occurs before the masses become involved in politics. Once a high level of political mobilization and participation occurs, elite consensus becomes harder to achieve because the elites will tend to be pulled apart by the vertical pressures of their various mass publics. Elite settlements are not impossible under such conditions, but they become much more difficult to achieve. Conversely, propitious conditions for elite unity include the existence of only a few elite factions, each with recognized leaders, relative isolation from mass pressures, and an understanding by the elites of the crucial importance of agreement. Such negotiated agreements unfortunately are most likely to occur after periods of prolonged violence. This is a fairly good description of the conditions faced by the framers of the U.S. Constitution in 1787, English elites in 1688, and Mexican leaders in the 1930s. Both Mexico and England illustrate the fact that the prolonged civil violence may even have occurred decades before the onset of elite unity, in the case of England thirty years earlier and Mexico fifteen to twenty years earlier. The memory of violence acts as a chastening influence on elites, making them more willing to cooperate.[5]

Once this type of basic political settlement occurs, it tends to last a remarkably long time. This is so because of the memory of the events that impelled the cooperation in the first place, particularly violence, and because the cooperation may become self-perpetuating. Cooperation may be institutionalized, creating a structure for further cooperation. That cooperation then begets further cooperation as trust grows among the elites.

But such a settlement does not necessarily last forever. New conditions arise that place a strain on the initial settlement. The U.S. Constitution "settled" the slavery issue for several decades, but as a new ethos developed in the industrial North that saw slavery as unacceptable, southern elites felt their economic and social interests threatened and hence tried to secede from the 1787 compact. The North resisted by force, and a civil war resulted. Although a civil war is not always the outcome of such stresses, every government eventually has to deal in some way with the political strains that accumulate as its society changes. A settlement that worked at one time may have to be revised, either slowly over several decades or quickly at some point. Hence adaptability is integrally related to elite unity.

The specific type of power with which we are most concerned in this study is political power, or the probability of influencing the policies and activities of the state.[6] This influence may extend even to the very existence of the state or at least to a particular regime. A fundamental question about elite unity is why it occurs. An important part of the answer is that changing conditions can transform the cost-benefit calculus of elite individuals. That is, trying to seize power through violence may become less attractive, and working peacefully within the existing system may become more attractive. The restructuring and strengthening of institutions of peaceful interaction often play an important role in the transformation of the cost-benefit calculations of elites and other political actors.

One of the great theoretical challenges of social science, and perhaps the characteristic that makes the development of social "laws" more difficult than in the physical sciences, is the complex interaction of structural determinants and free will. That is, to what extent is human behavior determined by factors in the environment and to what extent does human behavior occur independently of these factors? Physical phenomena appear to behave according to natural laws, and physical objects themselves are not faced with conscious choices, as far as we know. Water flows downhill, following the path of least resistance, without considering its course. Much of human behavior may, in fact, be comparable to the flow of water, that is, following the path of least resistance. But human behavior is different from the behavior of unconscious physical phenomena in at least two ways: the number of factors that influence human behavior appears to be greater, and humans can decide, as it were, to "flow uphill." They can exert their will and thereby act in ways other than automatically following the path of least resistance or the resultant of forces.

A major development in our understanding of human behavior in the past two centuries is the knowledge of the degree to which behavior is influenced by structural qualities of the environment in which humans find themselves. Although factors such as social class, level of education, and position of the nation in the international economic order seem to leave little room for human choice, we still believe that, at least at the individual level, there remains some space for choice. That choice may or may not be "rational," and it may be highly constrained. Yet, despite how far our knowledge of structural determinants advances, most social scientists probably believe that humans still have some degree of choice. Within political science, there has been a definite trend in recent years in the direction of examining the conditions under which elites try consciously to break out of historical patterns of violence, instability, or dictatorship and move toward more consensual politics. Several important findings have emerged from these studies.

In 1964 Robert Alexander described how Rómulo Betancourt and his colleagues in Venezuela learned from their mistakes. In their first period in power from 1945 to 1948, Betancourt and his leftist Acción Democrática party pursued radical public policies in an effort to reshape the political landscape of Venezuela. After three years, they were ejected from office by a military coup, and the country fell under repressive authoritarian rule for ten years. In 1958 Betancourt and his party came back into power, much chastened by their earlier experience. As a result of that experience, they had negotiated with conservative opponents a pact of understanding that put limits on reform and kept politics and public policy within a relatively narrow range for the foreseeable future.[7] Although not without difficulties, Venezuela has experienced a relatively peaceful succession of elected presidents since that time. (As of 1993, that elite consensus was showing signs of serious strain, indicating that although such agreements can last a long time, they do not necessarily last forever.)

In 1971 a volume appeared in the political development series of the Social Science Research Council that paid considerable attention to the importance of elite choices in resolving certain crises that face every political system as it deals with the political challenges produced by the economic and social changes of modernization.[8] A later volume in the series also offered elite compromise as an important factor in contributing to stable and nonviolent political change.[9] Elite choices were considered crucial to an acceptable and productive resolution of these issues.

Even though these crises were, to a large extent, imposed on societies by structural conditions such as the level of socioeconomic development, the exact way that a particular regime dealt with the crisis was, at least to some degree, a matter of choice by the political elites of the time. For example, in Britain, from the 1830s onward, the elites adapted to demands, first by the middle and then the working classes, for greater political participation in a series of reform acts that effectively resolved the country's crisis of participation. The dominant elites agreed on these measures, rather than running the risk that dissent would grow to such an extent that the entire monarchical-parliamentary system would collapse.[10]

The qualities that contribute to a stable regime are all, as we have said before, interconnected. A regime will tend to be stable to the degree that the *elites* are *united* in their commitment to the existing regime. They will tend to be committed to the degree that the regime is *effective* in achieving goals that are important in that society, such as economic growth. But since economic growth is not the only value that a society might be interested in, and because in its early stages economic growth can actually be politically destabilizing, an elite must be *adaptable* in responding to the pressures that come from society and that, sooner or later, will be reflected by divisions within the elite itself. The more highly *institutionalized* a regime is, the more stable it will tend to be because it will have established certain methods of interaction, such as the rules for executive succession and elite circulation in general. It will also have established the procedures for elite and mass political participation, whether democratic or not. With these qualities, a regime is more likely to achieve the strength both to forestall any attempt to overthrow it and to make it unnecessary to rule by brute force alone. A regime that must use large amounts of coercion to remain in power is obviously a regime under serious threat.

If a part of the elite believes it is being disadvantaged under existing arrangements, the dissenting group may make an appeal to mass groups in an attempt to gain their support and thus a larger share of political power. The dissident elite may invoke new "liberal" principles of politics that call for increased participation by nonelite groups. The motivation of these "subelites" will be a blend of sincere commitment to the new principles and self-interested calculation that the new principles (or a restoration of old principles) will help the dissidents obtain a share (or a monopoly) of political power. If one side wins a clear victory, this may result in a new equilibrium that may last for a significant time. However, if neither side wins a clear victory, and if the contending forces do not work out an agreement for interaction, the result is likely to be considerable political instability. This was the case in much of Latin America in the first fifty years after independence, from 1820 to 1870, when neither conservatives nor liberals could definitively gain the upper hand and when the two sides had not agreed on a method for acquiring political power.

One way out of the behavioral trap of institutionalized instability, in which powerful factions vie for control, is for the competing elites to make a conscious decision to act in the future only within some defined range of agreement, that is, to agree on basic principles of interaction. They may initially be brought to this point of compromise by a combination of factors, most of which we have already discussed at length. A particular group may come to power through force and be able to impose its will on the political system in general. The memory of violence may then play a crucial role in persuading members of the elite to accept and to stay within the new rules of engagement.

Present coercion and the memory of past violence were both important factors in convincing Mexican elites of both the early Porfirian and the postrevolutionary periods to accept the new regimes. In addition, both of these regimes were eventually effective in promoting economic growth in ways that created and satisfied economic elites. The approval of the United States also played a part in sustaining the Porfirian regime for decades. In the end, however, the failure of that elite to institutionalize the regime, especially the lack of agreement on the rules of succession to the presidency, eroded the unity of the elites. The Porfirian elite also did not display adequate flexibility or willingness to incorporate emerging elites such as Francisco Madero and his associates. The Porfirian regime might have endured for a while after Díaz's retirement or death—even if it had done nothing to settle the substantive complaints of workers and peasants—if it had been sufficiently open to new aspirants and if it had worked out a method for peacefully settling the succession. Neither political democracy nor economic justice was required to maintain the regime in power, at least for a while, if it had been able to work out its intraelite struggle peacefully. This argument has obvious antidemocratic implications, but I think it is an accurate portrayal of the reality in Mexico at that time. In 1910, demands for greater political democracy were not the primary motive of revolutionaries. With few exceptions—such as, perhaps, Madero—they mainly wanted a share of political power for its own rewards and for the ability it would give them to influence government policy. The main evidence for this assertion is that the revolutionaries proceeded to construct a political system that closely resembled the Porfirian system, with the exception that the presidency was regularly rotated.

THE UNITY OF MEXICAN ELITES

Before one discusses the elite of a particular society, it is useful to specify whether that elite is a single "ruling elite" that is tightly interconnected, as in C. Wright Mills's formulation of *The Power Elite,* or whether it conforms to Suzanne Keller's notion of a different "strategic" elite in each of several areas of life—politics, economy, culture, etc.[11] Although Mexico's various elites are smaller and in some ways more tightly interconnected than elites in the United States, several different elites are discernible in Mexico, and all of them are important in varying degrees to political outcomes, including political stability. Thus Mexico, like most countries, is characterized by plural elites rather than a single interlocking power elite. There are elites in different functional areas of life, such as politics, business, military, and labor. In some ways, it is true, the Mexican elites are more homogeneous and interconnected than in the United States. For example, many media leaders and intellectuals have been linked to the regime far more closely than have comparable individuals in the United States. Radicals in the United States would argue that Dan Rather and Tom Brokaw are merely supporters of the regime who occasionally question this or that public policy or action of a government official. However, they are considerably more independent than the comparable anchors of network newscasts in Mexico. Jacobo Zabludovsky, the anchor of "24 Horas," the major news program in Mexico City, reports the news in a way that is obviously biased toward the regime.

The same could generally be said for other Mexican elites, including intellectuals. A much larger proportion of intellectuals in Mexico have worked for the government than is true in the United States. Indeed, when the regime moves to the left, as it did under Echeverría in the early 1970s, it is usually trying to pacify not only workers and peasants but also, and perhaps even more important, the intellectual critics on the left who have grown impatient with the regime's lack of achievement in the area of social justice, as illustrated by the gross inequalities in income and wealth.

One type of elite has probably been less connected to the regime in Mexico than in the United States, at least in a sense. In the United States, top businessmen have moved in and out of government, especially since the 1920s. Such names as Andrew Mellon, Henry Morgenthau, Douglas Dillon, Robert McNamara, and George Schultz are only the most famous of a host of businesspeople who have held high positions in the federal government. That sort of lateral movement from business to government has been almost nonexistent in Mexico. This does not mean that business is alienated from the PRI regime—far from it. As we saw in chapter 3, the regime's policies were good for Mexican business, and business accommodated itself to the regime. However, movement of elites from business to government, as has been so common in the United States, has seldom occurred in Mexico.[12]

In any case, the independence of various elites is great enough to justify seeing them as distinct from one another. As distinct as they are, however, the stability of a political regime will depend on the degree to which it has the support of these different elites. By *elite unity,* I mean the elite members' actions and words that contributed to the maintenance of the regime rather than to its downfall. The vast majority of the Mexican political elite, including the "opposition," behaved in ways that contributed to the maintenance of the regime in power. They did so because conditions made it in their interest to do so. These conditions included the institutionalization of the regime, including rules of succession and a monopoly of coercive ability, the effectiveness of the regime in achieving economic growth from 1940 to 1982, and the adaptability of the regime in accommodating to political pressures from the left and the right. Elite unity is one of the major factors that determines whether a political system is stable or not.

At least as far as stability is concerned, it seems that the optimal elite is neither extremely closed nor extremely open. A tightly closed elite will be stagnant; it will not incorporate new members at a rate rapid enough to bring in new ideas and allow it to adapt to new conditions and new demands from below. It will not offer hope to outsiders who may aspire to membership in the elite. Hence it will tend to lose the all-important support of those just below the elite, the subelite. (In the United States, both term limits and campaign finance reforms are efforts to force the political system to open up to new entrants.) Conversely, an elite that is extremely open both to new ways and to new members may achieve many good things, but stability may not be one of them. For example, at least one scholar has argued that Argentine political instability was partly a result of the extreme heterogeneity of its political elite.[13] Thus other things being equal, extreme elite fluidity may contribute to regime instability.

The governing elite of any society is secure to the degree that individuals and groups in society believe that this elite and this regime deserve to be in power. A regime will also enjoy varying degrees of legitimacy in the view of different political actors. The executive and those around him or her may see the regime as thoroughly legitimate. If, however, significant numbers of the political elite begin to question whether a particular ruler or set of rulers deserves to be in power, their loss of support will produce an erosion of legitimacy that will be far more damaging to the regime than if a comparable number of nonelites questioned the regime.

The creation of a unified Mexican elite did not happen overnight. After the old political elite was overthrown in the Revolution of 1910, it took over twenty years for a new elite to consolidate itself. This process of consolidation was incremental, taking place slowly and step by step, although certain events stand out. The revolt in which Alvaro Obregón seized power from Carranza in 1920 was the last successful military rebellion in Mexican history, although uprisings occurred during the next decade. The ruling elite during this period was a combination of political and military, emerging primarily from the contingent of revolutionary generals. Factions of this politico-military ruling group clashed before each election, in 1923, 1927, and 1929. Each time, the governing group was able to put together a coalition that defeated the insurgents, although in 1923 it was a close call. Edwin Lieuwen says that in 1923 the insurgent troops and Obregón's government troops were almost equally matched, but Obregón was able to call on labor and agrarian irregulars. In the 1927 uprising, only about 20 percent of the troops rebelled. Another revolt occurred in 1929 as certain generals disagreed with Plutarco Calles's choice of Pascual Ortiz Rubio for president. With the creation of the revolutionary party in 1929, former president Calles was able to unite the competing elites into one organization that provided a framework for elite interaction and competition. But the discipline and cooperation required for elite unity still depended to a large degree on the forceful personality of the *jefe máximo* Calles. In 1935 President Lázaro Cárdenas broke Calles's personal power and centralized political power in the presidency. In 1938 Cárdenas reorganized the party along corporatist lines to include organizations of workers, peasants, the middle class, and the military. The elites and masses of those groups were thereby tied into the regime.

Thus by 1940 the Cárdenas administration had succeeded in uniting various factions within one political party and institutionalizing many of the more important political questions, especially the succession. In chapter 2 we argued that the institutionalization of the political system from 1929 to 1938 had a profound effect on the behavior of Mexican political elites. The creation of a broad political party that incorporated many of the major social forces, that provided a formal forum for presidential selection, and that afforded a mechanism for political recruitment contributed mightily to the continued willingness of most political aspirants to engage in politics peacefully within one party.

Some observers have argued that elite unity is the most important factor explaining the stability of the Mexican regime and that—contrary to appearances—institutionalization was not a major factor. One article says, for example, that "the system is held together not by institutions, but by the rigid discipline of the elites in not overstepping the bounds of the bargain." [14] But what enforces this rigid discipline? I believe that the political institutions created by the postrevolutionary elites played a large role in shaping elite behavior from 1929 to the present. The regime became broad enough to encompass many points of view and many personal ambitions. It became entrenched enough that most of those who wanted to play an active role in politics saw it in their interest to do so within the broad party and regime of the Revolution. Elite unity did not occur in a vacuum; it was as consistent as it was because of its interaction with the other factors discussed in this study. Thus the "rigid discipline" of the elites came about because of conditions that made political activists see their self-interest as staying within the regime. The predictability provided by institutionalized norms for interaction, the effectiveness of the regime in achieving certain results such as economic growth, and the flexibility of the regime in responding—at least to some extent—to various pressures all contributed to the decisions of political elites to remain in the system. Yet elite unity is not merely a dependent variable that is a result of other factors; to an extent, it can be seen as a distinct force of its own. Whatever the reasons that made it likely, it was not inevitable. Specific people made decisions to behave in particular ways. Just as Venezuelan and Colombian elites from the 1950s onward decided to cooperate, Mexican elites after the 1920s decided, by and large, to cooperate within an accepted set of institutional rules. However powerful the forces that encouraged them to behave in this way, they could have decided not to do so, and in fact some did defect, as we shall see later.

Elites might be considered "unified" or integrated along several dimensions, including social homogeneity, recruitment patterns, personal interaction, value consensus, group solidarity, and institutional context. Research on Mexico indicates that its political elite, at least for several decades after 1940, became more homogeneous. Increasingly, the elite came from a common background of social class and education (especially at the National University of Mexico and especially in law) and were increasingly urban.[15]

The composition and background of the Mexican political elite has changed considerably since the 1920s. From 1920 to 1940, political leadership was primarily political-military. Most presidents and many other political leaders, including state governors, had fought in the Revolution and in the various rebellions of the 1920s. After 1946, however, the new generation of political elites was increasingly civilian and educated. The first civilian president to serve a full term was Miguel Alemán (1946–52), and he represents the first major shift in the political elite from military to civilian rulers.

As the decades wore on, the educational level of upper-level politicians also changed. The percent of cabinet members who had university degrees grew, for example, from 69 percent under Cárdenas to 77 percent under Alemán and then to 96 percent under Echeverría before slipping slightly under López Portillo. Moreover, the type of education of the political elite shifted gradually in the decades after World War II. The percent of cabinet officials with law degrees rose throughout the 1950s but then fell to around 40 percent thereafter, whereas the proportion of those with other degrees, principally in economics and engineering, doubled from 27 percent in the 1930s to over 50 percent by the 1960s. Thus the political elite became not only increasingly educated but also increasingly "technocratic."[16]

As indicated by the background of the men who became president, since 1920 the Mexican political elite has changed in fundamental ways about every twenty-five years. From 1920 until 1946 (twenty-six years), every full-term president was a general; from 1946 to 1970 (twenty-four years), every president was a nongeneral politician with a background of elective office; from 1970 to 1994 (twenty-four years), every president had a background as a civilian bureaucrat without electoral experience. Broadly speaking, the transitions have been from soldier to politician to bureaucrat.

The rise of leaders with mainly technical training, often acquired in foreign universities and often in the field of economics, has been an important phenomenon of the past three decades. As early as 1963, Raymond Vernon pointed out that economic technicians were rapidly becoming indispensable as government played a larger role in the economy and as the techniques of economic management became increasingly complex.[17] In 1971 Roderic Camp also pointed to the growing role of technocrats.[18] In his major work on the Mexican political elite in 1979, Smith dealt at length with the rising técnicos and their potential conflict with políticos.[19] Some observers have argued that the recent transition from politician to bureaucrat is a major reason for the current divisions within the Mexican regime. They claim that the rise of the technocrat to political power threatens the stability of Mexico, or at least the continuation of the present regime, by upsetting the balance among técnicos, políticos, and militares.[20] Another point of view is that the major schisms in Mexican politics today are what they have always been, that the important distinctions are between the left and the right, not between those with one type of training and those with another.[21]

There is probably some truth to all these claims. Although the makeup of the Mexican political elite has changed in fundamental ways over the past fifty years, it was relatively homogeneous at any given time. That homogeneity may have been related to political stability by both reflecting and contributing to a common set of values among the political elite. The political generation of 1920–40 was dominated by those who had actually fought in the Revolution and who shared certain values. To one extent or another, they tended to be concerned with establishing civic order and pursuing some degree of social justice in the form of land distribution and labor rights. The next generation of political leaders, from 1940 to 1970, tended to come from similar backgrounds and to define the situation in a common way. They tended to see economic growth, rather than nationalism or social programs, as the primary way to solve Mexico's problems. The presidents that ruled from 1970 to 1994 did not have electoral experience before becoming president, and they tended to select associates who had similar technical training and bureaucratic backgrounds as themselves. It is true that by 1988, the continuation of this pattern of "technocratic" presidents would be a factor in elite division. However, it seems likely that the more fundamental division was in competing visions of political economy rather than competing career paths. (The two may be related, of course. Formal training in economics may give one a greater respect for the market and greater reluctance to interfere with market forces.) Thus despite changes in education and background over the years, the Mexican political elite tended to be somewhat homogeneous at a given time. This was a factor in its cohesion for over sixty years.

Another factor that contributed to elite unity was the institutionalized nature of the regime that produced a turnover in office each six years. This meant that the regime had enormous patronage to dispense to its supporters, which helped to maintain their loyalty. This was the case in all branches of government and party, including the government bureaucracy, state enterprises, legislature, and state and local governments.

This has always been one of the major uses of both the federal congress and the state legislatures. The federal Chamber of Deputies is renewed every three years with immediate reelection prohibited, and thus a new set of party loyalists could regularly be rewarded with largely ceremonial posts in the national legislature. Seats were routinely awarded to up-and-coming young politicians. The awarding of seats in the Chamber was also used as a means to balance the governing coalition. On average from 1943 to 1976, PRI seats in the Chamber were apportioned to the various sectors of the party in the following way: popular, 50 percent; labor, 25 percent; and peasant, 25 percent.[22] After 1960 the Chamber was also increasingly used to co-opt the opposition. The 1963 electoral law introduced the practice of proportional representation by which opposition parties were granted seats in the Chamber if they received at least 2.5 percent of the popular vote, even if they did not win any district seats. Thus the Chamber of Deputies performed at least four functions that served the ruling party, other than actually enacting legislation. It provided a training ground and career path for rising politicians, a sinecure for older loyalists, a forum for balancing the components of the governing coalition, and a place for allowing the opposition to play a role in the political system. The federal Senate performed a similar role as a training ground for party loyalists, but it did not provide a forum for the opposition, since no seat in the Senate was occupied by a member of the "real" opposition until the election of 1988, when four seats fell to Cuauhtémoc Cárdenas's group. The PAN won its first Senate seat in 1991.

The executive bureaucracy plays a similar role in providing jobs for supporters of the regime. The bureaucracy grew larger during each presidential term until recently. This was especially true of the Echeverría years, and this was one way that Echeverría tried to deal with the crisis of legitimacy in the early 1970s. Martin Needler, a close student of Mexican government, wrote in 1990 that even after the cuts of the 1980s, "The number of positions is out of all proportion to the work to be done." [23] Moreover, there is an almost complete turnover of positions with each new president (although many of the same individuals remain in regime positions).

Methods such as these provided for a relatively high degree of circulation of elites. This was not the case during the last years of the Porfiriato (1900–1910), when about two-thirds of high-level officeholders had held high positions in previous Díaz administrations. Or, looked at from the point of view of the aspiring individual, the chances were over 80 percent that a given member of the top political elite would reappear in a high position in the next presidential term. In other words, there was a very high degree of continuity among the political elite. The prerevolutionary elite tended to be stagnant, with the same people remaining in the same office for years or rotating from one office to another. As Smith says, "The system was static, rigid, and closed." [24]

The Revolution cut this degree of continuity in half. From 1920 until 1971, only about one-third of high officeholders had held high office previously. As Smith says, "During each presidential term, approximately two-thirds of the high national offices have been held by complete newcomers to the elite circles." [25] This is a relatively high rate of turnover. Top-level careers generally last for only one presidential term and seldom for as many as three (eighteen years). The rate of turnover from one presidential cabinet to another (about 75 percent) was far higher in Mexico than in many countries such as Britain, West Germany, and the Soviet Union during normal times. In fact, the rate of turnover of high offices was about the same in Mexico during normal times as in the Soviet Union during that country's periodic purges! Smith says, "Since the Revolution, the pattern of officeholding has borne more resemblance to a revolving door than to a game of musical chairs." [26]

How can such high rates of turnover be reconciled with our view of the Mexican political system as exhibiting a strong degree of continuity within the elite? Part of the answer lies in differing conceptions of the political elite. Smith defines it as those holding the *top* positions, and hence the rate of turn-over appears high, since few individuals remain in top positions for very long. If one conceives of it in broader terms, as including those individuals who have held positions at almost any level within the political system, then the Mexican political elite is much larger and therefore much more stable. Some people may spend several years at lower-level positions before joining Smith's elite.

Political elites in Mexico have come mainly from the middle class—"before, during, and since the Revolution." [27] However, at the same time, the Revolution also redistributed political power to previously dispossessed segments of the country's middle class, especially in the early decades, as power shifted to the north, to provincial towns, and to younger men. Power also shifted to military leaders (for a while), although after 1940, power shifted increasingly to university-trained lawyers and later to economists. Like the elites of most countries, the Mexican political elite is socially unrepresentative of the general population, and the higher up the political-status ladder one goes, the more socially unrepresentative the elite becomes—a phenomenon that Robert Putnam called "the law of increasing disproportion." [28] For example, although only a tiny portion of the Mexican population attended university, 83 percent of the Mexican cabinets from 1940 to 1970 attended a *particular* university—UNAM—compared with 72 percent of the British cabinets who attended Oxford or Cambridge. [29] Thus the early years are important in socializing the individuals who eventually enter the upper political reaches. The common background tended to link the elite together through personal connections and loyalties. Many professors at UNAM who had served in the government recruited their students for government careers, thus binding one political generation to another through shared values and personal ties.

The relatively high circulation of elites falters as one reaches the higher-level positions. Some members of the political elite last more than twenty years. In fact, 50 percent of those who were members of the political elite (by Smith's definition) had held political office for at least thirty years by the time they exited from the national elite. The typical member of the national political elite from 1940 to 1970 entered the political system at the average age of twenty-eight and stayed almost thirty years, until the average age of fifty-seven. [30] Thus, although he may have been a member of the top political elite for only one presidential administration, the typical person who wound up as a member of the elite had spent almost thirty years as a member of the governing regime at some level. Therefore, even though tenure near the top tended to be short, total political careers tended to be long. Moreover, those who made it to the very top were atypical in that they not only had been members of the regime for about thirty years but also had been members of Smith's national political elite for longer than the average elite member. That is, those who reappeared in three terms tended to be the very top elite.

This "combination of long apprenticeship, short supremacy, and early retirement'' at first glance might be seen as a likely source of resentment and hence instability.[31] However, this was not the case for at least two reasons. First many, if not most, Mexican government officials enjoyed the ability to ''enrich'' themselves while in office. Numerous observers have commented on the potential implications of corruption for political stability.[32] In less industrial countries, government service often provides important channels for socioeconomic mobility that the private economy does not, both because the private economy is not highly developed and because government regulates the private economy so closely that numerous opportunities exist for graft by those government officials who regulate business. Thus many of those who served long times at low levels and then departed the political elite were satisfied with the economic benefits they amassed during their tenure in office, often collecting enough to set themselves up in business with the capital thus obtained. Moreover, their continuing loyalty to the regime is maintained after leaving office because if they question the regime, there is the possibility that the government will investigate them for ''inexplicable self-enrichment,'' as the Mexicans euphemistically put it. Thus the fact that a party defector or adversary can be threatened with exposure increases the political control and cohesion of the party and the regime. The high level of official corruption is a source of ''tacit blackmail'' that discourages political opposition. A sufficient number of former officials have been prosecuted for corruption to make the point effectively to the rest.

Thus corruption can act as a stabilizing force by providing ''spoils'' for the members of the regime and also act as a check on defection by providing the regime with a weapon that can be turned against defectors. Moreover, if corruption is kept to a ''reasonable'' level, it can act as a necessary lubricant for an otherwise ineffective bureaucracy. Even members of the leftist opposition have been known to express some satisfaction that a bribe, to a police officer or other official, is an effective way of dealing with the bureaucracy (as well as a way to redistribute income to poorly paid officials). The regime can also use corruption as an excuse for failures in policy implementation, in the sense of ''if only the king knew.'' Thus society may see corruption as part of Mexican (or Spanish) culture and may believe that the government is doing its best to combat it. In fact, the anticorruption campaigns that tend to come in the first year of each new administration can help to bolster the image of that administration.[33] Thus as long as it does not exceed tolerable bounds, corruption can be seen as a stabilizing force. Even when it does exceed these bounds, as during the Alemán and López Portillo administrations, the efforts of the succeeding president to bring it back within acceptable limits can actually contribute to the legitimacy of the regime by giving the new administration an issue on which to be dramatically effective.

A second reason those who exit the political elite, having had their turn at the trough, do not rebel after leaving office is the hope that they or their children may return to government service at some time in the future. The high rate of turnover thus provides both real opportunity and the hope of opportunity. Therefore, it is relatively clear to most participants what they must do to thrive in the Mexican system: stay within the PRI; remain friends with as many others in the party as possible; avoid making enemies and mistakes; refrain from making public statements critical of the regime; and keep the corruption within bounds.

Those political activists who were not satisfied with the PRI were free to participate in politics outside the party as long as they did not challenge the regime in any serious way. They could join or organize opposition parties and might even be allowed to win the odd seat in the Chamber or in a local government. However, if they became too troublesome, then the regime's ability to employ coercion in the form of physical repression and rigged elections was adequate to the task. This was partly the result of another factor that enormously enhanced political stability: the incorporation of the military as a support of, rather than a threat to, the regime.

Political systems that are "unstable," in the sense that governments are removed through means other than elections and other regular political methods, are often characterized by heavy military involvement in politics. As a region, Latin America has been especially noted for military intervention in determining who occupies the top seats of government. Direct military intervention in politics has waxed and waned over the years since most Latin American states became independent. Military coups were relatively common in the first several decades after most of the Spanish-speaking countries of Latin America became independent in the 1820s. Mexico was no exception and, in fact, was one of the most military-plagued polities of the region until the 1850s. Once a particular elite established itself in power and economic growth took off, military intervention in politics tended to decline, and many Latin American countries enjoyed a period of political stability and economic growth from about 1860 to about 1930, with the military playing a less direct role in politics during this period. Mexico followed this pattern until the Revolution broke out in 1910. The new army of the Revolution, of course, assumed a large role in Mexican politics from about 1910 to about 1930. Thereafter its direct political involvement declined rapidly. At least four serious military rebellions occurred from 1923 to 1938, but the size of the military opposition to the government generally declined over this period. The percent of the army that rebelled from 1923 to 1938 was approximately as follows: in 1923 it was about 40 percent; in 1927 it was 20 percent; in 1929 it rose to about 30 percent; and in 1938 it fell to only 5 percent.[34] In 1940 when another revolutionary general and presidential candidate considered rebelling, he found little support in the military for open rebellion.

While numerous other Latin American countries continued to experience military coups that overthrew civilian governments, especially in the 1930s, 1950s, and 1970s, Mexico followed a different pattern. Why did the military refrain from overt involvement in politics during this time? Until a few years

ago, scholars who studied the military tended to believe that as a military became more professional, it tended to intervene less in politics. Professionalization of the military may be part of the answer, but at least for Mexico, three
other factors were important as well: the strength of civilian political institutions (including unity of the political elites); a weakening of the position of
the military; and absence of government interference in the internal affairs of
the military.

Changes do not tend to happen in isolation, and so the decline of the military
as a political force was hastened by the emergence of civilian political institutions. Samuel Huntington argued years ago that "the susceptibility of a political system to military intervention varies inversely with the strength of its political parties." [35] As Calles ended his presidential term in late 1928, he called
for the creation of a revolutionary political party that would provide a forum
for political participation to replace the violent contestation for the presidency.
When Cárdenas became president, he began to expand the bases of support for
the regime. As we saw in chapter 2, he encouraged the growth of labor unions
and peasant organizations, and then in 1938 he incorporated the new confederations into a restructured political party, the PRM. The military was represented
in the party from 1938 to 1942, but thereafter military men had to participate
through one of the other sectors, mainly the middle-class organizations
(CNOP).

At the same time that the government in general was being consolidated,
other forces were being strengthened as counterweights to the military, at least
in the early years. The earliest and most important was the armed peasantry,
which was important in combatting the military uprisings of 1923, 1927, and
1929. These groups were not actually used in battle during the 1930s, but their
existence was a constant reminder of the physical force available to the government in case of a military rebellion against it. Although less important, the
same could be said for the armed labor battalions. The 100,000-strong uni-
formed workers' militia (twice the size of the regular army) was a constant
reminder to the army of the need for caution, even though it never had to
be used. [36] After 1940, the regular political institutions—especially party and
presidency—were strong enough that irregular support such as armed peasants
and workers was no longer needed to deter the military from intervention in
politics. Thus the strengthening of civilian political institutions after 1929 was
a major reason that military involvement in politics declined.

Mexico's strong political institutions allowed the civilian government to be
relatively successful in maintaining its authority with a relatively low level of
coercion, when compared with some other Latin American regimes. For example, the Mexican regime was able to "pacify" the country during the tumultu-
ous decade from 1965 to 1975 with far fewer deaths (probably less than one
thousand) than in Brazil and Chile (several thousand) and in Argentina (perhaps
twenty thousand) during a comparable period of unrest. If turmoil in Mexico

had escalated, it is conceivable that the military might have given more serious thought to taking over the government directly.

A second reason that the military has not overtly interfered in politics in recent decades is that the Mexican military is relatively small, compared with the militaries of most Latin American countries. From 1920 to 1940, the size of the army was reduced by 75 percent, from 200,000 to 50,000, at the same time that the population doubled from 10 million to 20 million. The military share of the federal budget dropped from 60 percent in 1920 to 20 percent in 1940 and then to about 10 percent by the early 1950s.[37] After 1940 the army grew slowly until it reached about 90,000 by the mid-1980s. The air force and navy comprise about 30,000 members, for a total military force of about 120,000. Thus Mexico has a small military when compared to other Latin American countries. For example, as of 1984, Mexico ranked eighteenth of the twenty Latin American republics for military expenditure per capita, tied with Costa Rica, which has a national guard but not a regular army.[38] The military budget as a share of gross domestic product increased in the 1980s, partly in response to the revolutionary turmoil in Central America and the larger military role in the struggle against drugs. By the mid-1980s, Mexican military spending (at 1.6 percent of GDP) was about average for Latin America. Even though military size and expenditures increased in recent years, by this time the nonpolitical role of the Mexican military had become firmly established.

The Mexican military has been relatively small since 1945 for several interrelated reasons. First, the geopolitical position of Mexico strongly inclines the country toward a relatively small military. Located between the strongest military power in the world and the small countries of Central America, Mexico has little need of a large military for defense against invasion from either direction. It could be said, with only slight exaggeration, that Mexico cannot defend itself against the United States and has no need to defend itself against Guatemala, and thus it has no need of a large military for external defense. More precisely, it also generally did not need to defend itself against the United States, since this country had no major designs on Mexico after seizing one-half of Mexican territory in the war of 1845–48. The treaty of Guadalupe Hidalgo committed the United States and Mexico to peaceful resolutions of conflict if at all possible.[39] The two countries have had minor border controversies, such as the Chamizal dispute in southern Texas, but no major ones. In addition, Mexico has sought to use diplomatic persuasion rather than military might to enhance its influence in Central America. Thus the function of Mexico's military has been largely to help to maintain internal order rather than provide external defense or project national power abroad.

A third factor that helps explain why the Mexican military has not intervened directly in politics is that, by and large, politicians have not interfered in internal military affairs. In any civilian-dominated politician system, the military is controlled to some extent by civilian politicians. For example, the president may select the minister of defense and a few other military officials. President and parliament make decisions about the structure of the armed forces, provide their budgets, and determine their roles. But in all political systems, the military believes that there is a line that civilian politicians should not cross. One of the most salient examples is usually the matter of promotions below the very top positions. If a president tries to determine promotions within the military below the top levels, the military tends to see this as unwarranted interference, and it may become a factor in motivating portions of the military to try to overthrow the civilian government. This is especially true if the government is already unpopular among important segments of society and if turmoil is growing. For example, a populist government may become unpopular with economic elites for seeking to redistribute wealth, favoring labor in management-labor disputes, and the like. In an attempt to reduce the likelihood of a military coup, the government may then intervene much more actively in military promotions than in the past in order to place loyalists in key positions. That act, however, may backfire. It will tend to alienate top officers, who see one of their primary functions being eroded, as well as those officers who are failing to be promoted according to the new political criteria. Individuals from these two groups may then lead a coup against the government. This is often cited, for example, as one of the reasons why the military rebelled against Juan Peron in 1955.[40] This tends to become a circular process, with each factor reinforcing the other. As a government becomes shakier, it will tend to interfere more in military affairs in order to avert a coup, but that very interference may become a powerful motive for the military to stage a coup. With Mexico, the circle ran the other way. The government became increasingly institutionalized and stable and hence interfered in internal military affairs less and less, and thus a military coup became increasingly unlikely.

Usually, promotions are regular, merit-based, nonpersonalistic, and decided internally by the military. The Mexican government has generally not interfered in promotions within the military except to speed up the process during crisis times, apparently in an attempt to ensure the loyalty of the military. Camp wrote: "It can be reasonably hypothesized that Mexican political leaders use military promotions to assure greater loyalty among the officer corps. Further, it would seem probable that the greater the political instability of the regime— or the president's perception of it—the more likely that he will make use of the promotion process."[41] It should be noted, however, that Camp is talking about the *pace* of promotions, not the specific individuals who were promoted. Thus López Mateos, Díaz Ordaz, and Echeverría made an unusual number of promotions at crisis points of their presidencies: in 1960 after the railroad strike, 1968 after Tlatelolco, 1972 after paramilitary persecution of students and an increase in guerrilla activity, and 1976 after extremely conflictual land distributions and the economic problems at the end of Echeverría's term.

Finally professionalization, the factor that was traditionally offered as the explanation for military nonintervention in politics, may also play a role. The argument was that the more professional a nation's military became, the less likely it was to interfere in politics.[42] Professionalization consists of developing the military as an institution separate and distinct from civilian organizations, one in which recruitment and promotion are carried out according to military, rather than political, criteria. Officers and enlisted men are recruited and promoted according to their perceived ability to perform military functions, not their political allegiances. Thus professionalization often includes the establishment of separate schools and colleges for the training of officers, the creation of merit-based systems of promotion, and the development of training programs that emphasize skill at military activities such as the use of weapons rather than indoctrination of a particular political point of view. Every political regime, of course, tries to indoctrinate its military into the values of the regime. However, in a "professional" military, political views are supposedly secondary to the more important value of military leadership skills.

The Mexican military became increasingly professionalized after 1920. Military schools were established, where most officers would receive their education. Promotions were increasingly based on politically neutral criteria of merit, and the military increasingly turned its attention to learning its craft rather than interfering in politics. Nevertheless, all of this may not have the effect of keeping the military out of politics if that value is not explicitly enforced by military and civilian authorities. However, the Mexican military enforces almost total apolitical behavior among officers. It indoctrinates officers in military schools to accept civilian authority, and then almost everything in their subsequent environment reinforces that apolitical attitude. An officer who criticizes the civilian government is immediately punished. Depending on the severity of the offense, he might be reassigned to an undesirable post or cashiered entirely [43] (similar to the enforced retirement of a U.S. general in 1993 after he called President Bill Clinton "a draft-dodging, pot-smoking, gay-loving womanizer"). Thus the Mexican regime has labored to inculcate the attitude of noninterference in politics in its military. Without the other factors discussed above, however, professionalization alone would probably not have succeeded in keeping the military out of politics. The Argentine military, for example, has been highly professional for decades in many of the ways discussed above, but that has not been sufficient to keep it out of politics. It overthrew the government in 1943, 1955, 1962, 1966, 1970, and 1976. Most informed observers agree that Mexico has never even been close to a military coup since 1930. As David Ronfeldt wrote in 1984: "In most Latin American political systems the 'distance' from crisis to instability to coup is small. Mexico is different: Time after time its political system has demonstrated a profound capacity to absorb internal conflicts and crises without becoming unstable."[44]

This is not to say that the Mexican military played no role in politics after 1940. The military in every country has "political" functions to one degree or another; even the protection of the national community from outside conquest is a political act. However, the political functions of the military may go be-

yond this. According to one author, the Mexican military still has important
"residual political roles."[45] Two important roles are political communication
and management of conflict, not unlike the military in many other Latin American countries. Mexico is divided into thirty-five military zones usually corres-
ponding to state boundaries.[46] Zone commanders were often consulted by governors and presidents, especially on matters of public order. As late as the
1960s, the zone commander might even be appointed interim governor in the
event of a political crisis in the state. Zone commanders also provided the
president and the governor with an alternative source of political intelligence
about matters in the state. In addition, military officers have served in other
civilian positions at various times. For example, officers on leave have served
in such nonmilitary positions as mayor, chief of police, and director general of
roads in Mexico City as well as various federal bureaucratic positions. During
the 1950s and 1960s, military officers on leave or retired held from twenty to
thirty congressional seats.[47] Thus not only has the military been an important
pillar of the regime in its role as a military, but it has also buttressed the regime
through filling some essentially civilian positions. Surely they were not chosen
merely because the president thought they were they best men for the job.
Rather, they were no doubt chosen for their symbolic importance in demonstrating that the military was an integral part of the regime in every way and for
their personal and professional connections with the regular military forces.
The supporting structures of the regime are all interconnected. The military has
a large stake in the existing regime because military people are placed throughout that regime. By having a small and loyal military, as well as a military
presence in civilian positions, the regime is able to demonstrate to the potential
opposition the impregnability of the regime's position. Thus it would not be
precisely correct to say that the military has been excluded from politics; rather,
the military plays a small but integral part in the regime, a part that makes
more overt participation less likely.

Since 1970, however, it has appeared that a number of developments were
impelling an increase in what might be called national security thinking in
Mexico and thus an expansion in the importance of the military. For many
decades, Mexico's political leaders resisted thinking in such terms as "national
security." They saw the concept as part of the dangerous thinking that led
great powers to go perilously close to war out of an exaggerated sense of external threat. In addition, such thinking often led military regimes in South
America in the 1960s and 1970s to exaggerate civil threats, build up huge
militaries, and brutally repress their societies.[48] Following the student unrest of
the 1960s, guerrilla activity in the 1970s, development of its southern oil fields
in the late 1970s, and then revolutions and civil wars in Central America in the
1980s, the Mexican government has engaged in greater public dialogue about
national security and the role of the military.[49] However, by the early 1990s
that debate had quieted down or shifted back to the more traditional concept of
Mexican national security, namely the protection of its political and economic

independence, especially from the United States. The partial resolution of the Central American conflicts and the negotiation of a free-trade pact with the United States have worked to shift the debate once again back to the old terms that had characterized Mexico's fears at least since the Revolution. That is, the worst fear (or fondest hope) of many Mexicans was the prospect of a high degree of integration with the United States.

Therefore, the Mexican military has perhaps played a slightly more direct role in the political system than does the military in most industrialized countries, but a considerably smaller role than in most Latin American countries. This restraint was a result of several factors: the strength of civilian political institutions and the ability of those institutions to maintain civil order most of the time, the small size of the military, the noninterference of civilian officials in internal military affairs, and the professionalization of the military. For these reasons, the military has been a pillar of the Mexican political system rather than a threat to it.

Business elites, as we saw in chapter 3, were relatively content with the political-economic system that evolved after 1940.[50] Though they might have preferred a regime more ideologically committed to the virtues of private enterprise, business leaders became relatively comfortable with a government that provided tax breaks and other subsidies to encourage Mexican firms to thrive behind protectionist walls, a situation one author called "godfathered capitalism."[51] Mexican business thus had a captive market of domestic consumers who paid artificially high prices for products produced with little competition. If the hand of government regulation became too heavy for individual firms, exceptions could be obtained through negotiations often involving bribes.[52] Thus Mexican (and foreign) business found that it could coexist with this particular "revolutionary" regime.

Labor and peasant elites were co-opted into the regime even more thoroughly than was business. Organizations that cooperated in terms of wage settlements and other issues were recognized by the regime and incorporated into the PRI, and their leaders were usually selected by the government. The most notable beneficiaries of such a cozy corporatist relationship were the organization leaders, who usually profited handsomely from their ability to keep their members in line. In addition, some organization leaders were given seats in the Chamber of Deputies and in state legislatures. Even the rank-and-file members usually received more generous settlements than did those in nonrecognized organizations. The latter not only might receive smaller benefits, but if they became too obstreperous, they also might find themselves the objects of regime coercion.

Likewise, the media were kept in line in similar ways. The government used such positive incentives as access to government officials and regular payments for friendly treatment. The *embute* (envelope with money) has been used for decades. Reporters who cover a particular agency are given regular cash payments for consistently sympathetic articles and editorials. In fact, many "news" stories consisted solely of agency press releases. If the positive inducements of access and cash were inadequate to deter critical media coverage, the media might find themselves the victims of repression, like most other sectors of society. For example, the regime apparently inspired the removal of an overly critical editorial board at the *Excélsior* newspaper in the mid-1970s. If that level of intimidation was not enough, physical violence could be used. Killings of reporters became especially serious as politics became more pluralistic and conflictual in the late 1980s. For most of the postrevolutionary period, however, the Mexican media were tame appendages of the regime.

The willingness of most elites in the military, business, labor, and the media to cooperate with the regime was a result, therefore, of all of the qualities of the regime. Its highly institutionalized nature and set of rewards, including corruption, allowed for a circulation of political elites who benefited from the continuation of the system and who were deterred from opposing it by the regime's coercive ability. The economic growth that Mexico enjoyed from 1940 to 1980 satisfied various groups, especially the leaders of those groups. Generally, therefore, the regime was able to retain the loyalty of most elites in most sectors of society. This does not mean that no individuals tried to break out of the monopolistic hold that the regime had on power. The next section will look at the major defections in the history of the regime.

DEFECTIONS FROM ELITE UNITY

One way to study unity is to look at disunity, or defections. Let us, therefore, ask three questions in this section: What defections occurred from 1920 to 1990? Why did they occur? Why were they not destabilizing? If we can answer these questions, we should better understand the nature of Mexican elite unity. This section will show that despite the degree of stability Mexican politics have demonstrated on the surface, defections from the ruling group have regularly occurred since this regime came to power in 1920. Although it is difficult to assess motives for the behavior of political challengers, it appears that the defectors were impelled by some combination of personal ambition and ideological conviction. In each case, they saw both their career paths and their policy preferences blocked by the dominant tendency in the ruling party at the moment. Yet the defections were not calamitous and did not shatter the stability of the regime for the reasons explored throughout this book—the underlying strength of the regime achieved through institutionalization, effectiveness, adaptability, coercion, and U.S. support.

Defections from the regime have occurred frequently, but they have almost always been limited. Moreover, many who defected subsequently came back into the regime. Even most of those who defected permanently from the PRI followed a peaceful path, rather than taking up arms against the regime. Defectors may have believed that they were defrauded by PRI machinations, but they generally continued to play the electoral game or retired from politics rather than declare themselves in rebellion against the regime, as occurred so often in other Latin American countries. To a large extent, this was due to the continued unity of the Mexican political elite. Defectors were never able to attract enough support from other members of the political elite (or from the military elite) to allow them to believe that they could mount a serious physical challenge to the ruling group.

In almost every presidential election from 1920 on, former members of the ruling elite defected and challenged the ruling group. These defections usually occurred because a particular political leader believed that his career and policy preferences would not flourish, given the direction in which the regime was headed. In 1920, Obregón led a rebellion against his revolutionary colleague President Venustiano Carranza when Carranza did not select Obregón as the next president. This was the last time that a rebellion against the ruling group was successful. Then in 1923, General Adolfo de la Huerta rebelled against President Obregón over the choice of the next president. Next came a rebellion by Generals Francisco Serrano and Arnulfo Gómez in 1927 after Calles and Obregón had the constitution amended to allow Obregón to run for president again. This was extremely controversial and generated deep divisions among the politically aware population, partly because it violated one of the fundamental tenets of the Revolution—no reelection. Two revolutionary generals entered the race for president against Obregón. Serrano was a former secretary of war, and Gómez had been instrumental in putting down the de la Huerta rebellion of 1923. Both criticized Obregón for violating the principle of no reelection. When they became convinced that the election of 1928 was not going to be fair, they rebelled against the government. Both were soon captured and executed. While a law student, the future president Miguel Alemán had supported General Gómez for president in 1928. In fact, Alemán's father was a revolutionary general who was killed in the next rebellion against the government, in 1929. Yet neither his own youthful "indiscretion" nor his father's rebellion was held against the young Alemán. He later joined the ruling group and then enjoyed a rapid rise until his selection as presidential candidate in 1946. He brought into his administration numerous men who had participated with him as students in the 1927–28 campaign against Calles and Obregón.[53]

The feelings were so intense on the question of reelection and other issues that Obregón was assassinated by a Catholic zealot who opposed Obregón's antichurch policies and his reelection. As a result of the assassination, an interim president was appointed by Congress, and a special election was called for 1929. It was in this context that former president Calles and others organized the National Revolutionary Party (PNR) in 1929. The PNR offered a former governor of Michoacán, Ortiz Rubio, as its candidate for president, although Calles remained the *jefe máximo* behind the scenes. Many politically active people opposed a continuation of the Calles machinations, and so José Vasconcelos, a popular and scholarly former secretary of education under Obregón, ran for president in the election of 1929. Numerous young idealists worked in the Vasconcelos campaign, including many who later joined the ruling party and held high positions in the government. The group included a future president, Adolfo López Mateos, who was a high school student at the time. Camp lists almost fifty students and professors who supported the Vasconcelos campaign and who later became prominent in PRI and other regime institutions such as the national university. When he became president in 1958, López Mateos brought many of his former campaign-mates from 1929 into his administration, as Alemán had done earlier. In addition to López Mateos, other activists in the 1929 Vasconcelos campaign included a future secretary of government (the second-most powerful position in the regime), secretary of public health, federal attorney general, president of the federal senate, a governor, and various other members of the political elite in the coming decades.[54]

These examples point up several important aspects of the Mexican political system. First, the ruling party eventually became broad enough to attract a wide following, including many who had previously opposed it. Second, the official party became increasingly dominant, exercising a near-monopoly of the available political space, so that political activity took place largely within rather than outside it. Third, these examples demonstrate the relatively "forgiving" nature of the ruling group, who apparently believed it was better, wherever possible, to co-opt than to repress (or, perhaps more accurately, to use the two in combination). As long as the opposition was not violent and the break too harsh, the miscreants were welcomed into the party, and their future careers seemed not to suffer too badly as a result of their temporary defections. From 1935 to 1975, dozens of leading dissenters were strategically co-opted back into the official system, even though some of these had participated in more than one opposition movement against the government.[55]

Virtually all Mexican presidents practiced this policy of conciliation toward the opposition, although some more than others. This illustrates one of the major differences that Juan Linz detected between totalitarian and authoritarian systems. In the former systems, such as the Soviet Union, ideological differences could easily become the occasion for imprisonment, exile, or execution. In some authoritarian systems, on the other hand, such as Mexico after 1929, that was seldom the case, at least as far as middle-class political activists who refrained from violence were concerned. If they repented and were willing to work within the system, they were generally welcomed back.

Because the ruling party became so all-inclusive, it was naturally the source of much of the opposition. In addition, virtually all the opposition parties worked to some extent within the existing system, even when their activists strongly believed that they were being systematically defrauded from numerous political victories and even the eventual possibility of victory in the presidential race. The most important opposition party in modern Mexican politics has been the Party of National Action (PAN). By the late 1930s, a number of men who had worked within the regime for years became disenchanted by the populist tendencies of the Cárdenas government and broke with it to form the new conservative party. One of the leaders of this group was Manuel Gómez Morín, who with others formed the new party in 1939. Gómez Morín was a law professor at the national university (UNAM) for thirty years, eventually becoming rector of the university. Meanwhile, he held various high-level positions in the government.

The 1940 election was one of the most divisive in Mexican history, although it was relatively peaceful compared with the periods surrounding the elections of 1920, 1924, and 1928–29. After the populist policies of the Cárdenas period, a strong conservative backlash was to be expected. It was in this context that the conservative Party of National Action was created in 1939. Although PAN did not nominate a candidate for president in 1940, many PAN sympathizers supported the general who ran against the government candidate. Juan Andreu Almazán, one of the most powerful of the revolutionary generals, believed that he deserved the PRM nomination for president in 1940, but Cárdenas apparently decided to avoid the extremes of left and right (Múgica and Almazán) and selected the moderate General Manuel Avila Camacho. Almazán then bolted the party and ran for president as the candidate of a new party. A significant number of the political and economic elites joined Almazán, but it was not enough to take control. Why was this defection on the right not large enough to seize power?

The defectors themselves were not able to overcome the regime's coercive ability to control elections. Even though Cárdenas may have believed to some extent in the virtues of liberal democracy, he could not bring himself to contemplate a conservative victory, which to him would have been tantamount to a counterrevolution. Thus he used—or allowed his colleagues to use—the regime's ability to manipulate elections in order to control the outcome. Moreover, Almazán and his supporters could not persuade the U.S. government to provide them with military aid. As in previous crises since 1920, the U.S. government supported the regime, rather than aid those who wanted to replace it. As the U.S. government headed toward war in Europe and the Pacific, it wanted to avoid turmoil on its southern border. President Franklin Roosevelt and Secretary of State Cordell Hull discouraged Almazán and his supporters from contemplating an armed rebellion. Thus in 1940 the Mexican government had an almost complete monopoly on coercive ability because of the loyalty of most of the military and the friendly attitude of the United States.

It is also significant that major defections did not occur on the left in 1940. President Cárdenas was able to retain the loyalty of General Francisco Múgica even though he was not chosen for the presidency and even though the candidate selected was probably ideologically closer to Almazán than to Múgica. Thus Cárdenas was able to hold the left and center together, while losing much of the right in the 1940 election. If Múgica had decided to challenge Avila Camacho, either peacefully or violently, the outcome of 1940 might have been different.

The next major defection came in the election of 1946. Ezéquiel Padilla had served as secretary of foreign relations in Avila Camacho's cabinet. When he was passed over for the presidential nomination in 1946, he ran as an independent against Miguel Alemán. This election was not noted for great conflict. Like so many other defectors, Padilla was eventually welcomed back into the party and served in the 1964–70 Senate. In fact, with Padilla, as with other "opponents," it is possible that the opposition was merely for show so that the regime could appear to have won in a democratic election in which voters had a choice.

In the late 1940s, two leading members of the official party broke away and eventually ran as independent candidates for president. In 1945 General Miguel Henríquez Guzmán abandoned the official party and formed the Federación de Partidos del Pueblo Mexicano (Federation of Parties of the Mexican People). It remained dormant until 1951, when Henríquez decided to launch a presidential campaign. After two relatively conservative terms from 1940 to 1952, the regime's left wing thought that it was their turn for the presidency. Thus when Adolfo Ruiz Cortines, a moderate conservative, was selected as the candidate of the PRI, General Henríquez Guzmán launched his independent campaign with the help of many on the left, including some Cardenistas, although Lázaro Cárdenas himself refrained from endorsing Henríquez Guzmán. The fact that Cárdenas and other ex-presidents always supported the PRI candidates was a major factor in keeping the regime intact. The supporters of Henríquez Guzmán were the victims of violence, presumably at the hands of regime supporters, with at least twenty-two members of his party murdered during the election campaign. Henríquez Guzmán was awarded 16 percent of the vote.[56] The Henríquez Guzmán movement was probably the largest leftist opposition to contest a national election in Mexico between 1929 and 1988.

Meanwhile Vicente Lombardo Toledano, the labor leader during Cárdenas's term, had left the regime (after being removed from any real power) and created a new party on the left, the Popular Party. His old schoolmate, President Avila Camacho, persuaded him to postpone launching his new party and running for president in the 1946 election, but by 1952 he was ready to mount a campaign against the official candidate, Ruiz Cortines. He won only 2 percent of the vote, the PAN candidate Gonzáles Luna won 8 percent, and other candidates won about 15 percent, leaving the PRI's Ruiz Cortines with about 75 percent.

The 1958 election was unusually pacific. The economy had grown well, President Ruiz Cortines had been a peacemaker, and most parties supported the PRI nominee, Adolfo López Mateos, who won over 90 percent of the vote. The major opposition came from the conservative PAN candidate Luis Alvarez, who received just under 10 percent of the vote. Likewise, no major defections occurred in 1964 as the PRI candidate Gustavo Díaz Ordaz received 89 percent of the vote and the PAN candidate 11 percent. Despite the turmoil of 1968, the 1970 election was also relatively quiet, as the PRI's Luis Echeverría claimed 86 percent as against the PAN's 14 percent. In 1958, 1964, and 1970 other candidates (mostly leftist) were conceded less than 1 percent of the vote. Interestingly, we might have expected the conservative PAN to do well in the 1976 election, after the populist turmoil of the Echeverría years. However, internal divisions prevented PAN from nominating a presidential candidate, and so the PRI's José López Portillo received almost 99 percent of the vote, and other candidates (mainly on the left) got only 1 percent.

In 1982, the PAN came back in strength to gain 16 percent of the presidential vote for its candidate with the famous name of Pablo Emilio Madero (nephew of the revolutionary leader Francisco Madero). In that election, leftist parties also received about 16 percent of the vote. The Mexican Communist Party (PCM), never strong, had reconstituted itself as the Mexican Unified Socialist Party in 1981 and offered the former secretary general of the PCM, Arnoldo Martínez Verdugo, as its nominee.[57]

The 1988 election, as we shall see below, was one of the most hotly contested in decades. The PRI's presidential candidate officially received barely 50 percent of the popular vote; a candidate on the left was conceded 31 percent, and the PAN's candidate won 17 percent. The candidate on the left, Cuauhtémoc Cárdenas, had been a member of the PRI all his adult life, holding various offices within the regime, and was the son of Lázaro Cárdenas, who had reconstituted the party in the 1930s. This was the largest challenge to the PRI since 1952. Yet the party managed to claim the election, and its candidate, Carlos Salinas de Gortari, was inaugurated without major incident.

The factors that explain Mexico's political stability also help to explain elite unity itself as a factor that contributed to stability. First, coercion in the form of physical repression and fraudulent elections was used to varying degrees to enforce elite unity. As Daniel Levy and Gabriel Székely say, "That many of the electoral results were based on fraud is almost uncontestable, although we may never know the specifics in each case."[58] Defections did not grow larger because those who might be tempted to join the defectors recognized that a defection would probably not succeed in the face of electoral fraud and would stunt or end their careers. Second, the institutionalized nature of the regime with its regular rotation in office gave elites further incentive to stay in the game. In addition, the historical effectiveness and flexibility of the regime gave hope that better days would return. Finally, the United States gave no sign of support for the opposition. Thus every effort of both defectors and other opponents to mount a serious challenge to the regime was met by a relatively unified elite that saw its interests best served by remaining inside the fold rather than breaking away.

FROM CÁRDENAS TO CÁRDENAS: THE CRISIS OF 1988

The Mexican regime had faced defections in the past, but the defection of 1988 was the greatest challenge to the regime since 1968, 1952, or perhaps even the 1930s. Yet the regime once again demonstrated its remarkable resiliency. The great irony of the 1988 challenge was that it was led by the son of

the man who had done more than any other Mexican leader to create this strong
and highly institutionalized regime, Lázaro Cárdenas.

The Challenge from the Left

The government of Mexico has generally been accommodating to demonstrators. The streets leading into the Zócalo, or central plaza, of Mexico City are
closed off to vehicles on Saturday and Sunday so that people can walk unmo-
lested by auto traffic. This also makes demonstrations either for or against the
government easier to stage. Until recently, of course, most demonstrations
were for the government. Until the 1940s, the Zócalo was landscaped with
trees and flowers, like other plazas in Mexico. But the difficulty of maintaining
the vegetation in a square where thousands frequently gathered for political
rallies eventually persuaded the government to rip out all vegetation from the
Zócalo. The plaza now looks like a demilitarized zone, a vast expanse of one
square block of stone, surrounded by asphalt streets and encircled by four
blocks of austere stone buildings, with almost no trees or bushes to soften the
harsh visual impact. On the north side is the ancient cathedral of Mexico City,
built over a period of hundreds of years beginning soon after the Spanish Conquest in the 1520s. On the east is the National Palace, where the president of
Mexico has his offices and where such powerful bureaucracies as the Treasury
and Budget Office are located. On the south is the city hall of Mexico City,
which is actually a department of the federal government. On the west are
hotels and other businesses.

Late on the morning of June 25, 1988, thousands of demonstrators marched
down such streets as Madero and Cinco de Mayo toward the Zócalo. They
carried banners of the various parties and groups that supported the candidacy
of Cuauhtémoc Cárdenas for the presidency. The green-and-white banners of
the Authentic Party of the Mexican Revolution (PARM) mingled with the red-
and-white flags of the Mexican Socialist Party (PMS), the flags of the Popular
Socialist Party (PPS) and the new Party of the Cardenist Front for National
Reconstruction (PFCRN), and flags and posters for other groups that saw in
Cárdenas the hope for political change in Mexico. Several party posters had
Cuauhtémoc's picture in front of a black silhouette of his father, Lázaro Cárdenas, who is almost a popular icon in Mexico. The closing rally of Cuauh-
témoc's campaign in Mexico City was scheduled for June 25, one and a half
weeks before election day, because the PRI and PAN had already reserved the
Zócalo for their weekend demonstrations just before the election.

Both the size and the behavior of the crowd on this day demonstrated two
characteristics of Mexican politics in 1988. First, Mexicans had become politically more aroused. Hundreds of thousands were participating in marches and
rallies throughout the country, and the voter turnout on election day was probably higher than in recent decades, official returns notwithstanding. Second, the
political participation was largely peaceful. Words such as *mature* and *modern*

were frequently used in speeches and in the press to describe the behavior of the Mexican electorate in 1988. That maturity was certainly in evidence in the Zócalo on that June day. The rally was well organized (except for the long speeches), the crowd was receptive but calm, and one felt that Mexico was rapidly becoming less like Argentina and more like Canada.

Even when a light rain began to fall, the speakers made no concessions to the gods or to the crowd. The rally was scheduled for 10 A.M., and by about eleven, speakers began haranguing the crowd. The introductory speeches seemed to drone on interminably, as the crowd became increasingly restless and chanted "Cuauhtémoc! Cuauhtémoc!" and "Duro! Duro!" ("Remain Firm"). Estimates of the size of the crowd varied, but at least two hundred thousand people were present and perhaps far more. Strangers shared umbrellas and wry remarks about speakers who didn't know when to stop. The speakers called for change, for cooperation among opposition groups, and for an unaccustomed vigilance on election day to prevent the "PRI-government" from stealing the election.

The number and the length of the speeches were evidence that the Cárdenas campaign was not being advised by Madison Avenue. Finally, after two hours of speeches by his leading supporters, Cuauhtémoc himself came to the microphone. Cuauhtémoc Cárdenas challenges our traditional notion of that overused word *charisma*. Unlike most charismatic leaders, Cárdenas is not strikingly emotional or dynamic. He does not yell or carry on when he addresses a crowd of supporters. To watch Cuauhtémoc Cárdenas speak to the faithful is not to be reminded of Juan Perón or Gamel Abdel Nasser as much as Senator Eugene McCarthy during the U.S. presidential campaign of 1968, with his quiet, thoughtful manner. Cárdenas seems deliberately to avoid histrionics in order that emotion will not obscure his message. But in his own quiet way, Cuauhtémoc Cárdenas has charismatic appeal for many people. He seems to have special gifts of integrity and commitment, and most of all he has that most perfect of Mexican heritage and name.

"Cuauhtémoc" was not only the name of the last Aztec emperor before the Spaniards crushed that empire and its people but also the name of the only Aztec leader to rebel against the Spanish. He was killed for his efforts, and his martyrdom became a symbol of righteous rebellion against tyranny. More specifically, in the revolutionary iconography, "Cuauhtémoc" was a symbol of Indian and mestizo rebellion against the *gachupines,* or Spaniards. In like fashion, Cuauhtémoc Cárdenas is representative of the continuing ethnic tension in a Mexico that officially glorifies its Indian past but that in fact seems to value and reward more the Spanish and non-Indian parts of its heritage. For example, virtually all models in television commercials appear far more European than Indian. Cárdenas is seen by some of his supporters as a mestizo leader (his family is part Tarascan) who will deliver Mexico from those of full-blooded Spanish descent such as López Portillo, de la Madrid, and Salinas who, like Porfirio Díaz, seemed willing to deliver Mexico to the foreigners. It is notable that there are no statues in Mexico honoring either Hernán Cortés or Porfirio Díaz, whereas the Aztec leader Cuauhtémoc is commemorated by one of the most prominent statues in Mexico City.

But it is the Cárdenas family name that is the single most important factor impelling him into the leadership of the opposition. After six years of economic crisis, austerity, and mounting foreign debt—whose service alone consumed over half of the federal budget each year by 1988—millions yearned for a government that would pay more attention to the needs of the common people, would deal with the United States and multinational corporations more firmly, and would be less corrupt and more honest and democratic than recent PRI governments. Millions of Mexicans recall Lázaro Cárdenas as a president who tried to help the disadvantaged directly. As one American writer says, "Cárdenas was a Mexican name with the dynastic magic of a Kennedy or a Roosevelt in the United States."[59] (In fact, one Cárdenas supporter said that the only thing lacking in his name was "Guadalupe," Mexico's version of the Virgin Mary.)

Almost as if his parents had planned the day of his birth for its political symbolism, Cuauhtémoc Cárdenas was born in 1934 on May Day, the international day of the workers. This was just two months before his father's election and seven months before his inauguration as president of Mexico. He attended school in Mexico City and in the city of Morelia, Michoacán, where his father had been governor before becoming president. Cuauhtémoc studied engineering at the University of Mexico (UNAM) from 1951 to 1955 and received the title of civil engineer in January 1957. Although Americans often think of Mexicans as being nontechnological, it is interesting that three of the candidates for president in 1988 were educated as engineers—Cárdenas, Heberto Castillo, and Manuel Clouthier—and one, Carlos Salinas, as an economist.

It was rumored in Mexico that former president Lázaro Cárdenas wanted his son to pursue engineering postgraduate study in the United States but that the State Department under John Foster Dulles refused to issue a visa to the son of the Mexican president who had expropriated American oil companies.[60] In addition, Cuauhtémoc had probably attracted the State Department's attention on his own by vigorously protesting the U.S. intervention in Guatemala in 1954. In fact, he was president of the UNAM student committee that demonstrated against the U.S. action.

After obtaining his engineering license, Cárdenas went to France in 1957 and 1958 on a scholarship from the French Ministry of Foreign Affairs. He made technical inspections of various installations on a study tour with the Ministry of Reconstruction and Electricity. He also made inspection tours of Krupp and Siemens projects in Germany and of regional development projects in Italy.[61] He and his father were both interested in engineering, and his father had enjoyed a tour of the Tennessee Valley Authority in the United States during the 1950s.

After returning to Mexico, Cuauhtémoc went to work in 1959 for the Rio

Balsas hydroelectric regional development project, a complex similar to the Tennessee Valley Authority. After several years there as director of technical studies (1959–68) and as a member of the Rio Balsas Commission, he moved on to another regional development project, the Lázaro Cárdenas–Las Truchas Iron and Steel Complex, as subdirector general. During the 1960s and 1970s he was also active in professional associations for regional planning. For two decades, therefore, he pursued an engineering career.

In 1976 he entered politics with his election to the federal senate from Michoacán (for the period from 1976 to 1982). While still a senator, he was appointed under secretary for forestry in the Department of Agriculture and Water Resources in the López Portillo administration. Then from September 1980 to September 1986, he was governor of Michoacán, while still a member of the senate. Unlike in the United States where it is constitutionally prohibited to hold executive and legislative offices at the same time, in Mexico the practice is relatively common. This may contribute to elite unity by providing many members with several rewards at once.

During the 1970s, the Mexican government became increasingly technocratic in the sense that the highest positions were held more and more by people with advanced degrees in technical fields, especially in economics and especially from top U.S. universities such as Harvard and Yale. As an engineer, Cárdenas would certainly qualify as a technically trained person, but he was identified with the left, or "progressive," wing of the party rather than with the more market-oriented wing. Therefore, despite his heritage and his education, he began to feel increasingly alienated from the group that had taken control of the party and the government. Even earlier, Cuauhtémoc had shown independent tendencies. In the early 1960s he was active in the Movimiento de Liberación Nacional (MLN), a movement for reform within the ruling PRI. He was also a supporter of Fidel Castro. Patrick Oster, a Knight-Ridder correspondent in Mexico during the late 1980s, wrote:

About halfway through the administration of President Luis Echeverría Alvarez (1970–76), party elders began to get the idea that there was something radically different about this son of Lázaro Cárdenas. He began to show worrisome independence. Even worse, it appeared he was a man with a mission. In speeches, he sounded almost messianic. For a party that venerated public unity and obedience above all, there could be nothing worse.[62]

Descriptions often used by people who know Cárdenas well include "sincere," "authentic," and "man with a mission." Cárdenas seems to believe strongly that Mexico must return to the principles of the Revolution, principles that included social justice, land reform, and economic nationalism. This was not the direction that recent leaders of the regime intended to go. Nevertheless, President López Portillo was persuaded to give Cárdenas the governorship of his home state of Michoacán in 1980, where he was apparently a reasonably good governor. Like his father, Cuauhtémoc adopted a frugal personal style and had little tolerance for official corruption, especially corruption that robbed the people of state services.

As Mexico's economic crisis deepened in the 1970s and 1980s, the country's political elite became more and more divided over the best way to deal with it. First, the regime lurched to the left in 1982 by nationalizing the banking system in an effort to slow the flight of capital. After this temporary move to the left, the regime began what would become a much more sustained move to the right after 1982. By that year, Mexican fiscal policies had become characterized by huge deficits, debt, and inflation. In an effort to get these problems under control, the de la Madrid government cut spending, sold off some state firms, and generally tried to achieve greater fiscal discipline. The economic austerity strategy of the regime, which seemed to place much of the burden of modernization on the backs of the poor, was undoubtedly an important consideration prompting Cárdenas to launch his own candidacy for the presidency.[63] An additional factor may have been the recognition that with his background and ideological position, his career would not flourish in another market-oriented "technocratic" administration. Because of the policy orientation of the government, not only would Cárdenas likely not be selected by President de la Madrid to succeed him, but an economic nationalist and populist like Cárdenas would also probably not even be asked to serve in the next cabinet. Such interrelated career and policy considerations motivated Cárdenas and other PRI activists to form the "Democratic Current" within the PRI in the mid-1980s as a means to reform the party.

Cárdenas and others became concerned about the continued direction of public policy and the prospect of an official candidate who would continue those policies of economic "restructuring" and "modernization" that involved selling off state firms, inviting in more foreign investment, and cutting back on redistributive programs including subsidies for basic foodstuffs such as tortillas. Cárdenas and his supporters in the PRI thought that, at a minimum, the president and the party ought to open up the nomination process and allow various candidates to test their popularity. In this, Cuauhtémoc may have thought that his father's career offered a model. In 1933 various groups, especially supporters of the assassinated ex-president Alvaro Obregón as well as leaders of agrarian organizations, boosted the candidacy of General Lázaro Cárdenas for president. Before the *jefe máximo*, Plutarco Elias Calles, knew what hit him, the public support for Cárdenas was so great that Calles found it difficult to deny him the nomination. In 1987 the Democratic Current, a dissident faction within the PRI, insisted that the PRI nominating process be opened up. Cuauhtémoc and his associates may have believed that if the nomination process were broadened, Cuauhtémoc could gain enough support within the party and the country that President de la Madrid and PRI leaders would be forced to select him, as had happened with his father in 1933.

In fact, de la Madrid did agree to indulge the reformers to some extent in allowing several "pre-candidates" to present their cases and test their support within the party over a period of weeks. In August 1987, party chief Jorge de la Vega Domínguez announced that six pre-candidates would be allowed to do this; Cárdenas, however, was not on the list. As the leader of a large faction within the party, Cárdenas asked to be designated one of the pre-candidates. Fearful of the support that Cuauhtémoc was building and of his political philosophy of revolutionary nationalism, the party leadership refused to allow his candidacy or his appeal for sectoral support for the nomination. However, Cárdenas's supporters refused to accept any of the approved pre-candidates, and Democratic Current members marched around the Zócalo during their "100 Hours for Democracy," collected signatures, and filed petitions supporting Cárdenas. This was the first time since 1952 that PRI members in large numbers had defied their party and demonstrated openly for a nonofficial presidential candidate. After the march, Democratic Current leaders met with PRI leaders to request that Cárdenas be registered among the official candidates. Still the party leadership responded with a firm "no." Likewise, party leaders rejected the Democratic Current's appeal that its proposals for economic and social policies be included in the 1988 party platform.[64] The PRI's historical pattern of accommodation and co-optation had reached its limits. Thus denied a role within the official party, Cárdenas had little alternative but to break with the PRI.

Eventually three of the six pre-candidates emerged as the leaders. Alfredo del Mazo, governor of the state of Mexico and then minister of energy, was the only one of the three who had held elective office. Manuel Bartlett Díaz had run de la Madrid's election campaign in 1982 and then had been appointed minister of government. Carlos Salinas de Gortari was a Harvard-educated finance expert who had served as secretary of planning and budgeting. Despite the slight increase in openness in the nomination process, the president once again made the final choice. It is said that Mexico has "one man, one vote," but that the one man is the president. On October 5, 1987, the announcement was made that the PRI's candidate for president would be Carlos Salinas de Gortari, the budget secretary. From the point of view of Cárdenas and his supporters, this was the worst-possible choice, since Salinas presumably was one of the main architects of the administration's economic program. Therefore, his selection suggested six more years of a "technocratic" approach to public policy, which would emphasize the market, foreign investment and, in their view, continued hardship for workers and the poor.

Meanwhile, supporters of the Democratic Current were going in various directions. Some decided to continue trying to reform the PRI from within; among them was a cofounder of the Democratic Current, Rodolfo Gonzáles Guevara, an ex-ambassador to Spain who had been an outspoken member of the PRI calling for change. After the announcement that Salinas was the PRI's candidate, Gonzáles Guevara met with Salinas in a heavily photographed session, meant to emphasize that the ambassador had returned to the fold.[65] Thus did the regime try to get the elite to close ranks against the Cárdenas challenge.

After being shut out of the PRI nomination for president, Cárdenas decided to strike out on his own. In the first bombshell in what would become an election campaign of surprises, Cárdenas announced several days after the *destape* (the "unveiling," or the announcement by the president of the identity of his successor) that he would accept the presidential nomination of the Authentic Party of the Mexican Revolution (PARM). This was doubly surprising because for years the PARM had generally been a pseudo-opposition party and had recently shrunk almost to insignificance. The largest party on the left, the Mexican Socialist Party (PMS), had already chosen its presidential candidate in an open primary election. Its candidate, Heberto Castillo, immediately criticized Cárdenas's decision to accept the PARM's nomination because of the PARM's past association with the PRI. Castillo said that being a presidential candidate was apparently more important to Cárdenas than dealing with the problems of the country. But rumors began to circulate almost immediately that PMS leaders might be willing to negotiate an electoral coalition with Cárdenas.

Quickly Cárdenas received the presidential nomination of the PPS and the Socialist Workers Party (PST), which took the new name of the Party of the Cardenist Front for National Reconstruction (PFCRN). The various parties and groups that supported Cárdenas were placed under an umbrella organization called the National Democratic Front (FDN). Many called for the largest leftist party, the PMS, to likewise endorse Cárdenas, but Heberto Castillo insisted that since he had won the party's nomination in an open election, he would step down only if Cárdenas beat him in an all-left primary. Although rejecting the idea, Cárdenas agreed to a twelve-point program acceptable to the PMS, and Castillo then stepped aside and allowed the PMS to give Cárdenas its presidential nomination.[66]

A number of important *priistas*, most of whom were members of the Democratic Current, defected with Cárdenas. One of the most notable was Porfirio Muñoz Ledo, who had been secretary of labor, president of the PRI, and ambassador to the United Nations under Echeverría and López Portillo. He was widely regarded as the foremost political strategist in the Cárdenas group. Another important *priista* was Ifigenia Martínez Hernández, an economist who had been director of planning in the Treasury Department (SHCP) under Echeverría and a federal deputy under López Portillo. Both were elected to the federal Senate from the federal district in 1988 under the banner of Cárdenas's FDN. Many other members of the PRI at various levels also went over to the Cárdenas side.

The other candidate on the left was Rosario Ibarra de Piedra, the candidate of the Revolutionary Workers Party (PRT). The PRT is a Trotskyite party affiliated with the Fourth International. It was regularly anti-Soviet and opposed to the Mexican Communist Party. Rather than join the other parties on the left in nominating Cuauhtémoc Cárdenas as its presidential candidate in 1988, the PRT selected the well-known human rights activist even though she was not a member of the party. Rosario Ibarra had been active in pressing for human rights ever since her son had "disappeared" (that is, had presumably been murdered) because of his political activities in the 1970s.

The Challenge from the Right

To stand anywhere near a loudspeaker when Manuel "Maquio" Clouthier was giving a speech was to risk loss of hearing. Clouthier was described as dynamic, charismatic, and determined, but "subdued" was not among the adjectives usually applied to the conservative PAN's 1988 candidate for president. On Sunday, July 10, four days after the election, at least one hundred thousand PAN supporters marched up Insurgentes Avenue to the Monument to Mexican Independence, known as "The Angel." Four days after the election, no winner had been announced. The government was clearly "massaging" the results. The fact that the marchers doubled back to the west several blocks, to the Angel statue, suggested that the organizers wanted to have an impact on foreign tourists in the fashionable shopping area known as the "Zona Rosa," or pink zone. One important resource for which all major parties were competing in 1988 was international opinion, whether in the form of foreign correspondents, tourists, governments, or the international public in general. From the Monument to Mexican Independence, the demonstrators marched up Paseo de la Reforma to the Zócalo, the central square of Mexico City. There Clouthier delivered a fiery speech in which he denounced the electoral fraud and urged all Mexicans to boycott the government and socially ostracize the perpetrators. He said that Mexicans should "avoid them in restaurants . . . avoid their businesses, avoid their social clubs . . . isolate them completely," a strategy that was perhaps more realistic for the largely middle- and upper-class supporters of the PAN than for other partisans.

Clouthier said that no presidential candidate could legitimately claim victory at that point, a comment aimed as much at Cuauhtémoc Cárdenas as Carlos Salinas. At the end of the speech, as dusk came, the crowd turned to face the presidential palace and raised their hands in silent protest against the alleged electoral fraud of the regime. Their open palms were meant to indicate that *their* hands were clean, even if the regime's hands were not. Such dramatic gestures had become a hallmark of Manuel Clouthier.

After its creation in 1939, the Party of National Action became the leading conservative party. It thought that individual rights were being threatened in Mexico. It favored independent labor unions, encouragement of private enterprise and private schools, and restoring to priests their right to vote. Because the PAN opposed the antichurch measures of the revolutionary government, it acquired a reputation almost as a front organization of the Catholic church. Some feared that if PAN came to power, it would restore the church to its formerly dominant political and economic position in Mexico, but the PAN has denied such charges. It is true, however, that the PAN has a strong social Christian or Christian democratic wing that coexists uneasily with the probusiness wing of the party. Clouthier's background was almost completely in business, and he joined the party only in 1985. Although he had not previously been a member of the PRI, he had been the head of various national business associations that were closely allied with the government. Clouthier was so closely associated with the business wing of the PAN that a former PAN deputy, Jesús Gonzáles Schmal, who was defeated by Clouthier for the 1988 PAN presidential nomination, said that one of the tasks of the party would be to supplement Clouthier's candidacy with PAN advisors in order to make him a true PAN candidate, not merely a candidate of business.

The PAN's share of the popular vote has been increasing slowly in the past twenty years, reaching almost 17 percent in 1982, and has been especially strong in northern Mexico. In state and local elections in 1983, the PAN captured the mayoralties of Chihuahua, Durango, and other northern cities. By July 1986 many political observers expected it to win the governorship of Chihuahua, which would have been the first opposition governorship in the history of this regime. The PRI claimed victory, however, amid loud cries of electoral fraud from the PAN. Party activists protested the alleged fraud by acts of civil disobedience and even hunger strikes. That same year, the businessman Clouthier ran for governor of the state of Sinaloa but was defeated in an election that he also vehemently claimed was fraudulent. The regime's treatment of the PAN in these and other state and local elections stiffened the resolve of the *panistas* to guard the integrity of the 1988 presidential and congressional elections.[67]

After Clouthier became the presidential candidate of the PAN in 1988, that party took a more active position against alleged electoral fraud, and it even tried to learn from protest movements abroad. The party formed a group, led by party activist Norberto Corella, that studied methods of nonviolent protest. The group examined the marches and boycotts used by Martin Luther King in the United States and Mahatma Ghandi's nonviolent struggle for the independence of India. Corella himself visited the Philippines before the overthrow of Ferdinand Marcos to see what could be learned about civic participation.[68]

The PAN platform is somewhat similar to that of the Republican Party in the United States, with proper adjustment being made for the Mexican context. The primary political goal of the PAN is "democracy," by which it means fair elections, a true multiparty system, and human rights such as a truly free press and freedom of expression and assembly. The party says that it would cut the federal bureaucracy considerably, decentralize many functions to state and local governments, and allocate certain revenue sources to those levels. It favors independent organizations such as labor unions, agrarian organizations, and other civic associations, rather than having them tied into the PRI and government as is now the case. The PAN considers such corporatism to be inherently authoritarian and antidemocratic.

It would reduce the government's role in the economy by a significant amount, although it would retain PEMEX, the oil monopoly. It favors dividing up the *ejidos,* or collective farms, among the members and then protecting their rights against expropriation. A PAN government would renegotiate the foreign debt in an effort to get debt service payments down to a level that the country could live with. PAN leaders believe that they could have a more mature and fruitful relationship with the United States, since they would not be burdened with the ideological baggage of economic nationalism that has characterized the PRI. Finally they believe the Mexican government played a pernicious role in Nicaragua, encouraging the Sandinistas to construct a one-party regime with control of social organizations like the regime that has ruled Mexico for sixty years. The PAN also thinks that the Mexican government was not justified in demanding a level of democracy in El Salvador that it was not willing to practice at home.

In the view of some, Clouthier was a prototypical "norteño," which means he was individualistic, energetic, and entrepreneurial. He was generally thought to look more favorably on U.S. investment and influence than did the other major opposition leader, Cuauhtémoc Cárdenas. He did not hide his admiration for the United States. Born in 1934, Clouthier attended secondary school at the Brown Military Academy in San Diego, California. Increasingly Mexican leaders have studied abroad, just as many members of the U.S. elite in the nineteenth century studied in England, France, or Germany. Clouthier attended high school in the United States; Salinas attended graduate school there; and Cuauhtémoc Cárdenas did graduate work in France.

As a young businessman, Clouthier had a small produce business in Culiacán, Sinaloa. Later he worked as a date farmer and then owned a rice mill and a vegetable mill. He was fiercely proud of his entrepreneurial past. Once, when asked to comment on the report that he was the richest of the presidential candidates, he responded that the report may have been true. But he added: "I didn't steal it. I made it working."[69] This was an obvious allusion to the widely accepted allegations that most politicians and bureaucrats in the PRI leave office richer than when they entered.

After becoming a multimillionaire in business, Clouthier became active in regional and national trade associations and eventually was elected president of the Confederation of Employers of the Mexican Republic (COPARMEX) from 1978 to 1980 and then head of the Business Coordinating Council (CEE) from 1981 to 1983. It is said that he was profoundly shocked when President José López Portillo nationalized the banks in September 1982 and that the expropriation was a crucial event in persuading Clouthier to enter politics. He joined the PAN only in 1985 and ran for governor of Sinaloa in 1986. He believed that he actually won the election but that the regime stole it from him through electoral fraud. He then organized protests of various sorts, even disrupting the inauguration of the PRI winner, Francisco Labastida Ochoa, later that year.

Clouthier was very anti-Communist, but not in the common Latin American sense of mindless opposition to any change that threatens the privileges of the elite. He said he was opposed to "totalitarianism" or dictatorship in any form, whether of the left or the right. He was a "liberal" in the sense that he believed that the less the state interfered in people's lives, the better. He was an ardent advocate of private enterprise as the engine of economic development, although he accepted state ownership of such fundamental industries as petroleum. His attitude toward the U.S. role in foreign investment and in international politics, such as in Central America, was far more favorable than that of Cárdenas, Castillo, and perhaps even Salinas. He believed that Mexico needed more foreign investment from all countries, not less. But he was certainly no advocate of *anexionismo,* or *entreguismo,* as the practice of delivering Mexico into the hands of the United States is known. If Clouthier had become president of Mexico, the United States could have expected to be faced with a friendly but determined neighbor. Clouthier was killed in an automobile accident in western Mexico in 1989.

The other party on the conservative side was the Mexican Democratic Party, or PDM, which was founded in 1978. The PDM is a more conservative version of the PAN in that it is even more vehement in its call for private enterprise. With its roots in the Catholic history of Mexico, the PDM also calls for a return to the "Christian" way of life. By the nineteenth century, liberal Benito Juárez wanted to break the stranglehold that Catholicism had on the Mexican economy and culture. The reform laws of the 1850s and 1860s were enacted partly to free Mexico from the domination of the church in such areas as education and property ownership. The Porfirio Díaz regime achieved a symbiotic arrangement by which the church was allowed to dominate education and religion and keep most of its property as long as it supported the regime. The Revolution that began in 1910 was partly a reaction to the enormous power of the church; and the Constitution of 1917 took specific steps to reduce the influence of the Catholic church. Marriage was made a civil rather than a religious ceremony; public worship outside churches was banned; and all priests had to be native born.

The most ardent presidential opponents of the Catholic church were Alvaro Obregón and Plutarco Elías Calles. However, their attempts to weaken the hold of the church provoked a massive rebellion in large parts of the country as parish priests exhorted the devout to overthrow the infidel government. This Cristero War of the late 1920s cost thousands of lives and left an enduring mark on Mexican culture, as many old churches were razed to the ground. The passions of the Cristero civil war contributed to the assassination of ex-president and president-elect Obregón in 1928 by a devout Catholic who was known to be close to Catholic leaders. The early 1930s saw a reduction in conflict between church and state, but the attempt of Lázaro Cárdenas to intensify and expand "socialist," or nonreligious, education during his term led to a temporary increase in tension between state and church. During the ideologically charged 1930s, political Catholicism reemerged as sinarquism (order, or "without anarchy"). The National Sinarquist Union, most popular in the Bajío region around Guanajuato, eventually produced the Mexican Democratic Party (PDM) in the 1970s.

The party was created in 1978 and attracted a hard core of devoted followers who believed that the regime had isolated and excessively disadvantaged the church. In the 1982 presidential race, the PDM received 2.3 percent of the vote and thirty-four members of the Chamber of Deputies. By 1987 it also held nine *ayuntamientos*, or town councils, the most important of which was Guanajuato, the capital of Guanajuato state. In 1988, the presidential candidate of the PDM was Gumersindo Magaña Negrete. The party platform called for a "Christian" society as an alternative to both the selfish individualism of capitalism and the coercive statism of Marxist socialism. The PDM called for cutting back government bureaucracy to the minimum possible and for renegotiating the foreign debt to make it less burdensome. The party also has a populist facet and has called for encouragement of Mexico's traditional arts and crafts and better pay for artisans, as well as more educational scholarships for the needy. On religion, the PDM favors giving the church greater legal standing in general and specifically giving priests the right to vote. The support for the PDM seems to be mainly among people who yearn for a return to a "golden age" when the Catholic church exercised a far more pervasive influence on Mexican life. For the PDM in 1988, the question was not whether it would win the presidency but whether it would receive enough votes (1.5 percent of the total cast) to retain its official registry and whether it would win seats in the Chamber of Deputies.[70] In fact, it did not win 1.5 percent, and so it did lose its position as an officially recognized political party, at least until the next election.

The Media

Although the media in Mexico are not censored as heavily as in some authoritarian countries, it is well known that they are generally controlled by the government in various ways, ranging from government advertising and paid columns, a near-monopoly of newsprint, to physical intimidation and even murder. There are a few relatively independent outlets, such as the newspaper *La Jornada* and the newsmagazine *Proceso*, and the media in general are somewhat more independent than in the past. But by and large the Mexican media are heavily biased toward the government.

The imbalance in media treatment of the various candidates was indicated by a study commissioned by the independent Democratic Assembly for Effective Suffrage (ADESE), patterned after a similar group in the Philippines that was active in the protest against Marcos in the 1980s. According to their study, in fourteen newspapers surveyed on one day during the 1988 election campaign, the number of lines of type devoted to the various candidates was as follows: Salinas, 13,828; Clouthier, 2,828; Castillo, 2,817; Cárdenas, 2,127; Ibarra, 1,114; and Magaña, 961. A number of social leaders thought that this was strong evidence of unfairness and wrote an open letter to President de la Madrid about it. The group included such people as FDN politician Porfirio Muñoz Ledo, political scientist Enrique Krauze, writer Carlos Monsivais, and PAN leader Norberto Corella. They said that it was evidence of "electoral fraud" in that such unbalanced treatment in the media demonstrated regime pressure on the media to provide news in favor of the government. The same study indicated that the PRI spent as much on publicity in one day as opposition candidates spent in an entire year. Moreover, the study claimed that the PRI would spend two billion pesos, or $800 million, on the presidential campaign, 80 percent of which would come from the public treasury.[71]

One of the most notable examples of the cozy relationship between media and regime is the Televisa combine. Televisa is a major chain of television stations owned by a group of people who are very close to the PRI and the government, people such as Miguel Alemán Valdés, a son of the president from 1946 to 1952. Televisa broadcasts the popular evening news program *24 Horas,* anchored by the Dan Rather of Mexican television, Jacobo Zabludovsky. The major difference is that whereas Dan Rather is a thorn in the side of governments, Zabludovsky is widely regarded as a "point man" for the regime. The same combine owns *Novedades,* a major Mexico City daily newspaper, which in turn owns the *Mexico City News,* the major English-language newspaper in the capital. In the 1980s, the *News* became too critical for the regime's satisfaction, and pressure was put on the newspaper to tone down its editorials. As a result, over a period of months, a mass exodus of bright young American and British journalists left the *Mexico City News.* Several of them founded a new English-language weekly newsmagazine known as the *Mexico Journal.* The *Journal* was edited by Joe Keenan, a hard-hitting journalist who was one of the main targets of the pressure for censorship at the *News.* The *Journal* was owned and subsidized by *La Jornada,* a very independent newspaper that emerged from the enhanced press freedom of recent years in Mexico. The *Mexico Journal* sometimes pushed its analysis and criticism of the regime so far that both it and *La Jornada* could almost be seen as litmus tests of how far freedom of press would be allowed to go in the next few years in Mexico. However, sales of the *Journal* never reached adequate levels, and it ceased publication in 1989.

When violence is perpetrated against journalists, it is not always easy to determine when the government was behind it and when it resulted from a personal grudge of an offended target of the press, or some combination. For example, on April 2, 1990, a man walked into the *La Jornada* offices on Balderas Street in downtown Mexico City to deliver a package of propaganda for an extreme Marxist-Leninist group, the Partido Revolucionario Obrero Clandestino Unión del Pueblo (Procup). The receptionist had been given instructions not to accept any more of their propaganda. The two security guards of *La Jornada* took the package outside the building to try to return it to the man, and they were shot and killed by a second man. In its editorial the next day, *La Jornada* did not directly blame the government, but it said that the murders took place in an environment in which political murders had become relatively common and that the murders could be interpreted as an attempt to intimidate the newspaper.[72] It seems unlikely that the government would be in league with an extreme leftist revolutionary group, but nothing seems beyond belief to many in the heavily charged political atmosphere of Mexican politics. The murders seem more like a case of a leftist revolutionary group trying to use an independent newspaper to get its message out than a case of government-inspired violence. Nonetheless, murders of journalists became a matter of national concern as Mexican politics became more competitive and conflictual in the 1980s and 1990s.

The Regime's Response

In the 1988 election, the PRI faced a formidable pair of foes. The minor candidates—Ibarra and Magaña—could not be expected to do well against the PRI machine. However, the PRI faced two major candidates of movements that, for different reasons, believed that the regime had created the economic crisis of the 1980s and then had pursued the wrong strategy to resolve the crisis. Despite the unusual amount of opposition activity in 1988, however, the regime managed to claim victory in the election, inaugurate its presidential candidate on December 1, 1988, and maintain him in power. How did it do this in the face of such massive opposition?

First of all, the regime unquestionably employed coercion in the form of repression and electoral fraud. Numerous Cárdenas supporters were threatened, and several were even murdered during the election campaign and in the following years. The electoral authorities postponed announcement of the official results for a week after the election, and when the results were announced, the PRI's Salinas had won by the narrowest majority in history. Cárdenas claimed that his data showed that he had won a plurality of over 40 percent, compared with about 35 percent for Salinas.[73] Cloithier also maintained that the election had been so tainted by fraud that no one could claim victory and a new election should be held. Numerous protests were held over the following weeks, but Salinas was inaugurated on schedule on December 1. The protests were generally peaceful, and the regime remained united.

If the 1988 election was indeed stolen, as the opposition claimed, it was possible because the regime had had mechanisms in place for decades for that very purpose. The PRI had access to large amounts of money from undisclosed sources (presumably government revenues) to finance the campaign. The regime had enough influence over the media to ensure that a hugely disproportionate share of attention would be focused on the PRI candidate. The PRI trucked large groups of peasants and workers to the polls, where they cast their ballots under the watchful eyes of PRI representatives. PRI officials would, where necessary and possible, stuff the ballot boxes with handfuls of pre-marked ballots. In some areas, PRI officials would transport loyalists from one polling place to another to cast multiple ballots for the PRI. Ballots for the opposition would be summarily dumped into roadside ditches (see chapter 6 for further explanations of these traditional methods).

Yet the degree of monitoring of the election in 1988 was unprecedented. Opposition forces had swollen as a result of the economic crisis and the Cárdenas candidacy. They were prepared to observe the election carefully in order to prevent fraud, and hence they placed representatives in as many polling places *(casillas)* as possible. Therefore, although the PRI was able to do many of the usual things to ensure victory, the election was apparently so competitive that after the polling was over, the PRI could not claim a clear majority and perhaps not even a plurality. It resorted, therefore, to the ultimate weapon, a rigged count. The electoral authorities insisted that their computers broke down and that it would take several days to complete the vote count. Almost a week went by before the regime announced that Carlos Salinas had won by a tiny majority. Few observers in Mexico at the time doubted that the regime had used the time to ensure that the numbers added up plausibly. According to official returns, the candidates' shares of the vote were as follows: [74]

Carlos Salinas	50.74%
Cuauhtémoc Cárdenas	31
Manuel Clouthier	17
Gumersindo Magaña	1
Rosario Ibarra	.4

The opposition tried to challenge the results, but the electoral commission was dominated by PRI supporters. The opposition also mounted protests throughout the country, protests that were predominantly peaceful, although a few—especially supporting the PAN—involved civil disobedience, such as blocking highways.[75] Cárdenas instructed his supporters to protest peacefully and not to provoke the regime into a violent response. He was determined that his movement would not give the government a pretext for repression. To his surprise and disappointment, the regime held together and did not unravel, despite the obvious fraud and massive protests. It was clear to him that the regime retained a virtual monopoly on coercive ability and that violent protests would almost certainly lead to severe repression by the regime.

Moreover, as a leftist, Cárdenas could not expect any encouragement from the conservative Reagan administration in Washington. As in the past, the U.S. government contributed to the maintenance of the Mexican regime, this time by quickly acknowledging Salinas's victory. The U.S. ambassador in Mexico called to congratulate Salinas as soon as preliminary results were announced. As far as is known, the U.S. government had put no pressure on the Mexican government to hold a fair election. The Reagan administration had temporarily pressed Mexico for cleaner elections in the early 1980s when it had appeared that the primary beneficiary would be the conservative PAN. However, after a bit of turmoil in northern Mexico surrounding the elections in 1985 and 1986, and especially when the populist Cárdenas emerged as the main challenger to the PRI, the U.S. government quickly backed away from pushing Mexico on the issue, at the same time that it was exerting great pressure on the Sandinista government in Nicaragua to conduct competitive elections.

The fact that the institutionalized Mexican regime produced a new president in 1988, even if from the same party, helps explain why many Mexicans were willing to accept the PRI victory and did not join the opposition. In another political system in which the same leader was running for reelection, many in the political elite and nonelite who favored change might have gone over to the opposition. But many members of the political elite stayed with the regime at least through the election, in hopes that the new president would bring the changes that they favored. Thus the regular succession, even if within the same party, once again performed a stabilizing function. There was hope that the combination of institutionalized succession and the historical adaptability of the regime would once again provide at least a partial solution to the problems that Mexico faced in 1988. Again, the Mexican political elite had held together adequately to maintain the regime in power.[76]

However, this was the closest call since 1940, and it was not clear in 1988 whether the elite could remain unified through the coming six years. The nation would be watching the new president carefully. Would he be able to achieve the legitimacy, through his policies, that he had not achieved in the election? Would he be able to get the economy moving again after six years of economic disaster? Would he be able and willing to meet the demands for increased democratization of the Mexican political system? Would the Mexican political system remain stable through another presidential term?

NOTES

1. In fact, Argentine political history could be written as the story of the disunity of its elites. For example, see Peter Smith, *Argentina and the Failure of Democracy: Conflict among Political Elites, 1904–1955* (Madison: University of Wisconsin Press, 1974).

2. Gaetano Mosca, *The Ruling Class* (New York: McGraw-Hill, 1939); Vilfredo Pareto, *Sociological Writings* (New York: Praeger, 1966); and Robert Michels, *Political Parties* (New York: Dover Publications, 1966). All of these were originally published early in this century.

3. Peter Smith, *Labyrinths of Power: Political Recruitment in Twentieth-Century Mexico* (Princeton: Princeton University Press, 1979), p. 12.

4. G. Lowell Field and John Higley, *Elitism* (London: Routledge and Kegan Paul, 1980), p. 38.

5. Ibid., p. 120.

6. Robert Putnam, *The Comparative Study of Political Elites* (Englewood Cliffs, N.J.: Prentice-Hall, 1976), p. 6.

7. Robert J. Alexander, *The Venezuelan Democratic Revolution: A Profile of the Regime of Rómulo Betancourt* (New Brunswick, N.J.: Rutgers University Press, 1964). See also Daniel Levine, "Venezuela since 1958: The Consolidation of Democratic Politics," in Juan J. Linz and Alfred Stepan, *The Breakdown of Democratic Regimes: Latin America* (Baltimore: Johns Hopkins University Press, 1978), pp. 82–109. At about the same time, Colombia achieved a similar result—relatively peaceful politics—through a similar process of elite accommodation. See Alexander Wilde, "Conversations among Gentlemen: Oligarchical Democracy in Colombia," in Linz and Stepan, *Breakdown,* 1978, pp. 28–81.

8. Leonard Binder et al., *Crises and Sequences in Political Development* (Princeton: Princeton University Press, 1971).

9. Raymond Grew, ed., *Crises of Political Development in Europe and the United States* (Princeton: Princeton University Press, 1978).

10. Keith Thomas, "The United Kingdom," in Grew, *Crises,* pp. 44–97.

11. C. Wright Mills, *The Power Elite* (New York: Oxford University Press, 1956); Suzanne Keller, *Beyond the Ruling Class: Strategic Elites in Modern Society* (New York: Random House, 1963).

12. Roderic Camp, *Mexico's Leaders: Their Education and Recruitment* (Tucson: University of Arizona Press, 1980), and Roderic Camp, *Entrepreneurs and Politics in Twentieth-Century Mexico* (New York: Oxford University Press, 1989).

13. Jose Luis De Imaz, *Los Que Mandan, Those Who Rule,* trans. Carlos Astiz (Albany: State University of New York Press, 1970).

14. Susan Kaufman Purcell and John F. H. Purcell, "State and Society in Mexico: Must a Stable Polity Be Institutionalized?" *World Politics* 32 (2), 1980, p. 195.

15. Camp, *Mexico's Leaders.*

16. Martin Needler, *Mexican Politics: The Containment of Conflict,* 2d ed. (New York: Praeger Publishers, 1990), p. 83.

17. Raymond Vernon, The *Dilemma of Mexico's Development: The Roles of the Private and Public Sectors* (Cambridge: Harvard University Press, 1963), p. 136.

18. Roderic Camp, "The Cabinet and the Técnico in Mexico and the United States," *Journal of Comparative Administration* 3 (2), 1971, pp. 188–214.

19. Smith, *Labyrinths of Power.*

20. See Roderic Camp, "The Political Technocrat in Mexico and the Survival of the Political System," *Latin American Research Review* 20 (1), 1985, pp. 97–117, and Peter Smith, "Leadership and Change: Intellectuals and Technocrats in Mexico," in Roderic Camp, *Mexico's Political Stability: The Next Five Years* (Boulder, Colo.: Westview Press, 1985), pp. 101–17.

21. Juan D. Lindau, "Schisms in the Mexican Political Elite and the Technocrat/Politician Typology," *Mexican Studies/Estudios Mexicanos* 8 (2), 1992, pp. 217–35.

22. Smith, *Labyrinths,* p. 227.

23. Needler, *Mexican Politics,* p. 94.

24. Smith, *Labyrinths,* p. 156.

25. Ibid., p. 163.

26. Ibid., p. 164.

27. Ibid., p. 101.

28. Putnam, *Comparative Study*, pp. 33–36.

29. Smith, *Labyrinths*, p. 131.

30. Ibid., p. 176.

31. Ibid.

32. Samuel Huntington, *Political Order in Changing Societies* (New Haven: Yale University Press, 1968), pp. 59–71; see also Arnold Heidenheimer, ed., *Political Corruption: Readings in Comparative Analysis* (New Brunswick, N.J.: Transaction Books, 1978).

33. See Stephen Morris, *Corruption and Politics in Contemporary Mexico* (Tuscaloosa: University of Alabama Press, 1991).

34. Edwin Lieuwen, "Depoliticization of the Mexican Revolutionary Army, 1915–1940," in David Ronfeldt, *The Modern Mexican Military: A Reassessment* (La Jolla: Center for U.S.-Mexican Studies, University of California, San Diego, 1984), p. 55.

35. Huntington, *Political Order*, p. 409.

36. See Lieuwen, "Depoliticization," pp. 55–61.

37. Ibid., p. 56.

38. U.S. Arms Control and Disarmament Agency, *World Military Expenditures and Arms Transfers* (Washington, D.C.: Government Printing Office, April 1987), cited in Needler, *Mexican Politics*, p. 80.

39. Richard Griswold del Castillo, *The Treaty of Guadalupe Hidalgo: A Legacy of Conflict* (Norman: University of Oklahoma Press, 1990).

40. See Thomas Skidmore and Peter Smith, *Modern Latin America*, 2d ed. (New York: Oxford University Press, 1989), p. 90.

41. Roderic Camp, "Generals and Politicians in Mexico: A Preliminary Comparison," in Ronfeldt, *Mexican Military*, pp. 107–56, quote on p. 140.

42. For Latin America, and especially for Mexico, perhaps the best-known exponent of the thesis that increasing military professionalism diminishes political intervention is Edwin Lieuwen. See his *Arms and Politics in Latin America* (New York: Praeger, 1960) and *Mexican Militarism: The Political Rise and Fall of the Revolutionary Army, 1910–1940* (Albuquerque: University of New Mexico Press, 1968).

43. Camp, "Generals."

44. David Ronfeldt, "The Modern Mexican Military: An Overview," in Ronfeldt, *Mexican Military*, p. 11.

45. Ronfeldt, "The Mexican Army and Political Order since 1940," in Ronfeldt, *Mexican Military*, pp. 63–85.

46. Camp, "Generals," pp. 144–56.

47. Ronfeldt, "The Mexican Army," p. 70.

48. Ronfeldt, "The Modern Mexican Military," pp.18–22, and Penny Lernoux, *Cry of the People* (New York: Penguin Books, 1982), pp. 155–202.

49. Ronfeldt, "The Modern Mexican Military," p. 20.

50. For example, see Camp, *Entrepreneurs*.

51. Samuel Schmidt, *The Deterioration of the Mexican Presidency* (Tucson: University of Arizona Press, 1991), p. 22.

52. Morris, *Corruption*, pp. 51–53.

53. Camp, *Mexican Leaders*, p. 136.

54. Ibid., pp. 134–35.

55. Ibid., p. 33.

56. See Pablo Gonzales Casanova, *La democracia en Mexico* (México, D. F.: Ediciones Era, 1965), p. 307, and Roberto Newell and Luis Rubio, *Mexico's Dilemma: The Political Origins of Economic Crisis* (Boulder, Colo.: Westview Press, 1984), p. 95.

57. Daniel Levy and Gabriel Székely, *Mexico: Paradoxes of Stability and Change,* 2d ed. (Boulder, Colo.: Westview Press, 1987), pp. 71–81.

58. Ibid., p. 71.

59. Patrick Oster, *The Mexicans: A Personal Portrait of a People* (New York: HarperCollins, 1990), p. 94.

60. Cárdenas says, however, that he had no plans to study in the United States. Interview with author, July 1990.

61. Cuauhtémoc Cárdenas vita, personal collection of author.

62. Oster, *The Mexicans,* pp. 94–95.

63. Interview with author, July 1990.

64. *Mexico Journal,* Sept. 28, 1987, p. 8.

65. *Mexico Journal,* Oct. 14, 1987, p. 8.

66. Oster, *The Mexicans,* p. 107.

67. For detailed discussions of the elections of the mid-1980s, see Arturo Alvarado, ed., *Electoral Patterns and Perspectives in Mexico* (La Jolla: Center for U.S.-Mexican Studies, University of California, San Diego, 1987).

68. *Mexico Journal,* Feb. 15, 1988, p. 20.

69. Ibid., p. 23

70. *Mexico Journal,* Dec. 9, 1987, pp. 19–20.

71. *Mexico Journal,* April 4, 1988, p. 9.

72. *Proceso,* April 9, 1990, p. 12.

73. Jose Barberán, Cuauhtémoc Cárdenas, et al., *Radiografia del fraude: análisis de los datos oficiales del 6 de julio* (México, D. F.: Editorial Nuestro Tiempo, 1988).

74. Juan Molinar Horcasitas, *El tiempo de la legitimidad: elecciones, autoritarismo, y democracia en México* (México, D. F.: Cal y Arena, 1991), p. 219. Other sources give 50.36 percent for Salinas. The percentages vary depending, for example, on whether invalid ballots are included in the total count.

75. Luis Alvarez, president of the PAN at the time, claimed that each candidate got about one-third of the vote—about 30 to 34 percent each. Therefore, he argued, the regime cheated the PAN's Clouthier far more than it cheated Cárdenas in order to produce the 50-percent share for Salinas. Interview with author, July 6, 1990.

76. For a discussion of the role that personal networks play in Mexican political stability, see Samuel Schmidt and Jorge Gil-Mendieta, "La carrera por la presidencia de Mexico," *Administración Pública* 1, 1991, pp. 89–119, and Roderic Camp, "Camarillas in Mexican Politics: The Case of the Salinas Cabinet," *Mexican Studies/Estudios Mexicanos* 6 (1), 1990, pp. 85–107.

6

Carlos Salinas and the Revolutionary Regime

RETRENCHMENT OR REFORM?

When Carlos Salinas de Gortari became president of Mexico on December 1, 1988, he knew that the regime that had governed Mexico since 1920 was in serious trouble. Even by the official count, which few Mexicans believed, he had won barely 50 percent of the popular vote. For the first time, the opposition gained four seats in the Senate and almost 50 percent of the seats in the Chamber of Deputies, giving the PRI only a small majority of 263 of 500 seats in the chamber. The determined opposition continued to yell fraud and to demonstrate against the election outcome from July until inauguration day. On that day, as the new president began to deliver his speech to the assembled legislators, members of Cuauhtémoc Cárdenas's coalition walked out of the Chamber of Deputies in a bold display of protest against the regime.

Robert Pastor reported that on the eve of the inauguration, he suggested to Salinas that he read Arthur Schlesinger's description of Franklin Roosevelt's first one hundred days in office. "With a mischievous grin," notes Pastor, "he said that he had already *reread* it." [1] Salinas was determined to enter the presidency with a bold program for change that would revive the popularity of the regime. To reestablish that authority, Salinas and other regime leaders resorted to the traditional portfolio of devices. They sought maximum advantage from the support provided by the institutionalized party and the institutionalized presidential succession. They made structural changes in the economy, which they believed would lead once again to sustained economic growth. They also adapted to the political pressures of the day. The fact that the poor had suffered disproportionately from the economic woes of the 1980s necessitated the creation of a vast new social program, Solidarity. This redistributive program to satisfy the left was matched by a movement to the right to satisfy business, largely through proposing a free-trade agreement with the United States and

Canada. Regime leaders proved unusually adaptable in their efforts to rebuild support from both elites and others. Yet where necessary, the regime was also willing to employ coercion, in the form of repression and electoral fraud, in order to retain power.

Salinas's predecessor, Miguel de la Madrid, was the fourth Mexican president in a row to leave the office unpopular, with the regime vulnerable. The decline had begun with the repression near the end of Gustavo Díaz Ordaz's term in 1968, which left the country shaken and perplexed. Luis Echeverría managed to revive the popular bases of the regime to some extent, but his strident populism divided the country and frightened economic elites. The next president, José López Portillo, presided over a massive oil boom that restored the country's economy and largely reassured business until heavy spending and foreign borrowing began to weigh the economy down. Then the disclosure of widespread corruption in his administration once again disillusioned the Mexican people about their leaders. De la Madrid sought to restore a more moral tone to government, reminiscent of Adolfo Ruiz Cortines's anticorruption stance after the excesses of the Miguel Alemán years. De la Madrid also began the process of restructuring the economy to exorcise the worst aspects of protectionism to which Mexican business had become accustomed. But this reorganization was a wrenching experience, and the Mexican economy did not grow at all during the de la Madrid presidency.

To make matters worse, the regime was seen to be unusually ineffective during the severe earthquakes in Mexico City in the fall of 1985, which killed perhaps twenty thousand and left many thousands homeless. In fact, the calamity prompted the spontaneous emergence of various civic groups for self-help when the government failed to act. As a result of this and other government failures, especially with the economy, the conservative opposition grew bolder. It claimed more electoral victories and protested what it considered fraudulent defeats in northern states and cities. Finally, to add to the regime's mounting problems, when the PRI nominated Salinas in 1987, some discontented members on the left wing of the PRI broke away and mounted the opposition candidacy of Cuauhtémoc Cárdenas. The PRI encountered its toughest fight in decades in the 1988 election, barely pulling out a victory that was scarcely credible to most observers. In 1988, public opinion polls suggested that Mexico was faced with a "serious crisis of legitimacy" in which more than "three-fourths of Mexicans polled expressed negative views about the political system and about Mexican politics in general."[2]

When he became president, therefore, Salinas recognized that he must act with energy and dispatch if he was to save the regime. He used the factors that had proved so useful to the regime in the past: institutionalization, economic growth, adaptability, elite unity, coercion and Mexico's proximity to the United States. Salinas came into office with some strong disadvantages—loss of political legitimacy, a failed economy, the incredible election, a determined opposition. But he also assumed the presidency with one powerful advantage—

he was a new president. A major component of the institutionalized Mexican political system is the predictable presidential succession, which regularly brings in a new leader every six years. This almost always allows the new president a honeymoon period during which he can try to restore regime legitimacy and overcome some of the problems of the previous administration. If de la Madrid had run for reelection and had claimed victory in such dubious conditions, it seems likely that the turmoil of 1988 would have erupted into something far greater. But the institutionalized succession meant that the country had a new leader and that people could hope that Salinas would be more successful than de la Madrid had been at addressing the country's problems.

The institutionalized corporatist party had also helped Salinas to claim victory in 1988. Although the sectoral basis of the regime was weaker than in previous elections, the regime was still able to mobilize millions of voters through its domination of labor unions and peasant organizations within the official party. It is true that Salinas officially lost five states to Cárdenas—Baja California Norte, the Federal District, México, Michoacán, and Morelos—and may actually have lost others as well. Obviously, millions of Mexicans deserted the PRI and voted for opposition parties. Nonetheless, much of the regime's support held, and it was the PRI's influence over its constituent organizations that helped it to retain much of its traditional constituency. The importance of this sectoral support for the PRI was a major reason that, soon after taking office, Salinas moved against the leader of the oil workers union.

One of the ways that a new Mexican president traditionally establishes authority is to move energetically against corruption. Thus Salinas sent the army after the labor boss, La Quina. Then, "he moved with equal decisiveness to arrest businessmen for illegal trading and for not paying their taxes, well-known drug traffickers who had controlled local or even state governments, and a senior police official for his complicity in the murder of a controversial newspaperman."[3] Salinas arrested La Quina ostensibly because of the labor leader's notorious corruption and intransigent resistance to the necessary reform of PEMEX, the state oil monopoly. However, the new president moved swiftly against La Quina at least in part because the union leader had failed to deliver the votes of the oil workers in 1988. The action against him was intended to send a clear signal to other sectoral party leaders that similar defections would not be tolerated.

There was some evidence by 1988 that the sectoral bases of support in the party that Lázaro Cárdenas built had begun to fall apart and that the consensus that had held the PRI coalition together since the 1930s was showing signs of disintegration. To counteract this growing weakness in the sectors and localities, Salinas moved to concentrate power in the presidency. Always a powerful office, the presidency became even stronger under Salinas, and his personal will to act from the center became a critical ingredient in regime policies after 1988. In addition to punishing labor leaders who failed to control their sector for the regime, several times Salinas defied local authorities and overturned election results, sometimes in favor of the conservative PAN. Salinas increasingly overruled local leaders and relied more heavily on the *dedazo,* the pointing of the finger by the president, in selecting local candidates he thought would be more attractive to voters. Thus central control within the PRI increased after 1988 to offset growing regional differences of opinion and center-periphery conflicts in the party. Salinas also did not hesitate to use the army to ensure that his policies prevailed at the polls and within the party. Whereas many within the PRI agreed with this control-oriented approach, others reacted negatively and called for more freedom within the party to select and nominate candidates in a more open and democratic way, from the bottom up. Despite this, Salinas insisted on tight control of events from the center.[4] Thus Salinas was able to use the institutionalized succession and party to revive the fortunes of the regime.

Second, Salinas knew that the government must try to stimulate economic growth, which, as we have seen, had been one of the principal reasons for the endurance of the regime. Salinas faced two economic problems. The left wing of his own party and the populist challenge of Cárdenas demanded that Salinas address the needs of the poor and disadvantaged for more equal income distribution; at the same time, business wanted the free market to be given greater rein. Thus Salinas had to proceed in two directions at once, trying to make the Mexican economy both more efficient and more equitable.

Although he was no doubt a prime architect of the economic austerity policies under his predecessor de la Madrid, soon after becoming president, Salinas launched two major initiatives to address both problems. The first was a massive new social program to try to alleviate some of the discontent of the poor and, of course, to appeal for their votes in future elections. The new program, called Programa Nacional de Solidaridad, or PRONASOL (also called Solidarity), directed several trillion pesos (several billion dollars) at low-income people and the infrastructural needs of the country. It was aimed mainly at delivering public works projects—schools, roads, electricity, health clinics—to poor districts and at mobilizing local authorities to deal more effectively with these problems. Thus the PRONASOL approach was as much a result of political as economic imperatives. The Solidarity program was an obvious effort by the PRI to regain through redistributive programs some of its legitimacy as the revolutionary party and to arrest the appeal of the PRD. The effort proved relatively successful and helped the PRI to hold on to much of its left-wing and center-left intellectuals. Heavy social spending also contributed to PRI victories in various state and local elections during Salinas's term, as well as to regaining some of the seats in the Chamber of Deputies in the 1991 midterm election, seats that it had lost in 1988. Thus Solidarity, a departure from the PRI's unpopular austerity programs of the 1980s, represented a bold move by the new president.[5]

The second part of Salinas's strategy for economic recovery involved a serious effort to stimulate economic growth and restructure the economy. A central component of this effort was the sale to private investors of many of the state-owned firms that had become a drag on both the government and the economy. The de la Madrid administration had already significantly reduced the number of state firms from 1,100 in 1982 to 412 by 1988. The Salinas administration continued this process of privatization by halving the number of state firms again—to 221 by mid-1992. Privatization reduced the level of government subsidization of state firms from 13 percent of GDP in 1982 to a mere 3 percent by 1990. Most of the $20 billion in proceeds from the sale of state firms was used either to reduce the debt directly or to finance the Solidarity social programs.[6] However, this was a one-time revenue source on which the government could not continue to rely. Thus Salinas pursued other methods of growth stimulation.

Taking advantage of Mexico's location, President Salinas proposed in 1990 a North American Free Trade Agreement (NAFTA) with the United States and Canada to greatly reduce trade barriers over the coming years. In this way Salinas hoped to reorient permanently the Mexican economy away from inward-looking protectionism and start it on a path toward international competition and exports.[7] This two-pronged approach to the economy—Solidarity to help the poor and NAFTA to stimulate growth—apparently had positive effects. Salinas managed early in his term to revive the economy after seven years (1982–88) without economic growth. For the years 1990, 1991, and 1992, the Mexican economy grew at an average real rate of about 3 percent a year. The government debt, both domestic and foreign, declined from a crippling 62 percent of GDP in 1988 to a much more manageable 28 percent by 1992. Salinas's economic strategy also reflected, once again, the regime's adaptability.

In this new context, however, the Salinas government simultaneously had to pursue policies of economic growth and redistribution, which often appeared to be in conflict with each other. In addition, the regime had to deal somehow with the increasing demands for greater political participation. Public opinion polling had demonstrated that by the 1990s a large number of Mexicans wanted honest elections.[8] With a Ph.D. in political economy from Harvard University, Salinas knew all too well the dilemma that faces authoritarian regimes. Whether they try to liberalize quickly or to stifle reform, demands often built up faster than the existing regime can deal with them, and the result is sometimes the displacement of that regime. His strategy of preparing the PRI for this new challenge combined energetic economic and social policies with only moderate political liberalization. He seemed to believe that further movement toward democratization would have to wait until the PRI was capable of actually winning competitive elections.

Salinas's strategy was in a sense the opposite of Gorbachev's in the Soviet Union, who tried to liberalize politics before liberalizing the economy. That formula contributed to the collapse of the Soviet regime as freer politics led to a buildup of economic demands faster than the old economy could satisfy them.

Salinas followed a strategy more similar to the one followed by the leaders of Korea, Taiwan, and China. The leaders of these nations insisted that economic restructuring must precede political liberalization (and whether the latter would ever come in those countries was not entirely clear). Therefore, although the 1988 election suggested that the Mexican political system was being impelled toward a greater degree of democracy in which the regime would be forced to compete in more-or-less fair elections, Salinas sought to restore the PRI's image by concentrating on reviving the economy and by appealing to the groups that had traditionally provided electoral support for the revolutionary party—workers and peasants—as well as the growing middle class. It remained to be seen whether Salinas's order of reform would succeed. He was, however, relatively successful at recapturing some of the popular support that had fallen so low by 1988.

Judging from public opinion polls and state and local election results after 1988, the strategy at least partly succeeded. Polls after his election regularly showed that high percentages of the Mexican population approved of Salinas's performance as president. In one poll in early 1992, the president and his programs received an 80-percent approval rating, up from 62 percent in 1991. Salinas's bold actions on many fronts had made him a popular figure. For example, the North American Free Trade Agreement, one of the most important initiatives of his administration, was acceptable to a sizable majority of Mexicans. However, the president's popularity remained divided by class and geographic region. He was more popular in the commercial centers in northern Mexico than in Mexico City. The largest single bloc of votes in the country is in the Mexico City metropolis, and this area constituted the base of Cárdenas's populist support. Salinas's support, ironically, was stronger among the lower classes, whereas Cárdenas was often favored by better-off voters and economic elites, particularly in the south. Economic elites in the north tended to favor the market-oriented National Action Party (PAN) opposition. Nevertheless, northern voters were more likely to support both Salinas's policies and his leadership; in the Federal District, his policies were popular, but he personally was not. These developments represented a somewhat curious realignment of left and right opinion, although the peasants and workers continued, as they had traditionally done, to provide a solid source of support for the regime. Therefore, support for the PRI was divided geographically and by traditional right-versus-left ideologies. Some on the left wing of the PRI, as well as many independent leftists, came to favor Cárdenas's Party of the Democratic Revolution (PRD).[9]

It was essential that Salinas mend this rift in party and elite unity. To do so, he relied heavily on another common technique of the regime—coercion. As modern as Salinas may appear, to a large extent he employed all the classic approaches that the Mexican regime had used for decades. The Salinas government continued to use electoral fraud to win those elections it was determined to take. The regime allowed the opposition, especially the PAN, to win an occasional victory—two northern governorships and other state and local offices—but it was less conciliatory with Cárdenas's PRD which was, however, allowed to win occasional local electoral contests, such as in Guerrero and Michoacán in 1989. These elections were not decided by voters at the polls but by high-level negotiations between the president and his advisors and officials of the various parties. President Salinas also engaged in intense personal campaigning in an effort to increase regime legitimacy, campaigning that was reminiscent of populist leaders such as Luis Echeverría or Lázaro Cárdenas. In an effort to satisfy those who criticized the coercive nature of the regime, Salinas also created a national human rights commission to investigate charges of human rights violations. In this and various other ways, Salinas attempted to demonstrate that his government was committed to some degree of political liberalization.

The regime has generally feared the opposition on the left more than that on the right. It could always portray the right as reactionary and counterrevolutionary, arguing that conservatives would undo the gains of the Revolution. Containing the left was another matter. If the left was allowed to grow too powerful, it could undermine the very legitimating basis of the regime and its claim to be the embodiment of the goals of the Mexican Revolution. No one could have threatened that claim more forcefully than the son of Lázaro Cárdenas. Thus reestablishing elite unity after the defection of Cárdenas and his supporters from the PRI in 1988 posed a fundamental challenge. The PRI has chosen to play up the revolutionary credentials of the party in order to persuade defectors to return and potential defectors to remain. It also tried to frighten Mexicans into thinking a PRD victory would destabilize the country, discourage economic growth, and perhaps even launch another violent and bloody revolution.

Regime propaganda aside, however, it is more accurate to see the PRD as a moderate social democratic party. It is a combination of the left wing of the PRI (many of its leaders are former *priístas*) and the bulk of the independent socialist and Communist left. The real threat represented by the PRD since 1988 was not that its supporters were radical or revolutionary but that they were basically anti-PRI. PRD supporters have generally taken relatively moderate positions on most issues. For example, Cárdenas was not fundamentally opposed to either privatization or the NAFTA agreement, although he insisted that Mexico should bargain more forcefully so that the country would not be disadvantaged by trade with its much wealthier and more powerful northern neighbor. This was the cautious position adhered to by Salinas himself as late as October 1989 before he reversed his stance and wholeheartedly endorsed the trade agreement.[10] The real threat from Cárdenas and the PRD, therefore, was that they advocated a transition from the one-party dominance of the PRI to a system in which opposition parties were allowed to present their case to the people in fair elections.

Nevertheless the Salinas government seemed determined, at almost any cost, to concede nothing to Cárdenas and the left. It continued to charge that a Cárdenas government would undo much of what Salinas had tried to accomplish in modernizing the Mexican economy and opening it more to the market.[11] The regime portrayed the PRD as disloyal, violent, and perhaps even involved in drug trafficking while the regime's overwhelming control of the press enabled it to portray the PRI as the party of stability. Even when the PRD was allowed to win local elections, their representatives often faced uncooperative state and federal governments. PRD officials were made to appear incompetent by the federal government's withholding of money and other essential supports to which local governments were entitled. PAN officials reported similar difficulties. In addition, at least 130 murders of PRD supporters occurred from the time of the presidential election in 1988 to mid-1992, especially in the PRD strongholds of Michoacán, Guerrero, Oaxaca, Morelos, and the Federal District.[12] Thus while the Salinas government tried to adjust to some of the demands for liberalization of the political system, such as occasionally overturning patently unfair elections and by paying greater attention to social problems, at the same time it continued to employ many of the old techniques of control.[13]

As the Salinas administration tightened its grip on the political system after 1988, it particularly increased the centralization of power in the already powerful president's office and weakened the role of state and local officials and of the sectoral leadership in the party. Yet the Salinas government was not entirely successful in its goal of reconsolidating the authority of the PRI. Some *priístas* remained dissatisfied with the minimal movement of the regime toward political democracy. For example, the 1990 PRI national convention was punctuated by considerable internal criticism of the PRI's continuing undemocratic structure, particularly its method of selecting PRI candidates. The president and other PRI leaders continued to handpick most PRI candidates instead of using party primaries, as advocated by some members.

In addition, a few high-level defections continued to occur, although not many. The most prominent defection during the first four years of the Salinas presidency was that of Rodolfo Gonzáles Guevara, a former ambassador and a leader of the Democratic Current when Cárdenas was still in the party. Gonzáles Guevara complained that efforts to reform the party had been thwarted by labor leader Fidel Velázquez and others. A few others quit the PRI at the same time.[14] Undeterred by these defections, Salinas turned more often to the internal security forces to enforce his policies and increasingly used the military to put down electoral challenges. The army occupied government buildings in Michoacán to intimidate supporters of Cárdenas in his home state.[15] Salinas's approach appeared to be popular with many Mexicans, who were impressed by his show of strength in the face of adversity and by his willingness to act boldly.

One observer wrote in 1990, "It would seem that if the PRI regime could survive the tumult of the past decade, riding out the 1990s should be relatively easy." [16] There was much truth in the observation. After all, the regime had hung together through the worst economic time since the 1930s, and it had even survived the wave of democratization that swept the world in the 1980s. Thus by the early 1990s, the Mexican regime had survived two of the strongest challenges to the continuation of authoritarian regimes—economic difficulties and demands for democratization. It did so by relying on the strategies that had proved so successful for the regime in the past—institutionalization, economic growth, adaptability to the right and the left, coercion, corruption, and maintaining elite unity. By 1993, therefore, the prospects for the continuation of the regime seemed considerably stronger than they had after the election of 1988.

Yet the new variable with which the regime had to contend was the growing demand for democracy. Therefore, it is worth examining in more detail the pressures for democracy after 1988. To satisfy these growing demands, Salinas moved to reform the image of the PRI as a supporter of democracy by enacting a new electoral law in 1990 and recognizing more opposition victories. The next section explores in detail the content and implications of this potentially important contribution to the democratization of the Mexican political system. It examines the Mexican electoral system in order to show where problems existed in the past and how the regime claimed to be taking steps to overcome these problems.

THE ELECTORAL PROCESS AND DEMOCRACY IN MEXICO

Mexico and Liberal Democracy

As the twentieth century comes to a close, liberal democracy has become the model political form throughout the world. Although political scientists may differ somewhat on the details, many agree on the general meaning of the concept. Most theorists of liberal democracy agree that this type of political system is characterized, at a minimum, by three qualities—the opportunity for widespread political *participation,* the selection of leaders through fair and competitive *elections,* and the guarantee of civil and political *liberties* that make participation and elections meaningful. [17]

Not only is there broad consensus on what constitutes liberal democracy, there is equally wide agreement among scholars that Mexico is not in that category. Typical of scholarly discussion is one essay titled "Mexico: Sustained Civilian Rule without Democracy," which says: "Mexico has had no significant twentieth-century experience (and precious little prior experience) with democratic rule. Instead, Mexican politics has displayed considerable disdain for the public competition and accountability integral to liberal democracy." [18] However, a few months after the important election of 1988, Lorenzo Meyer, a leading Mexican political scientist, wrote: "The presidential elections of July 6, 1988 represent a watershed in the political history of postrevolutionary Mexico. They opened the door to a difficult transition, from stale authoritarianism to democracy. It is too early to say whether this transition will succeed.'' [19]

In the four years after the 1988 election, additional changes occurred in Mexican politics. In 1989, the opposition PAN won its first governorship (in Baja California Norte) and in 1992 its second (in Chihuahua). In addition, a PAN mayor was appointed interim governor of Guanajuato after a hotly contested election in that state. Both the PAN and the PRD controlled far more local governments than ever before. The press appeared to be freer to criticize the government, and various organizations were created to monitor human rights in Mexico. In addition, a new electoral law was enacted in 1990.

Liberal democracy is not merely an abstract idea. Its three defining qualities of political participation, human rights, and fair elections must be put into practice in concrete ways to be meaningful. One of the most important ways in which liberal democracy is operationalized is through elections. The rest of this chapter will examine the steps in the electoral process as a vehicle for evaluating whether any significant progress toward liberal democracy has been made in Mexico, especially under Carlos Salinas.

On the surface an electoral process may seem to consist mainly of the casting of votes and the counting of ballots. However, the voting process is composed of many steps, from the organization and recognition of political parties, through the determination of eligibility and registration of voters, to the actual casting of votes, tabulating results and any formal challenges of the results. The electoral process can be analyzed into ten steps, which occur in three stages: activities of parties and candidates; the ''creation'' of voters; and procedures, beginning with the vote itself, that produce the final outcome of the election. It will look first at the passage of the 1990 law and the problems it was meant to address. We will then examine the steps in the voting process, describe what problems occurred in the past at each step, and outline the major provisions enacted into the new law to address these problems. We will inquire whether the new law and other developments, such as efforts to improve human rights, helped to make Mexican elections fairer. Did these specific changes indicate that Mexico's semiauthoritarian, hegemonic political system was making progress toward liberal democracy?

Passage of the 1990 Law

Mexican electoral law was revised seven times between World War II and 1990. In 1946, political parties were prohibited from having ties to external organizations; this effectively outlawed the Mexican Communist Party for several decades. In addition, the standard for official recognition of parties was set at thirty thousand members nationwide, with at least one thousand registered members in at least two-thirds of the states. In 1954, women were granted the right to vote, and the threshold for official recognition of a party was raised to seventy-five thousand members, with at least 2,500 members in at least two-thirds of the states. In 1963 proportional representation was introduced for the Chamber of Deputies in order to give opposition parties a larger presence in that body. In 1973 the voting age was lowered to eighteen, and the threshold for proportional representation was lowered to make it easier for minority parties to gain seats in the Chamber of Deputies. In 1977 the number of seats in the Chamber of Deputies and the number allocated to proportional representation were both increased, and free television and radio time for all registered political parties was made available. In 1986 government financing of political parties was expanded and made a function of their share of the popular vote, and the majority party was made eligible for proportional representation (PR) seats. The number of seats in the Chamber was increased to five hundred, with two hundred allocated to proportional representation. None of these changes went very far in making Mexican elections more democratic. Instead, they were intended to give the opposition a bit more presence in government in order to make the regime appear more legitimate.

Although the 1988 national election was the closest in modern times, it was criticized by the opposition for being characterized by widespread fraud. In his inauguration speech, President Salinas promised a new electoral law that would ostensibly ensure a fairer electoral process. He was probably motivated by a desire to reduce political conflict, create an appearance of greater democracy for both domestic and international consumption, and calm the fears of foreign investors. To give the reform greater legitimacy, it was important that at least part of the *real* opposition (the Partido de Acción Nacional, or PAN, on the right, or the Partido de la Revolución Democrática, or PRD, on the left) support the reform and that the government not depend solely on the "satellite" opposition parties that had usually supported the PRI in the past—the Partido Popular Socialista (PPS), Partido Auténtico de la Revolución Mexicana (PARM), and Partido del Frente Cardenista para la Reconstrucción Nacional (PFCRN).

Hence in 1989 a constitutional amendment was enacted allowing for a new electoral statute. An indication of the new political reality in Mexico was that the PRI found it necessary to seek the support of the PAN in order to obtain the two-thirds vote required in the Chamber of Deputies to amend the constitution. In return for that support, Salinas gave PAN leaders a "letter of intent" indicating that their major concerns would be addressed in the new electoral law.[20]

In July 1990 the chamber passed the detailed new Código Federal de Instituciones y Procedimientos Electorales (COFIPE). The bill passed the Chamber by a vote of 369 out of a possible 500, with only 65 deputies voting against it. The PRI was able to get the votes of all deputies of the PPS, PARM, and PFCRN—all of which had supported Cuauhtémoc Cárdenas in the presidential election of 1988. The conservative PAN was deeply divided over certain provisions in the electoral law, and hence the PAN leadership allowed their deputies a free vote; 63 voted for the law, 29 voted against it, and two abstained.

To reduce electoral fraud, the law provided for the creation of a new, more accurate electoral roll of voters and the issuance of new voter identification cards with photographs and fingerprints. It also created a new electoral commission to oversee elections and mandated opposition party access to polling places during elections and to the commission's computers during the vote count.

The major complaints of both the PAN dissidents and the PRD was that the new law did not guarantee either the honesty of elections or the neutrality of electoral officials. For example, PAN Deputy Bernardo Bátiz said he voted against it because the government retained control over the electoral process.[21] The bill was also opposed by Cárdenas's PRD and the Grupo Independiente, a splinter faction of the PRD. In fact, both of these groups walked out of the Chamber in protest after the vote. The PRD was especially critical of the fact that the head of the new electoral commission would be selected by the president, although PRI deputies pointed out that the head of the commission had to be approved by two-thirds of the members of the commission, which meant that the president's choice would require the support of at least some of the opposition parties.

The PRD also objected to the "governability" clause, which gave any party receiving more than 35 percent of the national vote an automatic majority in Congress. The president wanted this provision because it would give the PRI a majority of seats in the Chamber even if it received less than 50 percent of the popular vote. The PRI thereby positioned itself to retain control of the Chamber even after conceding that it had not won a majority of the popular vote. This would allow the PRI at least to pass regular statutes, which require a simple majority in each house. However, the PRI pointed out that the majority party would need the support of minority parties for the two-thirds majority required to amend the constitution.[22]

The PRD also did not like the fact that the law continued the practice of disenfranchising Mexican citizens living abroad. Neither the PRI nor the PAN favored giving them the vote, saying it would be too difficult to ensure the honesty of the vote. It seemed more likely, however, that those two parties thought that they would not do very well among Mexican voters in the United States.

Despite opposition misgivings, the bill passed the Senate on August 14, 1990, and was signed into law by the president the next day, to go into effect for elections beginning in 1991.[23] Thus the new law was both promising and problematic. It seemed to address some of the concerns of the opposition about the fairness of elections, but the opposition continued to protest that the electoral process was fundamentally unfair and calculated to maintain the PRI in power. Were the changes merely symbolic, or could they make a real difference in Mexican elections? Let us outline an "ideal-type" electoral process, see what problems have occurred at each step of Mexican elections, and ask whether the new law and other developments after 1988 moved the country toward fairer elections.

The Electoral Process

The electoral process can be analyzed into three parts. One is the set of activities that *parties and candidates* engage in as they attempt to win elections. The second is the path of the *individual voter* and his or her vote. These two paths converge at the moment of the vote itself and then continue along a common path until any challenge of the *final results* is resolved in some way. Ideally, parties are allowed to organize, are given official recognition on the ballot, and are allowed (and perhaps subsidized) to campaign for office. Meanwhile, the government enacts laws establishing what category of individuals are eligible to vote, registers them, and maintains the voter lists. Citizens then vote, the ballots are counted, the results are announced, and any challenges to the electoral process are dealt with. In a liberal democracy, safeguards are put in place at each step to ensure that the elections are procedurally fair. Ideally, the law is explicit about eligibility and registration, the voter lists are maintained properly, the vote itself is monitored by neutral observers or a balance of partisans, the vote count is open to public scrutiny, the results are announced promptly, and an accepted method exists for challenging the results if irregularities have occurred.[24] Figure 6.1 illustrates the electoral process. Let us look at each step to see what is "supposed" to occur, what problems have occurred in Mexico in the past, and whether the 1990 law and other developments of recent years have made any changes in the reality of Mexican elections.

Parties and Candidates

1. *Organization:* A polity has taken a major step away from authoritarianism when its citizens are allowed by the authorities to organize themselves into political groups. In a highly authoritarian system, the government generally does not allow citizens to organize themselves into political parties with any notion of challenging the hegemony of the regime. We often associate such a blanket proscription with Communist regimes such as the Soviet Union from about 1920 until about 1990 or Cuba from 1960 until the present. However, numerous military dictatorships have similarly prohibited political meetings and the organization of political parties. For example, the Pinochet regime in Chile declared political parties illegal or "in recess" after its coup of 1973. Since the Revolution, Mexico has never banned parties in general, although in 1946 it did declare illegal any party with ties to external organizations, which was aimed primarily at the Mexican Communist Party. This party was finally allowed to participate in elections beginning in the 1970s, but because its electoral appeal was so small, it eventually merged with other parties.

The 1990 law had a possible effect on the organization of parties. In 1988,

Figure 6.1
The Electoral Process

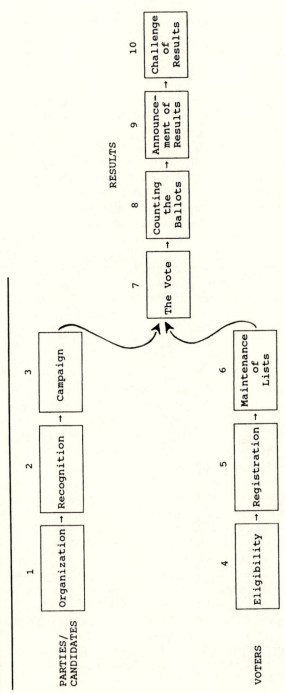

several small parties—PARM, PPS, PMS, and PFCRN—nominated Cuauhtémoc Cárdenas as their candidate for president while retaining their separate
identities on the ballot. Thus Cárdenas was able to gain the support of these
smaller parties without compromising their legal independence or ideological
distinctiveness. The new law appeared designed to prevent this type of in-
terparty cooperation in the future, requiring parties either to merge into formal
coalitions or to remain separate and to nominate their own candidates. That is,
no party could field a candidate already nominated by another party or by a
coalition.[25] Thus the kind of coalition that united behind Cárdenas in 1988 was
rendered illegal. The regime appeared to be betting that even though the factions on the left might be able to agree on a common candidate, they would
not be willing to submerge their identities within a coalition. It was possible
this this provision could weaken the opposition by preventing small parties such
as PPS or PARM from nominating a major candidate such as Cárdenas. However, the provision could have the opposite effect; it could give small parties
an incentive to coalesce or formally merge with the larger parties such as the
PRD. If that occurred, the regime's strategy would have backfired.

2. *Recognition:* It is one thing for a group to be allowed to call itself a
political party, to hold meetings, and to make plans to contest elections. Most
political systems, however, have thresholds that such organizations must cross
in order to appear on the ballot and thus offer its candidates to the voters. The
1990 law retained the same threshold as the prior law (1.5 percent), a threshold
that was actually set in 1977 when the PRI's main problem was the lack of a
sizable opposition. In the new context, in which the opposition is exerting more
pressure for fair elections, the 1.5-percent threshold turned out to be a two-
edged sword for the regime. On the one hand, the low barrier allows many
parties to receive official recognition, thus fragmenting and perhaps weakening
the opposition. On the other hand, it also made it easier for numerous parties
of the opposition to gain seats in the Chamber of Deputies than if the threshold
were higher, thus presenting the regime with a larger total opposition. However, to retain official registration, a party must not only obtain 1.5 percent of
the total national vote, but its support must be spread across at least one hundred congressional districts. This precludes parties that have only a regional
appeal from appearing on the ballot for national elections.

Another meaning of party "recognition" is representation in the legislature.
There are many ways in which electoral rules can encourage or discourage
additional parties. An electoral system with winner-take-all districts presents
higher barriers to new or small parties than does an electoral system characterized by proportional representation. It is commonly agreed that the plurality,
winner-take-all system of Britain or the United States favors a two-party system, whereas proportional representation tends to encourage multiparty systems
and coalition governments.

As the Mexican regime became increasingly embarrassed by the weakness
of the opposition in the prevailing system of majoritarian districts, it introduced

proportional representation for the Chamber in 1963. To induce a modicum of representation by opposition parties, the 1963 electoral law provided that any party receiving 2.5 percent of the national vote would get five seats in the Chamber of Deputies, as well as one seat for every additional .5 percent above the 2.5 percent, for a maximum of twenty seats. In the 1964 election, this provided the opposition with only thirty-five places in the three-hundred-seat chamber. After the turmoil of the late 1960s and early 1970s, it was decided to make it even easier for the opposition to win seats in the Chamber by lowering the threshold for PR seats to 1.5 percent of the national vote. In addition to that change, the 1977 law increased the number of seats in the chamber to four hundred, with three hundred to be elected in winner-take-all districts and one hundred chosen by proportional representation. Any party winning sixty or more districts (that is, the PRI) could not receive seats by proportional representation.

In 1986 the electoral law was amended again to increase the number of seats in the Chamber to five hundred, of which three hundred were district seats and two hundred were reserved for proportional representation. The 1986 law required that to retain its official registration, a party had to field candidates in at least one hundred of the three hundred congressional districts in the country. To guard against a situation in which it might win only a plurality of the popular vote and hence be left without a majority in the Chamber, the PRI inserted a provision that any party receiving a plurality of votes without winning a majority of seats would automatically be assigned enough additional seats through proportional representation to give it a majority. Hence the PRI would now be eligible for seats by proportional representation as well as from winning districts.

In the 1988 election, the PRI barely took a majority in the chamber, with 263 seats out of 500. PAN got 101 seats, PRD 50, and other parties the remaining 86 seats. Before 1988, PRI's problem had been to ensure a sizable opposition presence in the congress in a political system that generally did not allow real electoral competition; after this election, however, PRI had the opposite problem. Rather than being concerned with ensuring a significant opposition in Congress in order to legitimize the regime, its problem now was to ensure PRI control in a system that had suddenly become more competitive. The leaders of the regime obviously feared the possibility of being unable to command a majority in Congress. The problem for PRI was to protect its majority and its ability to govern. Unlike most of the previous laws since 1963, therefore, the 1990 law halted the trend of making it easier for minority parties to win seats in the legislature. Thus with PAN support, the PRI pushed through the "governability" clause, which would give a simple majority in the Chamber of Deputies to any party receiving at least 35 percent of the national vote. The PAN supported this proposal perhaps in part because its leaders believed the day would soon come when the PAN itself could receive over 35 percent of the popular vote.

Whether or not the governability clause is "fair" is a matter of opinion. In every political system, a tension exists between precision of representation and the ability of a government to make decisions.[26] Although some political systems seek to offer representation to very finely sliced ideological groupings, every political system must draw the line somewhere. Some mechanism for aggregation of votes to produce a governing majority is used in every system. For example, almost no British government since World War II was put into office by a majority of the popular vote, yet most of them commanded a sizable majority in the House of Commons. However, the resolution of the representation-governability dilemma introduced in the 1990 Mexican law was somewhat extreme. Few political systems routinely give a party a majority of seats in parliament when it has obtained only 35 percent of the popular vote. Therefore, on balance, the governability clause must be seen as a ploy to retain PRI dominance rather than an effort to move the system toward greater political pluralism.

3. *Campaign:* Even semiauthoritarian systems may allow political parties to organize and to be granted official recognition for the ballot. Things may tighten up, however, at the next step. For electoral campaigns to involve serious contestation with true uncertainty of outcome, a society must be characterized by a fairly high level of civil liberties, such as freedom of speech and press. If the press is mostly government owned or controlled, it will be difficult for the non-favored parties to get their message to the voters and stand a fair chance of winning. Likewise, if the government favors one party far more than others with financial help, this aspect of the election will tend to be unfair, even if other aspects such as the actual vote and vote count are "fair" in a formal sense.

The 1977 electoral law provided for free television and radio time, as well as some postal privileges, for all registered parties during political campaigns. The 1986 law provided that public financing of parties would be proportional to their percentage of the national vote. The 1990 law made no significant change in this area. As before, the new electoral law guaranteed each party some free radio and television time in proportion to its electoral strength. Also, each party could buy additional time at normal commercial rates. In addition, parties would receive government funds for their campaigns in proportion to their share of the vote. With regard to campaign resources, opposition parties were at a disadvantage in at least four ways. First, the PRI almost always had the advantage of incumbency. It can target public spending at areas that it particularly wanted to win. The opposition complained bitterly of the huge amounts of funds that the government spent in various states from 1989 to 1992 through Salinas's Solidarity program, which may well have swayed public opinion to a more positive view of the president and his party. Second, the amount of campaign funding that a party would receive from the government was a function of its percentage of the vote. Thus if the government party swelled its share of the vote through either outright fraud or more ambiguous methods such as pouring public funds into a state in the months before a close election, it not only might win the election as a result of such methods but also would receive a larger share of the available campaign funds after the election than it really deserved. The opposition parties were further disadvantaged by the fact that the funds were to be paid over a three-year period after the election, rather than during the election itself. Third, it was widely assumed that the PRI had access to almost unlimited government funds that were channeled to it secretly. Although Mexican budgeting has probably become more "modern" in recent decades, the president still had a significant slush fund that he could use at his discretion.[27] Thus the PRI was able to spend many times as much as the opposition on election campaigns. Fourth, although freedom of the press had apparently increased in recent years, it was widely recognized that the media in Mexico were still overwhelmingly favorable to the PRI. Televisa, the largest television network, was controlled by a group of men who are closely associated with the PRI and the government. (The son of former president Miguel Alemán was previously one of the owners.)

Examples of the massive imbalance in campaign resources abound. In Michoacán in 1991, the PRI spent $32 million (U.S.), or about $80 per vote gained. Projected on a national scale, that would come to $800 million for a presidential election. The PRI took 92 percent of the advertising space devoted to the elections. Its chief rival, the PRD, spent $650,000, or about $2.30 a vote. Thus the PRI spent thirty-five times as much per vote as the PRD! In Chihuahua, where it lost, the PRI spent $17 million, or about $52 per vote, while taking 81 percent of the advertising. In winning, the PAN spent $1 million, or $2.63 a vote.[28] This illustrates both that the huge inequality in resources between the parties continued after 1990 and that outspending the opposition did not always translate into victories. Nonetheless, the huge imbalance in campaign finance was an issue that would need to be addressed if elections in Mexico were to become fairer.

Although not part of the 1990 electoral law, mention should be made of another development that was important for the liberalization of the Mexican political system. In 1990, President Salinas created a National Commission for Human Rights (CNDH) to monitor and investigate alleged human rights abuses. This followed the assassination of a prominent human rights activist in Sinaloa and the murder of dozens of opposition political activists throughout the country, especially members of Cárdenas's PRD. The head of the commission was Jorge Carpizo, a Supreme Court justice and former rector of the national university. In addition, numerous other respected individuals (such as writer Carlos Fuentes) were appointed to the commission. In the first two years of its existence, the commission investigated numerous allegations of abuse by police and others and brought several charges against individuals. This sort of commitment by a government is an important factor in the liberalization process. Because of the problem of confessions extracted through torture, Salinas announced at about the same time that confessions would no longer be used as a basis for conviction in criminal cases. However, as demonstrated by the release of Amnesty International's study, *Mexico: Torture with Impunity*, in September 1991, overcoming this problem would not be easy, even assuming that the presidential office had the will to do so. As bad as torture is in itself, it also has a chilling effect on political activity. Mexicans knew that if they were arrested for political activities such as protesting electoral fraud, there was a significant possibility that they might be tortured while in police custody. In early 1993 Salinas appointed Jorge Carpizo as his new attorney general. By selecting a man with a good reputation for his human rights work as the chief law enforcement officer, Salinas appeared to signal an increased determination to come to grips with the problem of police torture of suspects and police immunity from prosecution. The attorney general oversees the federal judicial police, which had been notorious for its immunity from prosecution.

Although the national human rights commission said that its work would not involve politically related complaints (that being the job of the special election tribunal), the state of human rights in general has a powerful effect on people's willingness to engage in political activities. According to the government, for example, the heavy police and army presence at polling places is aimed at protecting the security of the electoral process, but it also intimidates both opposition voters and poll watchers. Cárdenas's PRD remained skeptical about the efficacy of the national human rights commission. A detailed report of political violence against PRD supporters said of the CNDH: "This Commission was conceived from the beginning as an organization without autonomy, dependent on the executive power and with a very limited and archaic concept of human rights. It only considers some individual guarantees, and explicitly excludes fundamental issues such as political rights, labor rights, and jurisdictional matters."[29] The report then went on to detail over one hundred cases of politically motivated murders of PRD supporters and hundreds of instances of other political violence from 1988 to 1992. Almost two-thirds of the cases listed occurred in the three southern states of Guerrero, Michoacán, and Oaxaca.

Another organization, the private Mexican Commission for the Defense and Promotion of Human Rights, charged in a 1992 report that fundamental freedoms were being "widely and systematically" violated in Mexico. Like the CNDH, the private commission did not focus explicitly on electoral abuses, but the general lack of personal safety of those who pursue their interests in ways that inconvenience the regime had implications for electoral fairness. The commission emphasized that rural people in general and Indians in particular were disproportionately subjected to violence, police repression, and the seizure of their lands. The greater repression, in the countryside might be part of the reason that the PRI finds it easiest to maintain its electoral support in those areas. Another human rights report, issued jointly by several large Canadian churches in 1992, said that Mexico continued to suffer "the traditional abuses, such as the assassination of peasant leaders, the torture of prisoners in detention, violations of labor rights, corruption in the judicial system, and virtual police and military impunity." Opposition critics claim that over four hundred assassinations and disappearances occurred during the six-year term of the governor of Chiapas from 1982 to 1988. Although the situation has apparently improved, Cuauhtémoc Cárdenas accused the PRI governor under Salinas, José Patrocinio Gonzáles, of "creating a state of barbarism and violence" in Chiapas.[30] Therefore, his appointment to the very powerful post of interior minister in early 1993 was greeted by ambivalence from the opposition. The Salinas government continued its ambiguous posture, therefore, by appointing a well-respected human rights activist as attorney general but a governor noted for repression as interior minister.

Another activity that has come to be associated with an open, competitive electoral campaign is public opinion polls. If a political system has become adequately liberal to allow valid opinion polls even in the absence of entirely free elections, the polls themselves can become a force for further liberalization and democratization in at least two ways. A poll that shows opposition parties gaining support can have significant self-fulfilling or snowball effects. Newspaper reports of opposition strength may convince even more voters that this election might be competitive and that the opposition actually has a chance, contributing to further support for the opposition. Serious public opinion polls appeared in the 1988 presidential-congressional campaign, and the growing support for the opposition as reflected in the opinion polls, especially for Cárdenas, may have been a factor in convincing many voters that he actually had a chance to win. Another way that valid opinion polls might contribute to a fairer election is that a regime may find it more difficult to "arrange" a final vote count that radically departs from the pattern reported in those polls that are considered reasonably objective. The regime realizes that the opposition and the press are likely to point to the discrepancy as evidence of skulduggery.

However, polls can cut both ways, of course; they can also be used to bolster the regime. It should be kept in mind that virtually any regime, even a relatively authoritarian one, enjoys some degree of support and that the support may be high and growing at a particular time. Although it is a salient value for many people, political democracy is by no means the only value with which a citizenry is concerned. People also want their government to be effective in reducing corruption, fostering economic growth, pursuing social justice, and protecting nationhood. Almost as soon as he came into office, Salinas began a series of dramatic actions that rapidly increased his popularity. Polls taken by various organizations in the first three years of his term showed that a healthy majority of voters thought he was doing a good job as president.[31] Likewise, polls taken before various elections since 1989 have shown the PRI to have a solid lead over the opposition. For example, a few days before the midterm elections of August 1991, a poll by an organization considered to be a serious, objective polling company indicated the following support:[32]

PRI   49%

PAN   13

PRD   11

Others/None   14

Don't Know   13

The final results gave the PRI about 60 percent of the vote, which is considerably higher than the opinion poll but not completely outside the realm of believability when compared with the poll. After all, the regime had poured millions of dollars into the Solidarity program of schools, roads, health care, and other programs since 1989. The same survey showed that 44 percent thought they were better off than they were the year before, while 53 percent expected their situation to improve further in 1992. It also showed that 62 percent had a good opinion of Salinas.

Hence a distinction could be made in the functions of polls. At a particular point in the liberalization process, they might foster fairness of elections without necessarily fostering competitiveness of elections. That is, the government might be willing to ease up on the opposition in the campaign and the election itself if polls indicate that the governing party will win in a reasonably fair election. However, at that point the regime may discover that, once it has liberalized, it is difficult to put the restraints back on, and it may be forced to maintain the more liberal approach even in a future election that it is less certain of winning. In that way, the presence of opinion polling will have contributed to a fair election the first time and a fair and *competitive* election the second time.

Probably in no society do people feel completely comfortable expressing their political views to strangers, and hence opinion polling may never be an entirely accurate indicator of public opinion. In a country like Mexico, with a long history of political repression, opinion polls may be commissioned by the government to give the impression that its popular support is greater than it is. Even independent polls might not elicit antiregime sentiment from respondents. One way in which polls may *not* contribute to fairer elections is that they may be biased in favor of the organization that commissions them. A spokesman for Nielsen of Mexico claimed that only ten to fifteen firms did quality work in that country and that the remainder "conduct studies tailored to what the client wants."[33] After some unfortunate experiences, the Gallup organization in Mexico (the Mexican Institute of Public Opinion, IMOP) decided to refrain from doing election-related work. Ultimately, public opinion polls in Mexico would not be credible until the elections themselves are credible. Therefore, the validity of such polls improves only to the degree that the political atmosphere in general improves.

These three areas illustrate how the center of gravity in Mexican elections has shifted in the past few years. Although the old problems of electoral fraud persist to some degree, they seem to have declined in salience relative to issues such as campaign resources and human rights. Even if Mexican elections were honest in the narrow sense that the vote and the vote count are conducted more or less properly, their validity would have to be questioned as long as the political atmosphere is suffused with intimidation and repression. The human rights reports by various organizations, ranging from the PRD to Amnesty International, indicated that such intimidation was continuing as late as 1993. However, the very existence of a wide range of human rights organizations that were paying attention to Mexico was progress of a sort. Thus by creating a national human rights commission, the regime may have contributed to a process of liberalization that it could not control even if it wanted to.

Voters

Let us now look at the path of the individual voter and see if any changes occurred in these steps.

4. *Eligibility:* The "electorate" does not exist a priori but is defined by each society at a particular time, and an important part of the history of democracy has been the expansion of the suffrage. Eligibility to vote is an evolving concept, and the general trend has been toward greater inclusivity rather than exclusivity. In Mexico, women were given the right to vote in 1954 and eighteen-year-olds in 1973. In 1990 the PRD argued for allowing Mexican citizens living abroad to vote in Mexican elections, but the PRI and the PAN opposed this change, and it was not part of the 1990 reform. Thus the 1990 law made no significant change in who was eligible to vote and, except for the PRD's advocacy of giving the vote to Mexican citizens living abroad, voter eligibility was not a major issue in Mexican politics in the early 1990s.

5. *Registration:* Virtually all political systems require that an individual register before voting, but the characteristics of the registration process vary greatly. It may be more or less difficult, may be required anywhere from several weeks to several minutes before voting, and may be more or less amenable to fraud by the voter, a party, or the government. Multiple registration of an individual or keeping people on the rolls after they have died can swell the vote of one party or another, usually the government party. Apparently this has occurred often in Mexican elections. The opposition has claimed that the regime maintained voter lists that were out of date and padded with PRI supporters and that discriminated against supporters of opposition parties. One common method was to make voter registration more difficult in areas that had voted heavily for the opposition in previous elections. The 1990 law provided for a new electoral roll that would take effect with the federal election of August 1991.

Nevertheless Vicente Fox, PAN candidate for governor of Guanajuato in 1991, claimed that the electoral authorities had discriminated against the opposition in delivering voter credentials. He said, "Anyone who indicated a preference for the PRI was given his voter credential immediately and those who were not aligned with the PRI were subjected to excruciating slowness."[34] Like the PAN, the PRD also claimed that the electoral authorities had been "selective" in the distribution of credentials. In fact, Cárdenas claimed that lower-level PRI officials had asked those in charge to withhold 15 percent of the credentials in areas less favorable to the PRI so that they could be used by PRI activists to cast multiple votes for their party's candidates. However, electoral officials claimed in 1991 that they had failed to distribute only about 8 percent of the credentials, mostly to people who had moved or died.[35]

Despite the new law, therefore, the registration of voters continued to be a problem in Mexican elections after 1991. The opposition claimed that a significant proportion of voters, especially opposition supporters, continued to be disenfranchised at this stage of the electoral process. However, it appeared that the proportion of eligible voters who did not receive their voting credentials in time to vote did decline after the new electoral law went into effect in 1991.

6. *Maintenance of Voter Lists:* Closely related to registration itself is what the electoral officials do with the list of registered voters. Even in advanced industrial democracies, electoral rolls are seldom entirely accurate at any given moment. However, in a system that is generally considered fair, the officials will try to ensure that only eligible individuals actually register and vote. To that end, the officials will periodically update information from each voter to be sure that the list is accurate. Where the previous step involves the original creation of the list, this step involves the maintenance of the list by the electoral officials. It includes, for example, the question of how long a name is kept on the list without being renewed in some way. A major change in the 1990 law was the requirement that a new electoral list be compiled for the elections in 1991. Ideally, this was supposed to eliminate from the rolls individuals who had died, moved from the district, been convicted of a felony, or should for any legal reason be removed from the rolls. As in the previous step, however, the opposition continued to claim that the rolls were not yet accurate enough.

The Results

The last stage in the electoral process includes the vote itself, the count, the announcement of results, and any challenges to the fairness of the process.

7. *The Vote:* The two tracks come together at the moment when individuals vote. For the vote to be fair, only eligible voters should cast ballots, and each one should cast only the number of ballots to which he or she is entitled. In most liberal democracies, the vote is secret in order to avoid illegitimate pressure on voters, only ballots cast by eligible voters should be in the ballot box, and all the valid ballots should be made available for the count. The ballot box should not be "stuffed" before the polls open (or at any other time), and valid ballots should not be thrown away and not counted.

This step in the electoral process has been the major point of contention in Mexican elections for decades. Opponents have claimed that the regime has stuffed ballot boxes, often with several ballots folded together, a device known as the "taco." They complain that the regime had its supporters vote several times at different polling places, often systematically transporting them from one polling place to the next in a procedure known as the "carousel." The opposition also claimed that the regime prevented opponents from voting by intimidation or by suddenly moving or closing the polls, a ploy called the "ratón loco," or crazy mouse. For example, in the November 1990 elections, the PRI claimed victory in 117 of 121 mayoral contests in Mexico state and 81 of 84 mayoral races in Hidalgo on the same day. Both the PRD and the PAN claimed that the government had stolen ballot boxes, expelled opposition observers from polling places, allowed people to vote without credentials, and even forced some to vote for the PRI. A PAN federal deputy said, "In general, the worst vice was the carousel voting—taking people from poll to poll with false credentials to vote several times."[36] The 1990 law supposedly would reduce this form of fraud by requiring that each voter be provided with a new identification card with photograph, fingerprint, and signature. The name on the card would be checked against the registration list at the time an individual votes.

An important link between human rights and fair elections is the monitoring of elections. Since the early 1980s, there has been a steady increase in the monitoring of elections by opposition partisans, journalists, and others. The 1988 presidential election was closely watched by Mexican and international journalists, and it was expected that the 1994 presidential election would be even more closely monitored. The new law did not explicitly allow international observers to monitor Mexican elections, a practice that has contributed to the fairness of elections in numerous other developing countries. Although the PAN generally favored allowing such observers, PRD leaders did not press for international observers during the debate over the electoral law. But after the state and local elections in the states of México, Hidalgo, Coahuila, and Yucatán in 1990, which they claimed were grossly fraudulent, the PRD began to demand the right to have international observers present during future elections. Cárdenas proclaimed in early 1991 that his party was setting up a process to monitor elections and demanded that the government allow international observers. He said that the continued refusal to allow observers would be evidence that the government was carrying out "obscure maneuvers to violate the results" of elections.[37]

Held at the same time as the federal midterm election in 1991, the election in the state of Guanajuato for governor and state legislature was one of the most closely monitored elections in Mexican history. The PAN expected to do well, and in order to protect its anticipated wins at the federal, state, and local levels in the state, the party mounted a major effort to monitor the election by having its partisans and other observers report any "anomalies" to a central command post on election day. More than one hundred complaints involving about two hundred polling places came in from around the state. Because only observed anomalies on election day itself were reported, the alleged irregularities did not include the campaign before or the count afterward. The complaints included multiple instances of each of the following, as well as others:

—many *casillas* (polling places) did not open on time;

—many *casillas* did not have all the proper officials present;

—PAN representatives were not allowed in several *casillas;*

—campaigning for the PRI went on in prohibited areas just outside the polling places;

—PRI representatives engaged in active solicitation of individuals to vote PRI, often with offers of free food and drink;

—several *casillas* had either too few or too many ballots for the list of electors for those *casillas;*

—many *casillas* did not have ballots for certain offices (each voter was entitled to cast four ballots for governor, legislature, federal chamber, and federal senate);

—some people with proper voter credentials were not allowed to vote, while some without credentials were allowed to vote;

—voters were brought in by PRI in minibuses, that is, allegation of "carousels";

—police were milling around the polling places for no apparent reason except presumably to intimidate voters and election officials; and

—many polling places were located in the homes of PRI activists.[38]

It is not easy to evaluate many of these complaints, and some of them may seem trivial to readers in liberal democratic countries, but they must be seen in the context of a history of noncompetitive and often rigged elections. Whether or not all allegations indicate illegalities, they demonstrate the social and psychological environment that still prevailed until 1993, at least to some extent, in Mexican elections.

Another effort to monitor the vote was the creation after the 1988 presidential election of a private monitoring group called the Council for Democracy, headed by lawyer-economist Julio Faesler and with a widely respected membership from all major parties as well as independents. One member, Julio Ortiz Pinchetti, commented after the November 1990 election in México state, "It is evident the government has abandoned its promise of clean elections."[39] As the above evidence indicates, it appears that a significant amount of voter fraud occurred in the elections held after the passage of the 1990 electoral law. The amount of fraud at this stage of the voting process may have declined, as the regime claims, partly as a result of better identification of voters and more complete monitoring of the elections. However, fraud was not entirely eliminated at this stage by the 1990 law.

8. *Counting the Ballots:* A completely fair election up to this point will mean little if officials engage in a dishonest vote count. To prevent this, liberal democracies construct various safeguards. In the United States, for example, several election officials representing a balance between the political parties are

usually present at each polling place. They conduct the election, open the ballot box at the end of the day, and verify that the number of ballots in the box corresponds to the number of voters whose names were checked on the registration list as they voted. Then ballots are either counted or prepared for the computer, all under the watchful eyes of the party representatives. Election officials do a practice run to verify that the computer and its program are operating accurately.[40]

As is well known, this is probably the most controversial step in the electoral process in Mexico. Opponents have alleged that ballot boxes have often been taken from the polling places by regime supporters to secret locations and tampered with. Later, piles of ballots have been found in garbage dumps or creek beds. Needless to say, the discarded ballots tended to be those marked for the opposition, not the PRI. To try to reduce this problem, the new law continued to guarantee opposition partisans the right to be present at the polling places from morning to night, including at the time of the vote count, and indeed opposition parties have placed observers in many more polling places in recent years. However, the opposition claimed that the PRI still sometimes engaged in the old practices of trying to prevent opposition representatives from observing the vote and the count. Therefore, although considerable improvement seems to have occurred in this step, some problems persisted after 1991.

9. *Announcement of Results:* Although this would appear to be the step that least lends itself to manipulation, it does offer potential for skulduggery. In the past, officials frequently waited several days to announce the results in order to give them time to rearrange the numbers. The 1990 law sought to address problems at this step in the process by providing that all parties will have access to the computers when votes are counted and by requiring that preliminary results be announced immediately.

The significance of this step in the process is illustrated by the fate of two of Cárdenas's supporters. On the night of July 2, 1988, four days before the hotly contested presidential election, two supporters of Cuauhtémoc Cárdenas were murdered on a dark street in Mexico City. A close and longtime associate of Cárdenas, Francisco Javier Ovando was in charge of the computer system that the opposition group would use to monitor the election on July 6; Gil Heráldez was his assistant. They were killed as they drove through the capital. Their deaths had the characteristics of a professionally arranged murder. They were shot at close range, and the only item taken from their car was a confidential directory with telephone numbers and addresses of various political associates. As of 1992, the murders had not been solved.[41]

The announcement of results comes in two stages—preliminary and official. The new law requires that preliminary results be released immediately, which means as soon as the votes have been counted and computers have added up the numbers, presumably within hours of the closing of the polls. The opposition wanted this provision in the 1990 law to avoid giving the government time to juggle the numbers in order to make them come out as the government wished, as allegedly occurred most notoriously in the national election of 1988. The opposition also demanded that final results be tabulated with opposition representatives present and announced as quickly as possible. After the 1988 election, the government claimed that its computer broke down, forcing it to postpone the announcement of the results for a week. The opposition claimed that the government did this in order to give itself time to "process" the numbers so that the PRI would win the presidency and a majority in the Chamber of Deputies. (In Mexico, the process of rearranging the numbers so that the vote comes out as the government wishes is called "alchemy.") If a government is going to cheat, it takes time to arrange the numbers so that the columns and rows add up logically and do not contain glaring inconsistencies. Therefore, requiring that preliminary and official results be announced promptly make a significant contribution to fairer elections.

In most political systems, the final results of an election are certified by an authoritative body. In the United States, the governing body at each level of government is responsible for elections of its officials. In Arizona, for example, the elected County Board of Supervisors "canvasses," or looks over, the results presented by the County Recorder and decides whether to accept the results as valid. A similar determination would be made for the appropriate elections by a city council, a school board, or the secretary of state of Arizona. In Mexico this official stamp was provided by the Federal Electoral Commission (CFE) until 1991, when it was replaced by the Federal Electoral Institute. Like the CFE before it, the Electoral Institute is in charge of elections from beginning to end. The General Council of the Institute consists of one representative from the executive, namely the Department of Gobernación, four representatives selected by the legislature (two selected by the congressional majority and two selected by the minority), and six representatives of the political parties. The latter are selected by a two-thirds vote in the Chamber of Deputies from a list submitted by the president.

Perhaps the major complaint of the opposition parties, especially the PRD, was that the new law, like the old one, gave the government control of the electoral process. A majority of representatives at every level are appointed or nominated by the chief executive (president or governor), who, of course, is usually from the PRI. In most liberal democracies, the government oversees elections, but apparently this is a stumbling block on the path to fairer elections in Mexico because the opposition parties believe that the government has not become sufficiently committed to fair elections.

10. *Challenge of Results:* The outcome of any election in any political system, no matter how fair and democratic, might justifiably be questioned. Thus most political systems have procedures by which the outcome can be challenged and aggrieved individuals can be given a hearing. In Arizona, for example, an official challenge must be made to the superior court within five days of the canvass. The challenger must provide evidence that something was wrong with the electoral process and that it made a difference in the outcome.

In the United States, of course, the courts are relatively independent of the other branches of government. In Mexico, disputes are handled by an electoral court. Very few of the challenges in the first two years after the new law went into effect were decided in favor of the opposition.

In fact, most challenges were still handled "politically." Ultimately, it seemed, the president still decided whether to overturn the official results of an election, according to some criteria known only to him. The most dramatic instances of such reversals came in Guanajuato and San Luis Potosí in 1991. After the PRI candidates for governor were declared the winners by state electoral officials, PAN supporters vigorously challenged the honesty of the elections with formal complaints and large public demonstrations. In Guanajuato, the PRI governor resigned, the PRI-dominated legislature appointed a PAN mayor as interim governor, and new elections were scheduled. In San Luis Potosí the PRI governor-elect did not take office but was replaced by a PRI official who was a close associate of President Salinas. It was widely assumed that the president was behind these decisions.

In the election in Michoacán in July 1992, the PRI candidate for governor was declared the victor, and he quickly received a telephone call of congratulations from the president as if to signal that that was the end of the matter. But the PRD claimed that at least one in three voter names was registered fraudulently and that 150,000 people were not allowed to vote because they had not been given their voting documents in time. In addition, the PRD said that the vote count was highly suspect in those polling stations that were not monitored by the PRD. In the polling stations that were monitored, the PRD said that it received more votes than the PRI. The PRI replied by saying that the PRD was to blame for not monitoring all polling stations, but it did admit that as many as 10 percent of otherwise eligible voters were disenfranchised because of lack of voting documents. After winning 52 of the 116 mayoralties in the state, the PRD said that its mayors would not recognize the authority of the PRI governor and that the PRD would engage in a campaign of protest marches. However, despite all these protests, the central government did not concede the election to the PRD in Michoacán. In the Chihuahua election on the same day as the election in Michoacán, the president called to congratulate the PAN candidate for governor as soon as preliminary results indicated his victory in that state. In all these cases, it appears that the final decisions on the outcomes were made by President Carlos Salinas and the central government, rather than by electoral officials.

CONCLUSION

This chapter has described the economic and political policies that the Salinas government employed as it sought to restore the weakened revolutionary regime. It argued that Salinas and his associates skillfully used the traditional techniques discussed throughout this book. Regime leaders made the most of the regular presidential succession to present the new president as a leader who would respond to problems in a fresh and energetic way. Salinas moved dynamically against some of the most notorious examples of corruption, established an important new social program funded in large part by huge sums of money raised from the sale of state firms, liberalized the economy considerably, and negotiated a free trade pact with the United States. The economy began to grow again after several sluggish years. The Salinas government also liberalized politics somewhat, by enacting a new electoral law that provided for a new electoral roll and new electoral identity cards. The president also overturned some state and local elections when evidence of fraud and opposition protests were overwhelming. The regime also took advantage of the fact that, as weakened as it was after 1988, it still had the capacity to mobilize voters and even to use electoral "alchemy" where necessary to stay in power.

Whether the regime could maintain social peace with this degree of "problem management" was, however, open to question. As skillful as Salinas and his associates had been in their first four years, it was not inevitable that this would be enough. The conditions in which the traditional factors operated had changed dramatically by the 1990s, and it was possible that the very factors that had allowed one party to remain in power for six decades would now threaten that hegemony. The next chapter will examine the altered conditions of the 1990s and ask what the prospects are for political stability and democracy in Mexico.

NOTES

1. Robert A. Pastor, "Post-Revolutionary Mexico: The Salinas Opening," *Journal of Interamerican Studies and World Affairs* 32 (3), 1990, p. 4.

2. Franz A. von Sauer, "Measuring Legitimacy in Mexico: An Analysis of Public Opinion during the 1988 Presidential Campaign," in *Mexican Studies* 8 (2), 1992, p. 277.

3. Pastor, "Post-Revolutionary Mexico," p. 4.

4. Stephen D. Morris, "Political Reformism in Mexico: Salinas at the Brink," *Journal of Interamerican Studies and World Affairs* 34 (1), 1992, pp. 31–40; John Bailey, "Populism and Regime Liberalization: Mexico in Comparative Perspective" (Paper Presented at Annual Meeting of the Midwest Political Science Association, Chicago, April 18–20, 1991), pp. 14–21.

5. Morris, "Political Reformism," pp. 32–34.

6. Ibid., p. 2.

7. Press Office of the Government of Mexico, *Mexico on the Record* (Washington, D.C.: Embassy of Mexico, 1992), vol. 1 (9), pp. 2–3. In fact, this publication itself was part of the Salinas offensive to improve the image of the Mexican regime.

8. Von Sauer, "Measuring Legitimacy," p. 269.

9. Bailey, "Populism," pp. 1–22; Morris, "Political Reformism," p. 39.

10. Bailey, "Populism," pp. 19–20; Ambler H. Moss, Jr., "A Democratic Party Approach to Latin America," *Journal of Interamerican Studies and World Affairs* 34

(2), 1992, p. 11; Judith Gentleman and Voytek Zubek, "International Integration and Democratic Development: The Cases of Poland and Mexico," *Journal of Interamerican Studies and World Affairs* 34 (1), 1992, p. 87.

11. For the argument that "international pressures, not the will of 'state managers,' determined the shape of the economic restructuring program," see Judith Teichman, "The Mexican State and the Political Implications of Economic Restructuring," *Latin American Perspectives* 19 (2), 1992, p. 89.

12. Human Rights Commission, Partido de la Revolución Democrática, *The Political Violence in Mexico: A Human Rights Affair* (México, D. F.: Partido de la Revolución Democrática, 1992), pp. 38–39.

13. Morris, "Political Reformism," pp. 27–57.

14. Ibid., p. 40.

15. Ibid., p. 38.

16. Pastor, "Post-Revolutionary Mexico," pp. 11–12.

17. For example, see Robert Dahl, *Polyarchy: Participation and Opposition* (New Haven: Yale University Press, 1971); G. Bingham Powell, *Democracies: Participation, Stability, and Violence* (Cambridge: Harvard University Press, 1982), p. 3; Guillermo O'Donnell and Philippe Schmitter, eds., *Transitions from Authoritarian Rule: Tentative Conclusions about Uncertain Democracies* (Baltimore: Johns Hopkins University Press, 1986), p. 8; and Larry Diamond, Juan Linz, and Seymour Martin Lipset, "Preface," in L. Diamond, J. Linz, and S. M. Lipset, eds., *Democracy in Developing Countries: Volume 4, Latin America* (Boulder, Colo.: Lynne Rienner Publishers, 1989), p. xvi.

18. Daniel Levy, "Mexico: Sustained Civilian Rule without Democracy," in Diamond, Linz, and Lipset, *Democracy in Developing Countries*, p. 459. Also see Diamond, Linz, and Lipset, *Democracy in Developing Countries*, p. xvii.

19. Lorenzo Meyer, "Democratization of the PRI: Mission Impossible?" in Wayne Cornelius, Judith Gentleman, and Peter Smith, eds., *Mexico's Alternative Political Futures* (San Diego: Center for U.S.-Mexican Studies, University of California, 1989), p. 325.

20. *Proceso*, July 16, 1990, p. 8.

21. Ibid., p. 11.

22. *Latin American Regional Reports, Mexico and Central America*, Aug. 23, 1990, p. 4.

23. Ibid., Sept. 23, 1990, p. 2.

24. This does not mean that "perfection" of or total agreement over electoral procedures is ever achieved in any polity. Debates may continue over recognition of parties, eligibility and registration of voters, campaign finance, and every other aspect of the electoral process.

25. Instituto Federal Electoral, *Código federal de instituciónes y procedimientos electorales* (México, D. F., 1991), Article 58.

26. For the argument that there is no necessary trade-off between proportional representation and governmental effectiveness, see Arend Lijphart, "Constitutional Choices for New Democracies," *Journal of Democracy* 2 (1), 1991, pp. 72–84.

27. See Dan A. Cothran and Cheryl C. Cothran, "Mexican Presidents and Budgetary Secrecy," *International Journal of Public Administration* 11 (3), 1988.

28. Based on a study by Instituto Mexicano de Opinión Pública, as reported in *Latin American Weekly Report*, Aug. 6, 1992, p. 10.

29. Human Rights Commission, *Political Violence*, p. vi.

30. *Latin American Regional Reports, Mexico and Central America*, May 7, 1992, p. 2. The uprising in Chiapas in January 1994 should be seen in this context.

31. E.g., *Los Angeles Times* poll, as reported in Wayne Cornelius, "Mexico: Salinas and the PRI at the Crossroads," *Journal of Democracy* 1 (3), 1990, pp. 61–70.

32. Centro de Estudios de Opinión Pública, as reported in *Latin American Regional Reports, Mexico and Central America*, Aug. 22, 1991, p. 6.

33. Quoted in Ted Bardacke, "Electoral Public Opinion Polls Become Politicians' Pawns," *El Financiero: Weekly International Edition*, Aug. 10, 1992, p. 16.

34. Quoted in Gerardo Galarza, "No hay avance, el elector no cuenta," *Proceso*, July 22, 1991, p. 22.

35. *Latin American Regional Reports, Mexico and Central America*, Aug. 22, 1991, p. 6.

36. Quoted in Marjorie Miller, "PRI Claims Victory in Mexico Elections," *Los Angeles Times*, Nov. 13, 1990, p. A8.

37. *Latin American Regional Reports, Mexico and Central America*, Jan. 17, 1991, p. 6

38. Partido de Acción Nacional, "Reporte de anomalias en la elección de Guanajuato," Guanajuato, August 1991.

39. Quoted in Jane Bussey, "Opposition Cries Foul in Mexico Elections," *Christian Science Monitor*, Nov. 15, 1990, p. 3.

40. Interviews with election officials, Coconino County, Arizona, February 16, 1991.

41. Human Rights Commission, *Political Violence*, pp. 67–68.

7

Prospects for Stability and Democracy in Mexico

POLITICAL STABILITY IN A NEW ENVIRONMENT

The circumstances in which the Mexican regime found itself in the 1990s had changed so much that the factors that had previously contributed to political stability could have the opposite effect as Mexico approached the twenty-first century. This chapter considers the prospects for continued stability and the potential for movement toward greater political democracy.

Institutionalization

This book has argued that strong institutions can make a powerful contribution to political stability. However, if the institutions do not adapt adequately to new demands emanating from society, they may undermine the ability of a regime to endure. As James March and Johan Olsen argue, "By constraining political change, institutional stability contributes to regime instability." [1]

By 1988 the fortunes of the regime had sunk so low that Carlos Salinas had little to lose and much to gain by attempting to reform the regime. By 1993 he had succeeded to some extent in doing that. [2] Salinas correctly read the mood of the Mexican people, who generally supported his programs for economic growth and change as public opinion polling suggested that a majority of Mexicans were more concerned about the economy than about democracy, at least at that time. [3] During Salinas's term, the regime found itself in the middle of political opinion, having to satisfy demands from both sides. In the short run, Salinas settled on a strategy of minimal political reforms, but as he moved into the last third of his term, it was not clear whether that would be sufficient to satisfy growing opposition demands for participation. However, Salinas seemed to be betting that his reforms would hold the bulk of the population with the PRI. He knew that the presidential election of August 21, 1994, would be the most closely monitored in Mexican history. Therefore, his strategy appeared to be to reinvigorate the regime so that it could actually win a relatively competitive election.

As shown in the previous chapter, the PRI benefited from the turnover of the presidency to a new man as a way of projecting an image of a party that could change. That same factor, the turnover of the presidency, could once again give the PRI additional credibility in 1994. That is, the prospect of another new president in 1994, even if a member of the PRI, might satisfy the demand of many Mexicans for change. Nonetheless, large numbers of Mexican voters were dissatisfied with a one-party political system, and it had become harder to keep the ruling coalition together. In 1988 the regime had difficulty keeping the labor unions in line and in fact lost the support of some. The peasantry was still the easiest sector for the PRI to control, partly because of its rural isolation, but even that support was shaky. As more and more people moved to the cities, the country was becoming less rural and more urban, and that could make it more difficult for the PRI to hold its voters in line. In the past, the PRI had found it easier to perform its electoral alchemy in the sparsely populated, rural areas that lay beyond the glare of press and opposition. Even assuming that elections are roughly "fair" in the sense that each vote represents a living person who casts a ballot for that party, the smaller the proportion of the population who live in the countryside, the harder for the PRI to maintain a large block of votes from that traditional source. Moreover, the opposition had become increasingly able to monitor elections even in rural areas.

But especially in urban areas, the opposition increasingly encouraged the use of poll watchers and foreign observers at election places to monitor the elections in order to make cheating more difficult. The government, on the other hand, was adamantly opposed to poll watchers, and as part of his "get tough" posture, Salinas claimed that foreign observers would violate the sovereignty of Mexico.[4] Closer monitoring of elections by the opposition forced the regime, however, to become more sophisticated and creative in its methods of manipulation, such as suddenly moving polling places so that voters did not know where to cast their votes or altering voting lists to exclude certain voters.[5] It was increasingly difficult to use some of the cruder techniques such as stuffing ballot boxes with handfuls of premarked ballots, or tacos, and so the regime developed more sophisticated techniques, which one opposition leader called "electronic fraud."[6] This involved, for example, manipulation of the computer count, as allegedly occurred in 1988. By 1991, the opposition was especially able to monitor elections in the cities, which was also where its greatest electoral support was found. Cuauhtémoc Cárdenas did not want a repeat in 1994 of the 1988 election, when he believed that he won at least a plurality of the popular vote but was cheated out of victory.

More competitive elections also weakened the PRI, with a decline in the number of electoral positions that the regime could hand out. For example, by 1993 the PRI had given up almost 50 percent of the seats in the Chamber of

Deputies, three or four Senate seats, three governorships, and about four thousand of nineteen thousand elected municipal posts.[7]

Thus neither the institutionalized party nor the institutionalized succession was as powerful a force for the stability of one-party rule as in the past. Although Salinas had reinvigorated the party and its popular support to some degree, the PRI was not the solid monolith it had appeared to be in previous years. In addition, the mere turnover of presidents, if always of the same party, might not be sufficient to satisfy a more politically aroused citizenry. And if elections became more fair, the PRI could lose the presidency, and the institutionalized succession within one party would come to an end. It was possible that the move to liberalize might pick up momentum that could not be controlled.

Adaptability

Salinas showed flexibility in a number of ways. To a certain extent he tried to accommodate critics on both the left and the right. Continuing a trend begun by Miguel de la Madrid, he moved Mexico further away from the statist-protectionist model of development that it had followed for decades. Salinas continued to reduce the role of the state through privatization of numerous state firms and through a lessening of government regulation in many areas of economic life. He also pushed Mexico toward greater engagement with the international economic system. At the same time he tried to restore the popular bases of the regime through such measures as Solidarity. However, both of these approaches had problems. First, to some extent they were in conflict with each other. Resources that are devoted to direct redistribution are not entirely available for investment in further economic growth.[8] Moreover, a large part of the funding for social programs came from the sale of state firms—a one-time event. In addition, taxes had already been raised considerably in the previous twenty years, and to raise them much more could threaten the very economic growth that Salinas was depending on to save the regime. If the government continued to spend large amounts on social programs even after the privatization money had run out, it could find itself once again resorting to foreign borrowing to finance its budget deficits, which is what got it into trouble in the first place. Yet people's taste for more government spending had been aroused and might be difficult to curb, especially with a strong leftist movement led by the popular Cuauhtémoc Cárdenas ready to criticize any retreat in this area. At the same time, the government might find its ability to move very far to the left in the form of populist redistribution blocked by the limits of its own resources and by a resurgent party on its right. By the early 1990s, the PAN was the largest opposition party in the Chamber of Deputies, and the president depended on a bloc of PAN members in the chamber to give him the two-thirds majority required for constitutional amendments. If the regime backtracked on its commitment to economic liberalization, it could expect severe criticism from the PAN. In addition, ratification of the North American Free Trade Agreement (NAFTA) would make it harder for future Mexican governments to shift policy from the right to the left, from an export-led, market-oriented approach to a more autarkic, statist strategy. Thus the regime's ability to adapt to emerging pressures might be more constrained in the future. Moreover, whereas the sale of so many state firms might help to make the economy more efficient, it also eliminated a significant amount of the patronage on which the regime had depended for political support. Thus Salinas's strategy of economic growth could eventually reduce the regime's support from both elites and non-elites.

Economic Effectiveness

After 1970, the relations between government and business in Mexico soured considerably. First came the major assaults, from the point of view of business, on private enterprise with the massive increase in the number of state firms, a step-up in land expropriations, the strident rhetoric of Luis Echeverría, and other actions. Then near the end of José López Portillo's term, when economic elites thought that the regime had become comfortably probusiness again, the president attacked businessmen for capital flight and then nationalized the banks. This action shocked the business community, which had come to think that the regime had permanently ended its proclivity for major nationalizations. The de la Madrid government (1982–88) actively moved toward policies that favored private enterprise, such as selling off two-thirds of all state firms, reducing government spending, and encouraging international trade, but it also engaged in some actions that worried business. These included the reiteration of the state's "rectorship" role in the economy and the expropriation of a large amount of urban property after the 1985 earthquakes to provide public housing for the homeless. In addition, some businessmen felt they were losing out in the new opening to foreign investment in the Mexican economy.[9]

Therefore, many businessmen began more openly to support the PAN. This support no doubt helped the PAN to do well in local elections in the early 1980s, at a time when the regime was deliberately allowing somewhat fairer elections anyway. Thus by 1988, business support of the PRI had weakened. The Salinas government was probably able to restore some of that support with its sustained market-oriented policies, but by this time, many businessmen had become skeptical of a regime that vacillated so dramatically back and forth on issues of importance to business. Steadiness in its probusiness policies had, after all, been a major factor in strong business support for the regime from 1940 to 1970. Salinas very much wanted to restore that support.

It is possible that the Mexican economy may have gotten through its worst phase in the 1980s. Under Salinas, the economy again grew at about 3 to 4 percent a year, although it dipped from 4.4 percent in 1990 to 2.6 percent in 1992, partly in response to the U.S. recession. Some economic indicators for

Table 7.1
Some Economic Indicators, 1988–1992

	1988	1989	1990	1991	1992
Real GDP Growth (%)	1.2	3.2	4.4	3.7	2.6
Inflation (%)	114.0	20.0	27.0	23.0	15.5
Exports ($bn)	21.0	23.0	27.0	43.0	46.0
Imports ($bn)	19.0	23.0	31.0	50.0	62.0
Current Account ($bn)	-2.4	-4.0	-7.1	-13.8	-22.8

Source: Economist Intelligence Unit, *Mexico: Country Report,* no. 1 (London: EIU, 1993), p. 3.

the first years of the Salinas administration are shown in table 7.1. Inflation was relatively low, at about 15 percent a year by 1992. However, the greater openness of the economy impelled imports upward much faster than exports, with the result that the country developed a yawning trade deficit of almost $23 billion by 1992.

Mexico's foreign debt fell from $100 billion in 1988 to $86 billion in 1990 but then rose to $104 billion by 1992 as increasing amounts of international funds flowed into a reviving Mexican economy. However, as a share of GDP, the foreign debt dropped from about 60 percent in 1988 to about 40 percent in 1992. The budget deficit shrank from 12 percent of GDP in 1988 to just 6 percent in 1989. Tariffs dropped from an average of 100 percent to 10 percent from 1988 to 1990, and the manufacture of products for export soared. Tighter enforcement of the tax laws raised revenues 13 percent during this period. All of this recharged the economy, raised nominal wages, and perhaps increased political support for the PRI.[10] Although economic growth in the neighborhood of 3 percent per year does not yet match the 6-percent average of the period from 1940 to 1981, it did offer promise of improvement after zero growth from 1982 through 1988. Also, since Mexico's population growth had apparently slowed to about 1.5 percent a year by the early 1990s, a given amount of economic growth would have a stronger effect on per capita income than in the past.[11]

The Salinas administration was obviously betting on free trade and other changes to improve the country's economy and to enhance the PRI's electoral chances in the more competitive political environment. However, the single-minded pursuit of a free market economic strategy might incur certain problems. Even if a North American common market worked out well for Mexico in general, the process was likely to be wrenching for many Mexican businesses and workers. Although many firms would flourish, some who depended on protectionism would shrink or disappear. In addition, the privatization of almost a thousand state firms had already diminished the regime's ability to use patronage as a means of maintaining political support. Moreover, deregulation of many aspects of business reduced the government's use of regulatory controls and corruption to retain business loyalty or acquiescence. Thus a free market approach may be good for the Mexican economy in the long run, but the strategy could create numerous problems in the short run, problems that could make it difficult for the PRI to maintain political support.

Although different studies project differing effects, most suggest that the economies of both the United States and Mexico would benefit from freer trade. It is expected, for example, that the effect of NAFTA on economic growth would be on the order of .5 percent for the United States and about 5 percent for Mexico.[12] This was expected, according to one study, to translate into about 600,000 extra jobs in Mexico and 112,000 jobs in the United States.[13] However, the effect is expected to be different for different sectors. In particular, the peasant sector of Mexican agriculture could be drastically affected if the corn industry is quickly exposed to international competition.[14] This could damage Mexico's rural economy, devastate the peasant sector of society, and impel hundreds of thousands more small farmers to migrate to the cities or to the United States in search of work. The major political result could be to further weaken rural support for the PRI.

Another way that freer trade could weaken the PRI regime is that the less-democratic Mexican government might feel that it could make more concessions in trade negotiations than could the more pluralistically constrained U.S. government. Those concessions, however, could weaken the PRI's electoral support in a context in which it might be faced with more competitive elections than in the past. Thus what was a "strength" at one point—a semiauthoritarian regime—subsequently becomes a weakness by tempting it to make concessions that later come back to haunt it.

What might be the political consequences of freer trade? One possibility is that liberal economics would lead to faster economic development, which in the short run could dislocate certain sectors and weaken the base of the regime. This could tempt the regime to rely even more on repression than in the past. Eventually, it is likely that economic development will produce a larger middle class, which may make stronger demands for liberal democracy. Although the path is not straight or easy, and setbacks often occur as elites employ repression in an effort to restrain the demands of the emerging middle and working classes, in the long run there seems to be a fairly high correlation between economic development and political democracy. Thus those political scientists who call modernization theory outmoded may be guilty of exaggeration.[15] Mexico's path in the immediate future cannot be predicted, but it seems likely in the long run—say the next twenty years—that economic growth will be accompanied by political liberalization, although the next few years could be rough. In fact, Cuauhtemóc Cárdenas argued that the Mexican regime offered the United States greater economic liberalization in return for the continuing U.S. acceptance of the current political regime.[16] It is true that governments sometimes have used greater repression to control the wage and other demands of workers and small farmers in order to generate the capital needed for faster economic growth. Thus regime leaders may consider government repression necessary to stifle the discontent that can result from the greater income inequality that often accompanies the early stages of industrialization. Ironically, therefore, economic growth could lead to either political liberalization or greater repression in the short run.

In many countries, privatization of state firms and the downsizing of the state are means of streamlining the state. However, it seems likely that as the Mexican regime gives up many of the controls that it exercised over the economy, including regulatory and licensing requirements and controls over wage levels and foreign investment, its hold over business and labor will weaken. In the short run, the effects of liberal economics or economic growth are indeterminate. As Peter Smith says, it is possible that "free trade and economic liberalization could loosen the social moorings of the present political system in Mexico and thus create objective conditions for a far-reaching political transition." But he goes on to say: "However, whether and how this opportunity is used entails the exercise of political will, skill, and management at the uppermost levels of power—especially the presidency. Given realignment of social forces, it would be just as conceivable for Mexico's leaders to resort to repression and install some new form of authoritarianism as it would be for them to embark on a quest for authentic democracy."[17] Thus even if the regime is able to put Mexico back on the path of economic growth, the implications for political stability in the short run are not easy to foresee, especially since economic growth could contribute to a further increase in demands for political democracy.

Elite Unity

The unity of the Mexican political elite was shattered in 1988 as it had not been for decades. Some defections had occurred in several of the elections between 1940 and 1982, but 1988 was clearly unusual. In fact, this was the first time since 1952 that a significant segment of the PRI defected and participated in a presidential election outside the ruling party. A part of the left wing of the regime defected with Cárdenas, and thus he took with him some of the revolutionary legitimacy on which the regime had depended. Defections from the PRI since 1988 have not been as great as during that election, but they have continued, the most notable being Rodolfo Gonzáles Guevara, who formally left the PRI in September 1990. A member of the ruling party for forty-four years, Gonzáles had held the job of secretary general of the PRI as well as numerous other high-level positions. Along with Cuauhtémoc Cárdenas, he had been a leader of the Democratic Current in the PRI in the late 1980s. After the departure of Cárdenas, Gonzáles remained in the PRI and organized a new dissident faction known as the Critical Current, which called for internal democratization of the party, honest elections, and a separation of party and state. He wrote newspaper articles accusing the government of electoral fraud and pressed for changes within the PRI, such as the use of secret-ballot primary elections.[18] He finally concluded, however, that the PRI would not reform itself adequately. Even though Gonzáles's defection was not followed by other major departures, his departure was not a welcome event for Salinas.

Moreover, the opposition political elite was better organized than ever before. The right had been reasonably well organized for decades, represented mainly by the PAN, but by the early 1990s it was stronger than ever. Previously the PAN was mainly a regional party, especially strong in the north, but by 1988 it had become a national force. The PAN candidate received 17 percent of the national presidential popular vote in 1988 by the official count and may actually have received more than that. It elected over one hundred members to the Chamber of Deputies in 1988, although it lost some of those in the 1991 midterm elections. The PAN was also granted three governorships during the first four years of Salinas's term. In 1989 the PAN's Ernesto Ruffo became the first opposition candidate to be elected a governor in the history of Mexico when the PRI recognized his victory in Baja California. In 1991 a PAN mayor was selected as interim governor of Guanajuato after a controversial election in that state. Then in 1992 the PAN's Francisco Barrio was elected governor of Chihuahua.

However, the PAN may continue to have difficulties in rural areas. One reason is that fraud is more common in rural than in urban areas, partly because local bosses (caciques) are in firmer control there. This is a result of the nature of the rural, peasant population and of the fact that the opposition is less organized there. As Juan Molinar Horcasitas puts it, "The opposition, with some exceptions, only goes as far as the pavement reaches."[19] Thus opposition candidates have seldom ventured into the highly rural areas, and the opposition parties have had few representatives at the polling places to provide evidence of fraud in subsequent litigation against the government. However, the PAN was much more organized by the early 1990s than previously.

The parties on the left were organized during the 1988 election as never before. The Mexican Socialist Party and several other parties gave Cárdenas their presidential nomination and competed under the coalition banner of the FDN. Within a year, parts of the coalition were reconstituted as the Party of the Democratic Revolution (PRD), with Cárdenas as its leader. The left at last had a party that could make a broad appeal with a popular figure at its head. The new party had, however, several debilities. It seemed to have difficulties establishing a network of local branches outside of Mexico City and Michoacán, partly no doubt due to harassment and intimidation by PRI supporters.

Salinas and the PRI were determined to weaken the PRD and Cárdenas at every opportunity. Salinas was willing to concede three governorships to the PAN between 1989 and 1992, but he recognized almost no major PRD victories during the same time. PRI leaders seemed to feel that they could deal with a challenge from the right more easily than from the left, since Cárdenas's candidacy threatened the PRI's identity as the party of the Revolution. In addition, the PRD had as much electoral support as it did partly because of Cuauhtémoc Cárdenas. As the son of the most popular leader in Mexican history, he had a special appeal for Mexicans. If he departed the PRD, it seemed likely that the left's electoral support would plummet to levels well below that of the PAN, which is where it was before 1988. It is hard to say for sure, of course, what the true level of electoral support for the left (or the right) might have been in the past if elections had been fairer, but if official results are a valid indicator of *relative* popularity among the opposition, the electoral appeal of the left in Mexico has always been limited.[20] However, it is also possible that the true appeal was always greater than indicated by official results and that Cárdenas's candidacy, and his call to revive the principles of the Revolution, may have enhanced that appeal even more. In any case, the regime behaves as if Cárdenas has enormous potential for popular support.

Given the failures of Mexican presidents since the 1970s, one possible interpretation of the present crisis of elite unity is that their fundamental debility was their lack of political skills.[21] Some authors have made much of the change that has taken place in Mexico between the "political" presidents who ruled before 1970 and the "bureaucrats" or "technocrats" who have governed since then.[22] The tendency in recent decades has been for the governing elite to be recruited from an ever-narrower segment of the population, especially from highly educated technocrats with degrees in subjects other than law. Moreover, many of these had no experience in electoral politics, where they might at least have met a wider range of people and improved their political skills. This may have the effect of alienating leaders from the people. It may also have the effect of fragmenting the regime. To a large extent the "technocrat-políticos" distinction is really a right-left ideological schism, with the technocrats (especially economists) tending to favor the market over government intervention in many cases and with many politicians continuing to favor state involvement in the economy to control foreign investment, redistribute income, and generally guide the economy and the society. In fact, one interpretation of the schism is that it represents not only a split over political-economic philosophy but also the competition for power between the two large blocs in Mexican politics, those that descend from the former presidents Lázaro Cárdenas and Miguel Alemán. That is, ideological cleavages are reinforced by personalistic loyalties.[23]

In recent years, Mexican government has been dominated by a more market-oriented (often called "neo-liberal") vision of political economy and a more technocratic style of governing. One way in which the technocrats have failed to take "politics" into account is in the makeup of their cabinets. A factor that contributed to the defection of Cárdenas and other members of the Democratic Current from the PRI in 1988 was that the "politicians" had been frozen out of cabinet positions and out of a role in selecting the 1988 PRI candidate. Where the cabinet had previously provided a forum for struggling "institutionally" for power, with the takeover by bureaucrats, cabinet appointment became a device for paying off debts of loyalty where dissent was not allowed. Hence, one could argue that the presidency became bureaucratically strong but politically weak.[24] In other words, a series of technocratic presidents mastered the technicalities of public policy but failed to adapt to the discontent that emerged from those policies, a failure that split the elite. However, at least one close observer believes that Salinas achieved a relatively balanced coalition in the makeup of his cabinet. Although he appointed mainly young technocrats to his "economic" cabinet, he tried to diversify the full cabinet to include more politicians who represented a broad coalition of forces. Roderic Camp says, "Salinas's cabinet has more electoral political experience than any presidential administration since 1970, and in fact, includes five governors."[25]

In any case, we should not exaggerate the significance of the recent succession of presidents who rose solely through appointive office. It is possible, of course, that Mexican presidents are as subject to "trained incapacity" as the rest of us. Officials like Echeverría, who rose through positions in which they specialized in pacification, might come to the presidency predisposed to see problems as being amenable to repressive solutions. Officials like de la Madrid or Salinas, who had held mainly financial positions, might tend to see the problems facing them as essentially economic.

Of course, this argument could cut either way. A fundamental strategy of the Mexican regime from at least 1935 has been to solve political problems through economic means, sometimes through distribution (Cárdenas, Echeverría, perhaps Adolfo López Mateos) and sometimes through growth (all the other presidents). Thus all presidents have tried to use the economy to pacify the polity, and technocratic presidents are no different than the "political" presidents in this way. Or one could argue that the technocratic presidents, especially the "finance presidents" from López Portillo to Salinas, have increased the proclivity of Mexican presidents to seek economic solutions to political problems even at times when political pressures have intensified dramatically. Thus technocrats might tend to define policy issues mainly in technical terms rather than seeing them in a broader way that includes other values, especially popular support for the regime. For example, technocratic presidents might be more concerned with technical matters such as budget deficits and foreign debt than with coordinating social peace. Whereas prior presidents might have paid more attention to politics, legitimacy, and coalition building, it is possible that recent presidents have focused too narrowly on managing the economy. This is not to deny the importance of economic effectiveness as a key criterion by which citizens evaluate their government. But if policymakers are concerned only with economic growth and not distribution, the result can be a loss of political support from those sectors that are negatively affected by the economic change. In fact, most recent Mexican governments have delivered neither economic nor political effectiveness. Nonetheless, numerous observers have argued that the ascendancy of technocratic presidents has had a negative effect on the political system.

On the other hand, to draw such a distinction between the withdrawn and inelegant "politician" Gustavo Díaz Ordaz and the gregarious, politically sensitive "bureaucrat" Echeverría is perhaps to emphasize an irrelevancy. It is possible that, on average, the "bureaucrats" are not as effective at manipulation of political symbols as the "politicians." For example, de la Madrid's lack of public activity in the first hours after the devastating series of earthquakes in the fall of 1985 was a major symbolic failure. As a good administrator, he may have been quite active behind the scenes in mobilizing relief efforts, but his lack of public activity was politically insensitive at best. Yet it is difficult to see how the other bureaucratic presidents were any less skillful or interested in symbolic politics than the "politicians." Salinas, in particular, seems to be aware of the need to be effective in both concrete and symbolic ways. In addition, he seems to be trying to address problems of growth and distribution simultaneously.

Moreover, it can be argued that in Mexico there is little difference between politics and bureaucracy. In Mexico's semiauthoritarian institutionalized system, politics are highly bureaucratized in the sense that advancement does not arise primarily from popularity with voters, since elections are not open, but from satisfying one's superiors within the system. Conversely, the bureaucracy is highly politicized in the sense that virtually the entire public work force is subject to political appointment rather than merit. This means that a bureaucrat's promotion depends heavily on his political skill in, among other things, picking winners among his superiors. That is, the clientelistic relations represented by camarillas seemed to be just as important under the "technocrat" Salinas as under previous "political" presidents, and in fact, several members of Salinas's cabinet had associations going back to Echeverría and López Portillo.[26]

It seems, therefore, that there has been little difference between "political" and "bureaucratic" presidents as far as their predilections and political skills are concerned. All have tried to solve the political problems of legitimacy and participation through economic means, whether primarily from growth or distribution. More important, their success or lack of it has been similar, no matter what their career trajectory. Both types of president were unable to resolve key issues of public policy emanating from the limits of the Mexican economic model. These limits had become obvious by the time of Díaz Ordaz and contributed mightily to the turmoil and loss of legitimacy that the regime suffered during his six years. This is analogous to the conclusion that James Malloy and others have reached with regard to the relative effectiveness of civilian democratic versus military regimes in Latin America. Most studies have discovered

little significant difference between the two types of regime in either encouraging economic growth or achieving distribution.[27] Likewise, in Mexico, "political" and "technocratic" presidents in recent years have had about equal success in dealing with problems of political legitimacy and economic well-being.
It is possible that some of the recent divisions among the elites within the PRI
stem from this split between políticos like Cárdenas and technocrats like Salinas. But more fundamentally, the division is the traditional split between the
left and the right over the best way to govern a society and how the costs and
benefits are to be apportioned.[28] Thus elite unity was fragmented both by the
rise of a new basis of political success within the regime (economic expertise)
and by divisions over economic strategy (market versus state and growth versus
distribution). The Salinas administration was able to hold the ruling elite together to a large extent, but these tensions would not soon disappear.

Coercion

The regime continues to use coercion in the form of electoral irregularities
and physical repression. Most elections are still not competitive, and political
intimidation and even murders still occur. Whether such activities emanate
from the central government (which Salinas denies) or from local rivalries, the
effect is the same. The Mexican regime still has a considerable capacity to
enforce its will by coercive means, and Salinas turned to the army several times
to enforce his will. In fact, Camp says that Salinas was the first president
since Alemán to combine military and police functions for internal security.
Comparing the two presidents, he wrote, "Similar military involvement into
what typically had been civilian responsibilities did not recur until the first
year of the Carlos Salinas administration, 1989."[29] Repression increased under
Salinas both because opposition increased and because his government, like
that of Alemán, intended to impose harsher discipline on workers.

In some ways, however, political freedom appeared to improve in recent
years. The wave of political liberalization and democratization that swept the
world in the 1980s and 1990s also affected Mexico. In particular, there was
increased attention to human rights within the country and by foreign entities
such as Amnesty International. Numerous groups emerged both in and out of
the country to monitor abuses and to press for greater progress on human rights
and electoral fairness, which, as we have seen, are closely connected. One
such organization was the Consejo para la Democracia, comprised of numerous
notables of various political persuasions. Headed by lawyer-economist Julio
Faesler, its founding members included, among others, Bernardo Bátiz, Carlos
Castillo Peraza, and Rogelio Sada Zambrano of the PAN; Marieclaire Acosta,
Samuel del Villar, Ifigenia Martínez, and Porfirio Muñoz Ledo of the PRD;
Rodolfo Gonzáles Guevara and Federico Reyes Heroles of the PRI; as well as
independents such as Jorge Castañeda and Enrique Krauze. Thus what is often
called "civil society" (political society outside of government) has become

more active in pressing for democratic reforms; this is especially true of non-governmental political elites. Therefore, increased scrutiny made it more difficult for the regime to engage in blatant electoral fraud and physical coercion, even if it wanted to do so. If the government carried out violations on the level of the 1968 Tlatelolco massacre, there would be serious repercussions from both the national and the international communities. Thus the regime's ability to maintain its power by force has been reduced. This trend may be intensified by the fact that a Democratic administration was in power in Washington after 1992, as discussed below.

The Salinas government seemed to go through at least two phases in its attitude toward political liberalization. At first it behaved with greater tolerance of opposition. In 1989 the PAN in Baja California Norte won the governorship and half of the seats in the state legislature. In 1991 the government intervened after disputed elections in Guanajuato and San Luis Potosí, replacing the recently elected PRI governors with interim appointees (with a *panista* in Guanajuato) until new elections could be held. Then in 1992 another PAN governor was elected in Chihuahua, and the recently elected PRI governor of Michoacán was replaced by another PRI governor. During this time, the opposition was allowed to win numerous local offices as well. In other words, the regime displayed a certain amount of flexibility during the first two years of the Salinas administration.

Then the government's strategy seemed to change. In November 1992, state and local elections were held in various states. Reminiscent of the old days, the PRI claimed a clean sweep in Puebla and Sinaloa. In Tamaulipas it conceded only one of the 19 seats in the state legislature and 3 of 43 municipal posts. In Oaxaca the PRI claimed victory in 538 of 570 town halls. The opposition cried fraud, and the conflict quickly deteriorated into violence. The situation was especially interesting in Tamaulipas. In that state, the PRD and the PAN had agreed to support the same candidate for governor (Jorge Cárdenas González, the mayor of Matamoros), and he had fought a strong campaign. After the PRI candidate was declared the winner, riots broke out during which the offices of the city election commission were burned, destroying most of the election ballots. A number of opposition supporters fled across the border into Texas, which could hardly enhance Mexico's image in the eyes of international investors, including the large *maquiladora* community of Tamaulipas, but Salinas refused to annul the election as he had done in several previous cases.

Instead, he continued his hard line by appointing José Patrocinio González Garrido, the former governor of Chiapas, as minister of the interior, the department that oversees elections as well as law and order. Meanwhile, Beatriz Paredes, an Interior Department official who had taken part in negotiations with the PRD, was removed from her post and sent to Cuba. At the same time, an Interior Department official was put at the head of the Federal Electoral Institute, the country's highest electoral authority. All this was interpreted as an attempt by the president to strengthen his control of the regime before the time came (in late 1993) to select his successor for the election of August 1994. Salinas was faced with severe internal divisions within the PRI as well as a much more determined opposition. Therefore, his hard-line moves could be seen to be directed as much at the PRI itself as at the opposition.[30] Thus although the regime appeared to ease up in some instances, in general it tenaciously and even brutally held on to power, using electoral fraud and physical repression when necessary.[31] Moreover, that monopoly of power meant that a given event had a different meaning in Mexico than in liberal democracies. Whereas NAFTA could be debated and modified in the United States and Canada, the Salinas government tried to suppress dissent over the terms of the treaty. Thus one possible connection between economic and political liberalization was severed as the Mexican regime prevented an open discussion of the fundamental question of whether Mexico should even move in the direction of a more open economy.[32]

Location

The United States has always played an important role in Mexican history. After the United States became an independent country in the late eighteenth century, Mexican liberals tended to view their northern neighbor as a model for their own political and economic development. The United States was instrumental in discouraging France from intervening militarily in Mexico in the 1860s. Then during the reign of Porfirio Díaz, U.S. investment played an important role in shaping the economic development of Mexico. Politically, the primary goal of the United States in Mexico has almost always been stability, rather than democracy. It is true that the United States did support Benito Juárez and the liberals in Mexico in the 1850s and 1860s, but that was more to gain transit rights and to prevent a European power (France) from wielding influence in Mexico than to support liberalism itself. During the long reign of Porfirio Díaz, there is little evidence that the United States tried to influence Díaz in the direction of fair elections or civil liberties. Then after Francisco Madero came to office in 1911, the United States had an opportunity to support liberal democracy in Mexico, but instead it was more concerned with order, and so the U.S. ambassador worked for the overthrow of Madero when he became convinced that Madero was too weak to maintain order (and perhaps because he thought that Madero's policies would threaten the property of U.S. citizens in Mexico). It is difficult to say whether Madero's government would have survived even with U.S. support, but its fall and Madero's murder were certainly made more likely by U.S. collusion with the rebels.[33]

One of the few times that U.S. policy seemed to be motivated largely by the desire to encourage democracy in Mexico was in 1913–14, when Victoriano Huerta was president of Mexico and Woodrow Wilson was president of the United States. Wilson represented the progressive wing of the Democratic Party and, unlike many Republicans, believed that liberal democracy was appropriate for all societies. Against the wishes of American business, State Department officials, many Republicans, and even some Democrats, Wilson refused to recognize Huerta's government. In 1914 he ordered the occupation of Veracruz to demonstrate the U.S. determination that Huerta resign. Although perhaps not the determining factor, the U.S. repudiation of Huerta made it easier for the Constitutionalist forces of Carranza and others to defeat Huerta.[34]

After the failure of the United States to support democracy in Mexico under Madero in 1911–13, and its policy toward Huerta, which may have been motivated in part by a concern for democracy, the United States took virtually no substantial action to support the forces that seemed to be trying to establish a more democratic political system in Mexico. The rare exception came in the early 1980s when the PAN opposition was viewed with some sympathy by the administration of Ronald Reagan because the PAN was conservative and shared some U.S. foreign policy objectives. After that brief flirtation with Mexican democracy, the U.S. government continued to support the Mexican regime throughout the presidencies of Reagan and George Bush. The Reagan administration recognized the Salinas victory immediately in 1988, and the Bush administration continued close relations with the Salinas government, including rapid negotiation of the free trade agreement. Insofar as is publicly known, the U.S. government made no serious demands on the Mexican government in recent years for greater electoral fairness or attention to human rights.

The United States has put stability over democracy not just in Mexico but in most of Latin America as well. As one observer noted, "It was characteristic of the Cold War era to prefer stability over progress toward democracy and human rights whenever Washington felt that a choice had to be made."[35] However, with the end of the Cold War and with a Democratic administration and Congress in power in Washington, it was possible that the U.S. fixation with political stability in Mexico would change. It was conceivable by the early 1990s that the U.S. government might try to exert more influence on Mexico and other Latin American countries to be more attentive to human rights, especially as part of the price of free trade. The administration of Bill Clinton was likely to be more interested in human rights violations in Mexico, in protecting the environment, especially along the border, and in cooperative efforts to manage the drug problem in the hemisphere. Now that the Cold War is over, there may not be such insistence by the United States on conservative stability in the region as the bulwark against supposed Communist influence. If U.S. policy does not change after the collapse of the Soviet Union, the U.S. claim that its anti-left policies in Latin America were motivated by a concern for national security will be laid bare. The argument that radicals in Latin America and in the United States made for decades—that the antipopulist position of the United States in Latin America was motivated far more by a desire to protect U.S. business interests than to contain any alleged Communist threat in the hemisphere—will gain credibility.

It seems probable, however, that with the removal of the Soviet threat, the

U.S. government will take a more tolerant position toward populism and perhaps even toward instability because the stakes are no longer seen to be so high. It is conceivable, therefore, that the U.S. government may give less support to the PRI regime in the 1990s than in the past. Yet democracy may still not be at the top of the U.S. agenda. The Democratic administration may, like Salinas, choose to emphasize economic growth over political liberalization. Clinton promised Salinas that he would support passage of the NAFTA treaty, and so the United States may continue to put democracy in Mexico second to economic concerns and to overlook the imperfections of the Mexican political system. However, a key factor was how boldly these issues would be portrayed in the American press in 1994. Like the Mexicans, the American people have often been ambivalent about supporting democracy. The U.S. administration may choose to point to the electoral reforms of the 1990 law and the increasing number of opposition victories in state and local elections as evidence of progress, even though the law was crafted in part to enable the regime to continue to win elections, especially the presidency and the congress.[36]

Although the Clinton administration may not be as active as was the administration of Jimmy Carter in the area of human rights, it seems likely that it might move somewhat further in that direction than did Reagan and Bush from 1981 to 1993. This may be partly a result of ideological commitment and partly a reaction to pressure from human rights groups, to which a Democratic administration may be more responsive than were the Republican administrations.[37] The Democratic administration may not be so single-mindedly intent on free trade as were the Republican administrations and for that reason may be more willing to press Mexico on human rights. Thus because of increased attention by monitoring groups and perhaps the U.S. government, the Mexican regime may find it difficult in 1994 to repeat the experience of 1988, when it engaged in obvious electoral fraud and put off announcing the election results for a week while rearranging the numbers.

In addition, concern over immigration may replace communism as the major factor influencing the U.S. government attitude toward Latin America. Immigration to the United States increased dramatically in the 1980s as a result of such events as the turmoil in Central America, the devastated Mexican economy, and the overthrow of the Aristide government in Haiti. It seems likely, therefore, that the United States will still be concerned about stability and order in Latin America in the 1990s, but as a way of slowing emigration rather than containing communism. Both economic growth and political democratization (or at least maintenance of a regime that is not so brutal as to drive large numbers of people out of the country) may contribute to that goal. It is possible, therefore, that the U.S. government will press for greater democracy in Mexico if it sees the failure of the regime to liberalize as a factor contributing to turmoil and emigration. In fact, in the 1990s, mass migration from authoritarian or poor countries became a major political issue in numerous industrial nations such as the United States, Germany, and France.

For all of these reasons, the factors that contributed to Mexican political stability in the past may now have the opposite effect. An institutionalized succession within the same party may now alienate more people than it satisfies. The ideology of the Revolution, likewise, may prove insufficient to hold the various factions together within the single corporatist framework fashioned by Lázaro Cárdenas in the 1930s. The regime's ability to adapt to pressures from society may be constrained by structural factors over which the regime has little control. For example, the movement to freer trade and a more market-oriented economy may create both opportunities and problems for the Mexican economy and polity. At least in the short run, increases in unemployment and bankruptcies are likely to occur. Privatization will displace thousands of employees who were probably loyal supporters of the regime. The government can no longer alternate between growth and redistributive policies with such nimbleness as in the past. Also, it can no longer be sure that it can arrange electoral outcomes and intimidate opponents in the new international environment of greater scrutiny of electoral results and civil liberties. Finally, the acquiescence of the U.S. government in electoral irregularities and human rights abuses cannot be taken for granted any longer by the Mexican regime.

Each of the factors that contributed to political stability contained within it the potential eventually to contribute to instability. The institutionalization of a particular set of political arrangements may have developed a rigidity that could convince many Mexicans that the regime could never be flexible enough to adapt to a new set of demands for which this regime was not designed, such as political democracy. Moreover, economic change eventually has the potential for destabilizing a regime, no matter how it occurs. If an economy does not grow, the regime eventually is seen as incompetent. If it does grow but with gross inequalities, that growth could weaken the supports of the regime. And even if it grows and a large and prosperous middle class develops, these groups will probably demand an end to one-party rule in a world context in which virtually all "modern" nations have a political system characterized by liberal democracy—that is, civil liberties and competitive elections. This is not to say that a simple linear relationship exists between economic growth and political democracy. However, once a nation passes a certain level of economic development, the likelihood of moving toward greater political democracy does seem to increase. As a noted student of the process wrote, "Economic factors have significant impact on democratization but they are not determinative." Yet he goes on to say, "Most wealthy countries are democratic and most democratic countries . . . are wealthy."[38] It is possible, however, that the crucial threshold, if such exists, is closer to $6,000 per capita income in 1990 than to the $2,000 per capita income of Mexico. Therefore, even if there is a close relationship between economic development and political democracy in the long run, it is conceivable that Mexico has a considerable way to go before its economic development provides a firm basis for political democracy.[39] But as Mexico becomes wealthier, more urban, and more middle class—assuming that happens in the coming decades—it seems likely that the one-party regime will become less acceptable to a larger number of Mexicans.

Coercion also becomes less viable in the context of a growing urban middle class of informed citizens, especially in a global environment concerned with human rights and political democracy. The drug problem, however, confounds the situation. The "militarization" of the drug problem under the influence of the United States contributes to the power of the military, relative to civilian authority. This is perhaps a larger problem in some other Latin American countries trying to consolidate democracy, but it could also counter any general trend in Mexico away from repression; it is easier for the government to disguise political repression as antidrug activities. Nonetheless, repression in general seems less tolerable to Mexicans in the 1990s than in previous decades, and so the regime may not be able to use drug trafficking as a pretext for repression as much as it would like.

Finally, elite unity itself can become a force for political change in either of two directions. If the elite remains united behind the one-party semiauthoritarian regime, then the regime will fail to adapt to growing demands for political participation and democracy, thus contributing to a buildup of frustration and potential violence. On the other hand, if the elite supports a historical compromise permitting movement to a new, competitive, multiparty regime with fair elections, then we could say that this particular regime has died while the overall political system has been transformed peacefully.

Thus because of changed conditions, the Mexican regime may find that the old practices have new consequences in the 1990s. As we have seen, both economic and political conditions have changed. One of the most important changes is the degree to which many Mexicans are demanding a more open political system. One should not exaggerate these demands or overlook the possibility that other values such as political stability, patronage, the avoidance of violence, and economic growth are also important considerations among the Mexican population. However, the call for democratization has been a salient value in Mexico in recent years. Let us now examine what the opposition has called for and what the regime has conceded in this area.

PROGRESS TOWARD DEMOCRACY?

The Mexican system has made some progress toward democracy. In terms of the activities of parties and candidates, the Mexican electoral system has been relatively open for several years. Virtually every political persuasion is allowed to organize and to offer its candidates to the voters, and this was not changed in the 1990 electoral law. Likewise, in terms of official recognition of parties and for purposes of campaign finance, free media exposure, and being listed on the ballot, the 1990 law retained the threshold of 1.5 percent of the vote. The same level was retained for proportional representation in the Chamber of Deputies. Finally, the human rights situation has improved, at least insofar as several organizations now exist to monitor and investigate abuses, and press freedom seems to be relatively high compared with the past.

On the negative side, however, threats, abuse, and political murders still occur. More than thirty journalists were murdered during the 1980s, and although many of the killings were attributed to drug traffickers and not directly related to politics, such a pattern no doubt has a chilling effect on press freedom in general. Although the number of killings declined toward the end of the decade, a recent survey indicated that with four journalists murdered in 1990, Mexico had the third-highest rate of murders of journalists in the world for that year. It was also revealed in 1991 that the offices of the national human rights commission had been wiretapped. This is an extremely serious breach that could undermine people's belief that they are safe in going to the commission to denounce human rights violations.[40] Various human rights reports also indicated that serious problems persisted.[41] Thus the human rights situation in Mexico remained decidedly mixed in the 1990s.

Another dubious development was the provision in the 1990 law that prohibited more than one party from offering the same candidate. This seemed designed to make coalitions in general less attractive, and in particular it seemed to be aimed at preventing a repetition of 1988, when numerous parties nominated Cuauhtémoc Cárdenas as their presidential candidate. Whereas its obvious purpose was to weaken the opposition on the left by keeping it fragmented into several small parties, it could have the opposite effect, encouraging the smaller parties to merge officially into one large opposition party. The governability clause, which gives the largest party an automatic majority in the Chamber, is also designed to make coalitions less likely. This puts a serious obstacle in the path often followed by emerging parties in other countries as they evolve toward the status of a governing party. In addition, the massive imbalance in campaign resources between the PRI and the opposition parties has continued, including the advantages of incumbency and the attention of the media. Overall, therefore, progress in this area was spotty, and serious problems remained to be addressed as of 1993.

At the stage in which an electorate is "created," both progress and problems can also be discerned in Mexico's recent efforts. The new law did not change the eligibility of voters, but Mexico was already up to prevailing world standards in this regard. With the usual exceptions, all adults eighteen years and older are eligible to vote. A new electoral roll was also created, which almost certainly was more accurate than the previous one, although the opposition continued to argue that it favored the PRI to some extent. The opposition alleged that the government's discrimination against opposition supporters was now a more sophisticated form of fraud: the delivery of new voter credentials. They also claimed that electoral authorities were slow in distributing voter credentials to opposition supporters. The remaining problem in this area, therefore, was proper enforcement of the existing law.

In the final stage of elections, from the vote itself to formal challenges of the results, the law provided for the use of voter identification cards that made scrutiny of the act of voting easier. This, combined with the steady increase of opposition and neutral monitoring of the polling places, seems to have reduced the PRI advantage to some extent. Monitoring increased not only in quantity but in quality as well. The creation of a "monitoring central" for each election, as in Guanajuato in 1991, may be the wave of the future. In addition, the creation of the national monitoring group, the Council for Democracy, raised the visibility of the observation process. The remaining problems with monitoring were that opposition observers were still not allowed in some polling places and that international observers were not officially allowed anywhere—because Salinas said they would challenge Mexico's national sovereignty. Thus even if informal international monitors were present, their observations would not be admissible in subsequent legal inquiries into irregularities. The 1990 law allowed opposition representatives to be present during the vote count and called for the announcement of preliminary results as soon as the ballots were counted. However, the law was not always followed, and after various state and local elections the opposition continued to complain that PRI representatives had absconded with ballot boxes for several hours. The criticism at this step in the process went to the heart of opposition complaints. The opposition, especially on the left, was convinced that the electoral process from beginning to end remained controlled by an electoral commission a majority of whose members were selected by the regime. Thus, the ultimate decision about electoral outcomes continued to be made by the president and not by a neutral organization.

As we have seen, many factors contribute to political change. Because changes in the law and formal procedures are not everything, it might be useful to summarize some of the other factors impelling Mexico in the direction of liberalization. The environment within which recent political events have occurred has been almost the classic context for discontent and change. During most of the 1980s, Mexico suffered a sustained economic crisis, in large part because of major increases in government spending that, after oil prices fell, were impossible to sustain without massive foreign borrowing. Real wages fell by over 50 percent from 1982 to 1988, and unemployment rose in a country already plagued by consistent problems in providing jobs for its rapidly growing population. To make matters worse, huge earthquakes devastated the capital in 1985. The government response was seen as inept and inadequate, and partly for that reason civic participation and self-help surged in the aftermath of the earthquakes.

Discontented with what they saw as the government's neoliberal policies for dealing with the prolonged economic and social crisis, Cárdenas and numerous other members of the political subelite broke away from the PRI and created a relatively united left, which offered a populist program and a presidential candidate with the most recognized name in Mexican politics. The conservative party also put forth a dynamic candidate in Manuel Clouthier, and the degree of cooperation between forces of the right and the left in the 1988 campaign and afterward was unprecedented. With the help of the domestic and international media, the opposition's organization and determination allowed them to monitor elections after 1988 far more than in the past. In addition, the international environment favored at least some degree of political change, as numerous governments in Europe, Latin America, and Asia became less authoritarian and more democratic in the 1980s and 1990s. Although the Republican administrations in Washington apparently did not put pressure on the Mexican regime to democratize, it was clear that brutal repression would not be appropriate at a time when the United States was trying to take some credit for the liberalization of much of Latin America and the world. Moreover, a Democratic administration in Washington after 1992 seemed likely to press Mexico on human rights and fair elections more than had the Republican administrations. Hence most forces—domestic and international—appeared to push the Mexican regime in the direction of liberalization.

As significant as these other factors are, however, law and formal procedures can also be important in a context in which they interact with other factors. Thus the relationship between law and other determinants is circular. For example, by demonstrating will and capacity, the opposition may persuade a regime to make legal concessions, many of which the regime may not even intend to follow in practice. But once laws are in place, they become a resource that the opposition can use, in conjunction with other developments such as a freer press, a more congenial human rights environment, and increased international attention. The law can be used as a standard by which to judge regime behavior as that behavior is held up to domestic and international scrutiny. In other words, citizens can insist than the law be enforced. The law can form the basis both for registering protests and for proposing yet more changes that will make abuses more difficult to perpetrate in the future. By the early 1990s, critics in Mexico were able to point to specific laws, electoral and otherwise, in their efforts to force the regime to loosen its grip on power. The initial impetus for political change may have come from broader forces such as those discussed above, which allowed the opposition to obtain legal changes at least partially to their liking. But once in effect, the new laws themselves become a tool for pressing for further change, both in practice and in law. Thus the law and other factors interact in a mutually reinforcing way.

One change notable in Mexico's electoral process is that complaints of election irregularities seem to have followed a curvilinear pattern in recent years. It appears that fraud charges increased dramatically during the 1980s and perhaps peaked in about 1990, not because fraud had necessarily increased but because opposition monitoring of abuses had flourished. In fact, the electoral debate increasingly turned in a new direction beginning in the early 1980s. Instead of simply ensuring opposition representation in Congress, as in the past, the primary issue now became the fairness of the elections themselves. The PAN won numerous local elections in northern Mexico in the early years of the de la Madrid presidency (1982–88) and looked forward to winning some state elections in the north. When the regime suddenly slammed the door on this process of liberalization in the mid-1980s, preventing victories in state elections that the PAN was convinced it had won, PAN supporters became increasingly vehement in their denunciations and determined in their monitoring of electoral fraud. That set the scene for the federal election of 1988, when the honesty of the election emerged as the central issue for the first time since 1952 or perhaps even 1940. Then beginning with the midterm elections of summer 1991, the quantity of complaints seemed to decline, and the nature of the complaints appeared to change. Although almost every type of "irregularity" continued to be used by the government to some extent, opposition complaints of blatant fraud seemed to decline, especially for the major vices that had been so prominent in the past—grossly fraudulent voting (taco, carousel) and vote count (dumping piles of opposition ballots in creek beds, taking a week to manipulate the count).[42] This suggests that the cruder forms of fraud may have declined and that the government had been forced to find new and perhaps more sophisticated ways of cheating.

Increasingly, the opposition shifted its focus from individual violations to the broader nature of the political system. Critics complained that the government used its resources to "buy" votes through public spending in areas where PRI support had declined. For example, in the 1990 election in the state of México, the opposition accused the regime of buying votes by pouring almost $100 million into the state for roads, schools, water systems, and other benefits in the year before the election (a practice not unknown in more "advanced" political systems). In addition, the opposition increasingly complained about the continuing use of government funds, equipment, and personnel during the campaign and election—practices common in the United States until the Hatch Act of the 1930s. Hence the focus of attention has increasingly shifted from fraud at the ballot box to issues that are in the "gray area" of politics, or from illegal practices to activities that may be legal but controversial.

Do these changes add up to significant progress toward fairer elections? The picture is mixed no matter what criteria are used. If small, incremental changes are considered important because they signal the pluralization of power in a hitherto one-party regime, and because they may be the harbinger of larger changes to come, then we could say that significant progress has been made. Elections were much more closely monitored than before 1988, old-style fraud appeared to have declined, election outcomes were generally much closer than in the past, and the opposition were winning more, especially at the state and local level. The PAN and the PRD won thousands of local positions, dozens more seats in state legislatures and control of two of them, three governorships, and record numbers of votes for president in 1988. The regime had to take opposition views into account to an extent almost unheard of in Mexican politics. And for the first time since 1911, there was actually a serious possibility that the opposition could win the Mexican presidency in an election in the not-too-distant future.

However, if one accepts electoral change as significant only if elections have become as free of procedural disputes and as characterized by competitive outcomes as they generally are in North America and Western Europe, then Mexico had not made significant progress by 1993. The PRI continued to win virtually all elections, and the opposition argued that electoral fraud was the major device that produced that outcome. The PRI still controlled the presidency, both houses of congress, twenty-eight of thirty-one state governments, and the vast majority of local governments. The progress had been small, the concessions were calculated and grudging, and some regression occurred (for example, the opposition lost many seats in the Chamber of Deputies in the midterm elections of 1991). The fact that the government was not willing to give up ultimate control of the electoral process in the 1990 law suggests that the regime was not willing to risk losing control of the presidency, congress, and most state and local governments.

In no liberal polity anywhere in the world has the ruling party been in power without interruption for sixty years. In virtually all liberal democracies, the opposition occasionally wins control of the national government, even if only for brief periods, as in Sweden. Comparing Mexico with liberal democracies throughout the world suggests that the regime must have engaged in electoral legerdemain over the decades to have remained in power so long and that it probably still did so as late as 1993. As mentioned previously, only the Communist Party of the Soviet Union had been in power longer than the PRI, and by 1991 the latter had survived even that venerable party. To some degree, therefore, election outcomes in the long run are an indicator of the fairness of those elections. With virtually no exceptions, sooner or later—usually within a couple of decades—ruling parties are turned out of office in polities where elections are fair. (Even the LDP in Japan was finally replaced in August 1993, after thirty-eight years in power.) Thus although the opposition in Mexico was certainly winning more elections than in the past, they were probably not winning as many as they would if the elections were fairer, and they had not won national power.

The essential question is not whether this or that election technique is employed but whether a regime intends to allow meaningful elections. Judging by the results from 1988 to 1993, the Mexican government chose to be very selective in its enforcement of fair elections; in fact, one could characterize the Mexican situation in the early 1990s as "selective democracy." Therefore, in a sense, no amount of procedural change would force fair elections if the regime did not intend for them to occur. Law does not equal practice, nor is it a substitute for political will. It was even possible that the regime would benefit more than the opposition from the electoral changes in that such changes might make it easier to present a democratic facade to the rest of the world. In addition, by resisting at every turn, the regime could prolong the process of liberalization for years, keeping the opposition tied up in procedural battles over a few more seats in the Chamber of Deputies, state legislatures, or city councils. It occasionally granted the opposition a governorship as a sop of co-optation to keep them in the game. Through 1993, only the conservative PAN, which shared the PRI's belief in economic liberalization, had been conceded any state governments. Even these changes, however, were small and grudgingly conceded at every step. If Mexico is democratizing, it would have to be called "democratization in very slow motion." In fact, it might more accurately be called "limited power sharing," rather than democracy.

However, even if the regime did not *intend* to allow the democratization process to go very far very fast, it was possible that the reforms would take on an unintended momentum of their own. Each concession might make it harder for the regime to perpetrate fraud. Laws certainly matter if a government enforces them, but they may also make a difference simply by being on the books if they provide the opposition a legal basis on which to argue that fraud is occurring. The construction of a new electoral roll provides the opposition with an access point in the process of trying to force the regime to be more honest. Requiring voter identification cards gives the opposition something tangible to use to monitor the act of voting. Allowing the opposition to observe the computer in operation as it tabulates the vote, and committing itself to immediate release of preliminary results, reduces the government's room for maneuver and makes it more difficult to rearrange the numbers in private. Each of these changes might make it harder for the regime to cheat without doing so in the glare of publicity, and in the late twentieth century, that is not an inconsequential consideration. Therefore, whether the regime intended to or not, it might be weaving a web of legal constraint around itself that would make it increasingly difficult to behave as in the past. The opposition was trying to move Mexico toward democracy through law while the regime was trying to resist democratization through both law and practice. The elections of 1994 could tell us which strategy would prevail. Whatever regime leaders have in mind, however, the process of liberalization can develop a dynamic of its own, as change often has a way of doing. Especially today, when the world context contributes to a "democratization demonstration effect, " when the movement for human rights and press freedom in Mexico has proceeded so far, and when the electoral laws are relatively supportive of fair elections, it would be difficult for the PRI in 1994 to repeat its creative performance of 1988. As Laurence Whitehead wrote, "Once a governing elite accepts the theoretical hegemony of liberal institutions, once it pays lip-service to popular sovereignty expressed through open elections, a process of habituation is set in motion which tends over time to turn the 'facades' into more real structures."[43]

CONCLUSION

From 1920 to the early 1990s, Mexico experienced a degree of political stability that was unique in Latin America. This book has argued that the stability was largely a result of the institutionalization of the regime, its effectiveness in achieving economic growth, its adaptability to demands from society, the high degree of elite unity, its willingness to use coercion, and its location next to the United States which provided support for its regime and economic relief in the form of investment and emigration. These conditions created what has been called "the perfect dictatorship." However, the conditions within which these factors operate have changed dramatically in recent years, and each factor that previously contributed to stability may now contribute to instability. If the political system is to remain stable, the regime must be adaptable enough to respond to the widespread demand for liberal democracy, which includes conceding governorships, state legislatures, the congress, and eventually even the presidency itself to opposition parties if they win these offices in fair elections. In that case, Mexico would in effect have a new regime within a continuing, stable political system. At the end of the twentieth century, democracy may be the only route to continued political stability in Mexico.

Like Lyndon Johnson, who did not want to be "the first American president to lose a war" (he apparently forgot the War of 1812), or Winston Churchill, who "did not become the king's first minister to preside over the dissolution of the British Empire," no Mexican president wanted to be the one to preside over the disappearance of the revolutionary regime that had held power for seven decades. It is not surprising that the president and the regime resisted a change of this magnitude. However, Carlos Salinas had the opportunity to play a historical role. He could either be like Porfirio Díaz, the recalcitrant conservative who refused to adapt to demands for more democratic participation and who thereby provoked the Mexican Revolution, or he could be a creative, "transformational" leader like Rómulo Betancourt, who went beyond "normal" behavior in an effort to lead his society to a new level of development.[44]

NOTES

1. James March and Johan Olsen, *Rediscovering Institutions: The Organizational Bases of Politics* (New York: Free Press, 1989), p. 168.

2. Peter H. Smith, "The Political Impact of Free Trade on Mexico," *Journal of Interamerican Studies and World Affairs* 34 (1), 1992, especially pp. 14–20.

3. John Bailey, "Populism and Regime Liberalization: Mexico in Comparative Perspective" (Paper Presented at Annual Meeting of the Midwest Political Science Association, Chicago, April 18–20, 1991), pp. 2, 15.

4. Stephen D. Morris, "Political Reformism in Mexico: Salinas at the Brink," *Journal of Interamerican Studies and World Affairs* 34 (1), 1992, p. 41; Robert A. Pastor, "Post-Revolutionary Mexico: The Salinas Opening," *Journal of Interamerican Studies and World Affairs* 32 (3), 1990, pp. 12–22.

5. Judith Gentleman and Voytek Zubek, "International Integration and Democratic Development: The Cases of Poland and Mexico," *Journal of Interamerican Studies and World Affairs* 34 (1), 1992, p. 86.

6. Interview with Luis Alvarez, president of the PAN, July 6, 1990.

7. Economist Intelligence Unit, *Mexico: Country Report,* no. 1 (London: EUI, 1993), p. 6.

8. However, the degree of trade-off between efficiency and equity should not be exaggerated. It is true that one cannot redistribute more than is available as a result of growth, but certain kinds of social programs, such as education and job training, can contribute to economic growth. See Robert Reich, *The Work of Nations* (New York: Vintage Books, 1991).

9. Daniel Levy and Gabriel Székely, *Mexico: Paradoxes of Stability and Change,* 2d ed. (Boulder, Colo.: Westview Press, 1987), p. 64.

10. Pastor, "Post-Revolutionary Mexico," pp. 3–6.

11. Economist Intelligence Unit, *Mexico,* p. 3.

12. Jamie Ros, "Free Trade Area or Common Capital Market?" *Journal of Interamerican Studies and World Affairs* 34 (2), 1992, pp. 53–91.

13. Gary Hufbauer and Jeffrey Schott, *North American Free Trade Agreement* (Washington, D.C.: Institute for International Economics, 1991), reviewed in Benoit Brookens, "Book Reviews," *Journal of Interamerican Studies and World Affairs* 34 (2), 1992, pp. 189–92.

14. Sidney Weintraub, "U.S.-Mexican Free Trade: Implications for the United States," *Journal of Interamerican Studies and World Affairs* 34 (2), 1992, pp. 29–52.

15. For example, Smith, "The Political Impact."

16. Cited in ibid., p. 8.

17. Ibid., pp. 19–20.

18. Majorie Miller, "Dissident Quits Mexico's Ruling Party," *Los Angeles Times,* Sept. 15, 1990, p. A14.

19. Juan Molinar Horcasitas, *El tiempo de la legitimidad: elecciones, autoritarismo y democracia en México* (México, D. F.: Cal y Arena, 1991), p. 9.

20. Of course, in a political system without fair elections, it is impossible to say for sure how much real electoral appeal any party has. However, one close student of Mexican elections believes that absolute figures for the opposition are more accurate than for the PRI because the PRI finds it easier to increase its vote than to decrease the vote for the opposition by using such devices as the carousel and taco. See Molinar Horcasitas, *El Tiempo,* p. 9.

21. The following relies heavily on my introductory essay "Pacification through Repression and Redistribution: The Echeverría Years in Mexico," in Samuel Schmidt, *The Deterioration of the Mexican Presidency: The Years of Luis Echeverría* (Tucson: University of Arizona Press, 1991).

22. See Schmidt, *Deterioration,* p. 152.

23. Samuel Schmidt, "Lo tortuoso de la democratización mexicana," *Estudios Interdisciplinarios de América Latina y el Cáribe* 4 (1), 1993.

24. Schmidt, *Deterioration.*

25. Roderic Camp, "Camarillas in Mexican Politics: The Case of the Salinas Cabinet," *Mexican Studies/Estudios Mexicanos* 6 (1), 1993, p. 104.

26. Ibid.

27. James Malloy, "The Politics of Transition in Latin America," in James Malloy

and Mitchell Seligson, eds., *Authoritarians and Democrats: Regime Transition in Latin America* (Pittsburgh: University of Pittsburgh Press, 1987), pp. 235–58.

28. Juan Lindau, "Schisms in the Mexican Political Elite and the Technocrat/Politician Typology," *Mexican Studies/Estudios Mexicanos* 8 (2), 1992, pp. 217–35.

29. Roderic Camp, *Generals in the Palacio: The Military in Modern Mexico* (New York: Oxford University Press, 1992), p. 26.

30. Economist Intelligence Unit, *Mexico*, p. 7.

31. Andrew Reding, "Mexico: The Crumbling of the 'Perfect Dictatorship,'" *World Policy Journal* 8 (2), 1991, pp. 255–88.

32. Adolfo Aguilar Zinser, "Authoritarianism and North American Free Trade: The Debate in Mexico," in Ricardo Grinspun and Maxwell Cameron, eds., *The Political Economy of North American Free Trade* (New York: St. Martin's Press, 1993), pp. 205–16.

33. Lorenzo Meyer, "Mexico: The Exception and the Rule," in Abraham F. Lowenthal, ed., *Exporting Democracy: The United States and Latin America* (Baltimore: Johns Hopkins University Press, 1991), p. 99.

34. See ibid., p. 101.

35. Ambler Moss, Jr., "A Democratic Party Approach to Latin America," *Journal of Interamerican Studies and World Affairs* 34 (2), 1992, p. 7.

36. See chapter 6; also see Gentleman and Zubek, "International Integration," pp. 79–87, and Smith, "The Political Impact," pp. 5, 14.

37. For example, Amnesty International, *Mexico: Torture with Impunity* (London: Amnesty International Publications, 1991).

38. Samuel Huntington, *The Third Wave: Democratization in the Late Twentieth Century* (Norman: University of Oklahoma Press, 1991), pp. 59–60.

39. For a recent discussion of the possible connections (or lack of them) between economic development and political change, see Smith, "The Political Impact," and Nora Hamilton and Eun Mee Kim, "Economic and Political Liberalisation in South Korea and Mexico," *Third World Quarterly* 14 (1), 1993, pp. 109–36.

40. *Latin American Regional Reports: Mexico and Central America*, May 9, 1991, p. 6.

41. For example, Amnesty International, *Mexico*, and Human Rights Commission, Partido de la Revolución Democrática, *The Political Violence in Mexico: A Human Rights Affair* (México, D. F.: Partido de la Revolución Democrática, 1992).

42. There are regional differences as well. Although charges of blatant fraud have declined in northern Mexico, they continue to be high in the south-central part of the country, such as in Morelos. See *Latin American Regional Reports, Mexico and Central America*, May 9, 1991, p. 6. Likewise, most of the politically motivated murders seem to occur in southern Mexico.

43. Laurence Whitehead, "The Alternatives to 'Liberal Democracy': A Latin American Perspective," *Political Studies* 60, 1992, pp. 146–59.

44. James MacGregor Burns, *Leadership* (New York: Harper and Row, 1978). Salinas's selection of Luis Donaldo Colosio, head of the Solidarity program, as the PRI nominee for president demonstrated his willingness to consider social issues in the 1994 campaign. In addition, after first trying to quell the January 1994 Zapatista guerrilla rebellion in Chiapas by armed force, Salinas pursued a more conciliatory policy by negotiating with the rebels and committing the government to economic aid and electoral reform.

Selected Bibliography

Alexander, Robert J. 1964. *The Venezuelan Democratic Revolution: A Profile of the Regime of Rómulo Betancourt.* New Brunswick, N.J.: Rutgers University Press.

Almond, Gabriel, Scott Flanagan, and Robert Mundt. 1973. *Crisis, Choice, and Change: Historical Studies of Political Development.* Boston: Little, Brown and Company.

Ames, Barry. 1970. Bases of support for Mexico's dominant party. *American Political Science Review* 64:153–67.

Amnesty International. 1991. *Mexico: Torture with Impunity.* London: Amnesty International Publications.

Ankerson, Dudley. 1984. *Agrarian Warlord. Saturnino Cedillo and the Mexican Revolution in San Luis Potosí.* DeKalb: Northern Illinois University Press.

Ashby, Joe C. 1967. *Organized Labor and the Mexican Revolution under Lázaro Cárdenas.* Chapel Hill: University of North Carolina Press.

———. 1985. The dilemma of the Mexican trade union movement. *Mexican Studies* 1 (2):277–301.

Bailey, John J. 1988. *Governing Mexico: The Statecraft of Crisis Management.* New York: St. Martin's Press.

Barkin, David. 1975. Mexico's albatross: the United States economy. *Latin American Perspectives* 2 (2):64–80.

Barry, Tom, ed. 1992. *Mexico: A Country Guide.* Albuquerque: Inter-Hemispheric Education Resource Center.

Basañez, Miguel. 1981. *La lucha por la hegemonía en México, 1968–1980.* Mexico: Siglo XXI Editores.

Basurto, Jorge. 1982. The late populism of Luis Echeverría. In Michael Conniff, ed., *Latin American Populism in Comparative Perspective,* pp. 93–111. Albuquerque: University of New Mexico Press.

Bennett, Douglas, and Kenneth Sharpe. 1979. Agenda setting and bargaining power: the Mexican state versus transnational automobile corporations. *World Politics* 32 (1):57–89.

Bermeo, Nancy. 1992. Democracy and the lessons of dictatorship. *Comparative Politics* 24 (3):273–91.

Brachet-Márquez, Viviane. 1992. Explaining sociopolitical change in Latin America: the case of Mexico. *Latin American Research Review* 27 (3):91–122.

Brandenburg, Frank. 1964. *The Making of Modern Mexico.* Englewood Cliffs, N.J.: Prentice-Hall.

Brown, Lyle C. 1964. General Lazaro Cardenas and Mexican presidential politics, 1933–40: a study in the acquisition and manipulation of political power. Ph.D. diss., University of Texas.

———. 1979. "Cardenas: creating a campesino power base for presidential policy. In G. Wolfskill and D. Richmond, eds., *Essays on the Mexican Revolution: Revisionist Views of the Leaders,* pp. 101–36. Austin: University of Texas Press.

Bunce, Valerie. 1981. *Do New Leaders Make A Difference? Executive Succession and Public Policy under Capitalism and Socialism.* Princeton: Princeton University Press.

Burling, Robbins. 1974. *The Passage of Power: Studies in Political Succession.* New York: Academic Press.

Burns, James MacGregor. 1978. *Leadership.* New York: Harper and Row.

Burton, Michael, and John Higley. 1987. Elite settlements. *American Sociological Review* 52 (3):295–307.

Camp, Roderic Ai. 1980. *Mexico's Leaders.* Tucson: University of Arizona Press.

———. 1984. *The Making of a Government: Political Leaders in Modern Mexico.* Tucson: University of Arizona Press.

———. 1985. *Intellectuals and the State in Twentieth-Century Mexico.* Austin: University of Texas Press.

———, ed. 1986. *Mexico's Political Stability: The Next Five Years.* Boulder, Colo.: Westview Press.

———. 1989. *Entrepreneurs and Politics in Twentieth-Century Mexico.* New York: Oxford University Press.

———. 1992. *Generals in the Palacio: The Military in Modern Mexico.* New York: Oxford University Press.

Cárdenas, Cuauhtémoc. 1988. *Nuestra lucha apenas comienza.* México, D. F.: Editorial Nuestro Tiempo.

———. 1990. Misunderstanding Mexico. *Foreign Policy,* Spring:113–30.

Cárdenas, Lázaro. 1972. *Obras I: Apuntes, 1913–1940.* México, D. F.: UNAM.

———. 1986. *Obras I: Apuntes, 1941–1956.* México, D. F.: UNAM (originally 1972).

Carpizo, Jorge. 1978. *El presidencialismo Mexicano.* Mexico: Siglo Veintiuno Editores.

Cleaves, Peter, and Charles Stephens. 1991. Businessmen and economic policy in Mexico. *Latin American Research Review* 26 (2):187–202.

Collier, David, and Deborah Norden. 1992. Strategic choice models of political change in Latin America. *Comparative Politics* 24 (2):229–43.

Collier, Ruth Berens, and David Collier. 1991. *Shaping the Political Arena: Critical Junctures, the Labor Movement, and Regime Dynamics in Latin America.* Princeton: Princeton University Press.

Contreras, Ariel José. 1983. *México 1940: industrialización y crisis política.* Mexico: Siglo Veintiuno Editores.

Cornelius, Wayne. 1973. Nation-building, participation, and distribution: reform under Cárdenas. In Gabriel Almond, Scott Flanagan, and Robert Mundt, *Crisis, Choice, and Change: Historical Studies of Political Development,* pp. 392–498. Boston: Little, Brown and Company.

————.1990. Mexico: Salinas and the PRI at the crossroads. *Journal of Democracy* 1 (3):61–70.

Cornelius, Wayne, Judith Gentleman, and Peter Smith, eds. 1989. *Mexico's Alternative Political Futures*. La Jolla: Center for U.S.-Mexican Studies, University of California, San Diego.

Cothran, Dan A. 1986. Budgetary secrecy and policy strategy: Mexico under Cárdenas. *Mexican Studies* 2 (1):35–58.

Cothran, Dan A., and Cheryl C. 1988. Mexican presidents and budgetary secrecy. *International Journal of Public Administration* 11 (3):311–40.

Cumberland, Charles C. 1968. *Mexico: The Struggle for Modernity*. New York: Oxford University Press.

Dahl, Robert. 1971. *Polyarchy: Participation and Opposition*. New Haven: Yale University Press.

Davies, James C. 1962. Toward a theory of revolution. *American Sociological Review* 27:5–19 .

de Mora, Juan Miguel. 1982. *Esto nos Dió López Portillo*. México, D. F.: Anaya Editores.

Denitch, Bogdan, ed. 1979. *Legitimation of Regimes*. Beverly Hills: Sage Publications.

Diamond, Larry, Juan Linz, and Seymour Martin Lipset, eds. 1989. *Democracy in Developing Countries: Volume 4, Latin America*. Boulder, Colo.: Lynne Rienner Publishers.

Dix, Robert H. 1984. Why revolutions succeed and fail. *Polity* 16:423–46.

Duff, Ernest. 1985. *Leader and Party in Latin America*. Boulder, Colo.: Westview Press.

Evans, John S. 1982. The evolution of the Mexican tax system since 1970. *Technical Papers Series*, no. 34. Austin: Office for Public Sector Studies, Institute of Latin American Studies, University of Texas.

Evans, Peter, Dietrich Rueschemeyer, and Theda Skocpol, eds. 1985. *Bringing the State Back In*. New York: Cambridge University Press.

Felix, David. 1982. Income distribution trends in Mexico and the Kuznets curves. In Sylvia Ann Hewlett and Richard S. Weinert, eds., *Brazil and Mexico: Patterns in Late Development*, pp. 265–316. Philadelphia: Institute for the Study of Human Issues.

Field, G. Lowell, and John Higley. 1980. *Elitism*. London: Routledge and Kegan Paul.

Fitzgerald, E.V.K. 1978. The state and capital accumulation in Mexico. *Latin American Studies* 10 (2):263–82.

Foix, Pere. 1971. *Cardenas*. 3d ed. México, D. F.: Editorial Trillas.

Foweraker, Joe, and Ann L. Craig, eds. 1990. *Popular Movements and Political Change in Mexico*. Boulder, Colo.: Lynne Rienner Publishers.

Garcia Marsh, Alma Maria. 1982. Ideology and power: a study of the Mexican state under Porfirio Diaz (1876–1911) and Lázaro Cárdenas (1934–1940). Ph.D. diss., University of Texas.

Garrido, Luis Javier. 1989. The crisis of presidentialism. In Wayne Cornelius, Judith Gentleman, and Peter Smith, eds., *Mexico's Alternative Political Futures*, pp. 417–34. La Jolla: Center for U.S.-Mexican Studies, University of California, San Diego.

Gentleman, Judith. 1984. *Mexican Oil and Dependent Development*. New York: Peter Lang.

Gentleman, Judith, and Voytek Zubek. 1992. International integration and democratic development: the cases of Poland and Mexico. *Journal of Interamerican Studies and World Affairs* 34 (1):59–97.

Glade, William. 1965. The enigma of Mexico's dilemma. *Economic Development and Cultural Change* 13:366–76.

Godwin, Kenneth. 1977. Mexican population policy. In Lawrence Koslow, ed., *The Future of Mexico*, pp. 145–68. Tempe: Center for Latin American Studies, Arizona State University.

Goodwin, Jeff, and Theda Skocpol. 1989. Explaining revolution in the contemporary third world. *Politics and Society* 17 (4):489–509.

Grayson, George W., ed. 1990. *Prospects for Democracy in Mexico*. New Brunswick, N.J.: Transaction Publishers.

Greene, Thomas. 1990. *Comparative Revolutionary Movements*. 3d ed. Englewood Cliffs, N.J.: Prentice-Hall.

Grindle, Merilee S. 1977. *Bureaucrats, Politicians, and Peasants in Mexico: A Case Study in Public Policy*. Berkeley: University of California Press.

———. 1977. Policy change in an authoritarian regime. *Journal of Interamerican Studies and World Affairs* 19 (4):523–55.

———. 1986. *State and Countryside: Development and Agrarian Politics in Latin America*. Baltimore: Johns Hopkins University Press.

Gruening, Ernest. 1928. *Mexico and Its Heritage*. New York: Century Company.

Gurr, Ted Robert. 1970. *Why Men Rebel*. Princeton: Princeton University Press.

Haber, Stephen H. 1989. *Industry and Underdevelopment: The Industrialization of Mexico, 1890–1940*. Stanford: Stanford University Press.

Hall, Peter K. 1984. Mexico's economic crisis and need for a new development strategy. *Australian Outlook* 38 (1):26–32.

Hamilton, Nora. 1982. *The Limits of State Autonomy: Post-Revolutionary Mexico*. Princeton: Princeton University Press.

Hamilton, Nora, and Timothy Harding, eds. 1986. *Modern Mexico: State, Economy, and Social Conflict*. Beverly Hills: Sage Publications.

Hansen, Roger. 1973. *The Politics of Mexican Development*. 2d ed. Baltimore: Johns Hopkins University Press.

Hanson, James. 1977. Federal expenditures and "Personalism" in the Mexican institutional revolution. In James W. Wilkie, ed., *Money and Politics in Latin America*, pp. 19–37. Statistical Abstract of Latin America Supplement 7. Los Angeles: UCLA Latin American Center Publications.

Hellman, Judith Adler. 1983. *Mexico in Crisis*. 2d ed. New York: Holmes and Meier.

———. 1988. Continuity and change in Mexico. *Latin American Research Review* 23 (2):133–44.

Hirschman, Albert O., 1963. *Journeys toward Progress: Studies of Economic Policy-Making in Latin America*. New York: Twentieth Century Fund.

———. 1970. *Exit, Voice, and Loyalty: Responses to Decline*. Cambridge, MA: Harvard University Press.

———. 1971. *A Bias for Hope: Essays on Development and Latin America*. New Haven, CT: Yale University Press.

Horowitz, Irving Louis. 1979. "The norm of illegitimacy. In Bogdan Denitch, ed., *Legitimation of Regimes*. Beverly Hills: Sage Publications, pp. 23–35.

Human Rights Commission, Partido de la Revolución Democrática. 1992. *The Political*

Violence in Mexico: A Human Rights Affair. México, D. F.: Partido de la Revolución Democrática.

Huntington, Samuel. 1968. *Political Order in Changing Societies.* New Haven: Yale University Press.

Huntington, Samuel, and Clement Moore, eds. 1970. *Authoritarian Politics in Modern Society: The Dynamics of Established One-Party Systems.* New York: Basic Books.

Huntington, Samuel, and Joan Nelson. 1976. *No Easy Choice: Political Participation in Developing Countries.* Cambridge: Harvard University Press.

Johnson, Chalmers. 1982. *Revolutionary Change.* 2d ed. Stanford: Stanford University Press.

Krauze, Enrique. 1987. *Lázaro Cárdenas: general misionero.* México, D. F.: Fondo de Cultura Económica.

———. 1987. *Plutarco E. Calles: reformar desde el orígen.* México, D. F.: Fondo de Cultura Económica.

Latin American Regional Reports, Mexico and Central America. 1990–92.

León de Palacios, Ana Maria. 1975. *Plutarco Elias Calles: creador de instituciones.* México, D. F.: Instituto Nacional de Administracion Pública.

Levy, Daniel. 1989. Mexico: sustained civilian rule without democracy. In Larry Diamond, Juan Linz, and Seymour Martin Lipset, eds., *Democracy in Developing Countries: Volume 4, Latin America,* pp. 459–97. Boulder, Colo.: Lynne Rienner Publishers.

Levy, Daniel, and Gabriel Székely. 1987. *Mexico: Paradoxes of Stability and Change.* 2d ed. Boulder, Colo.: Westview Press.

Lieuwen, Edwin. 1960. *Arms and Politics in Latin America.* New York: Praeger.

———. 1968. *Mexican Militarism: The Political Rise and Fall of the Revolutionary Army, 1910–1940.* Albuquerque: University of New Mexico Press.

———. 1984. Depoliticization of the Mexican revolutionary army, 1915–1940. In David Ronfeldt, ed., *The Modern Mexican Military: A Reassessment,* pp. 51–61. La Jolla: Center for U.S.-Mexican Studies, University of California, San Diego.

Linz, Juan. 1964. An authoritarian regime: Spain. In Erik Allardt and Stein Rokkan, eds., *Mass Politics: Studies in Political Sociology* (New York: The Free Press), pp. 251–83.

Linz, Juan J., and Alfred Stepan, eds. 1978. *The Breakdown of Democratic Regimes: Latin America.* Baltimore: Johns Hopkins University Press.

Lowenthal, Abraham, ed. 1991. *Exporting Democracy: The United States and Latin America, Case Studies.* Baltimore: Johns Hopkins University Press.

Lustig, Nora. 1992. *Mexico: The Remaking of an Economy.* Washington, D.C.: Brookings Institution.

Malloy, James. 1987. The politics of transition in Latin America. In James Malloy and Mitchell Seligson, eds., *Authoritarians and Democrats: Regime Transition in Latin America,* pp. 235–58. Pittsburgh: University of Pittsburgh Press.

March, James, and Johan Olsen. 1984. The new institutionalism: organizational factors in political life. *American Political Science Review* 78 (3):734–49.

———. 1989. *Rediscovering Institutions: The Organizational Bases of Politics.* New York: Free Press.

Martínez de Navarrete, Ifigenia. 1960. *La distribución del ingreso y el desarrollo económico de México.* México, D. F.: Instituto de Investigaciones Económicas.

————. 1967. Income distribution in Mexico. In Enrique Pérez López, ed., *Mexico's Recent Economic Growth*. Austin: University of Texas Press, pp. 133–71.

Martínez Hernández, Ifigenia. 1989. *Algunos efectos de la crisis en la distribución del ingreso en México*. México, D. F.: Facultad de Economía, UNAM.

Medina, Luis. 1978. *Del cardenismo al avilacamachismo*, vol. 18 of *Historia de la revolucíon Mexicana*. México, D. F.: El Colégio de Mexico.

Mexico, Government of. 1987. *The New Mexican Electoral Legislation*. México, D. F.: Federal Electoral Commission.

————. 1991. *Código federal de institucíónes y procedimientos electorales*. México, D. F.: Instituto Federal Electoral.

Meyer, Lorenzo. 1991. Mexico: the exception and the rule. In Abraham F. Lowenthal, ed., *Exporting Democracy: The United States and Latin America*, pp. 93–110. Baltimore: Johns Hopkins University Press.

Meyer, Michael, and William Sherman. 1987. *The Course of Mexican History*, 3d ed. New York: Oxford University Press.

Michaels, Albert. 1966. Mexican politics and nationalism from Calles to Cardenas. Ph.D. diss., University of Pennsylvania.

————. 1970. The crisis of Cardenismo. *Journal of Latin American Studies* 2 (1):51–79.

Middlebrook, Kevin. 1985. *Political Liberalization in an Authoritarian Regime: The Case of Mexico*. La Jolla: Center for U.S.-Mexican Studies, University of California, San Diego.

Millon, Robert Paul. 1966. *Mexican Marxist: Vicente Lombardo Toledano*. Chapel Hill: University of North Carolina Press.

Molinar Horcasitas, Juan. 1991. *El tiempo de la legitimidad: elecciones, autoritarismo y democracia en México*. México, D. F.: Cal y Arena.

Morris, Stephen D. 1991. *Corruption and Politics in Contemporary Mexico*. Tuscaloosa, AL: University of Alabama Press.

————. 1992. Political reformism in Mexico: Salinas at the brink. *Journal of Interamerican Studies and World Affairs* 34 (1):27–57.

Moss, Ambler H., Jr., 1992. A democratic party approach to Latin America. *Journal of Interamerican Studies and World Affairs* 34 (2):1–17.

Needler, Martin. 1976. Review essay: Daniel Cosío Villegas and the interpretation of the Mexican political system. *Journal of Interamerican Studies and World Affairs* 18 (2):245–52.

————. 1990. *Mexican Politics: The Containment of Conflict*, 2d ed. New York: Praeger Publishers.

Nef, Jorge. 1988. The trend toward democratization and redemocratization in Latin America: shadow and substance. *Latin American Research Review* 23 (3): 131–53.

Newell, Roberto, and Luis Rubio. 1984. *Mexico's Dilemma: The Political Origins of Economic Crisis*. Boulder, Colo.: Westview Press.

O'Donnell, Guillermo, and Philippe Schmitter, eds. 1986. *Transitions from Authoritarian Rule: Tentative Conclusions about Uncertain Democracies*. Baltimore: Johns Hopkins University Press.

Padgett, Vincent. 1966. *The Mexican Political System*. Boston: Houghton Mifflin.

Pastor, Robert A. 1990. Post-revolutionary Mexico: the Salinas opening. *Journal of Interamerican Studies and World Affairs* 32 (3):1–22.

Pastor, Robert A., and Jorge G. Castañeda. 1988. *Limits to Friendship: The United States and Mexico.* New York: Alfred A. Knopf.

Paz, Octavio. 1972. *The Other Mexico: Critique of the Pyramid.* New York: Grove Press.

Peeler, John. 1985. *Latin American Democracies: Colombia, Costa Rica, Venezuela.* Chapel Hill: University of North Carolina Press.

Portes Gil, Emilio. 1954. *Quince años de política Mexicana.* México, D. F.: Ediciones Botas.

Proceso, 1988–93.

Purcell, Susan Kaufman. 1973. Decision-making in an authoritarian regime: theoretical implications from a Mexican case study. *World Politics* 26 (1):28–54.

Purcell, Susan Kaufman, and John F. H. Purcell. 1980. State and society in Mexico: must a stable polity be institutionalized? *World Politics* 32 (2):194–227.

Pye, Lucian. 1990. Political science and the crisis of authoritarianism. *American Political Science Review* 84 (1):3–19.

Ramírez, Miguel D. 1989. *Mexico's Economic Crisis: Its Origins and Consequences.* New York: Praeger Publishers.

Reyna, José Luis, and Richard S. Weinert, eds. 1977. *Authoritarianism in Mexico.* Philadelphia: Institute for the Study of Human Issues.

Reynolds, Clark. 1970. *The Mexican Economy.* New Haven: Yale University Press.

Ronfeldt, David. 1984. The Mexican army and political order since 1940. In David Ronfeldt, ed., *The Modern Mexican Military: A Reassessment,* pp. 63–85. La Jolla: Center for U.S.-Mexican Studies, University of California, San Diego.

———. 1984. *The Modern Mexican Military: A Reassessment.* La Jolla: Center for U.S.-Mexican Studies, University of California, San Diego.

Salinas de Gortari, Carlos. 1982. *Political Participation, Public Investment, and Support for the System: A Comparative Study of Rural Communities in Mexico,* Research Series No. 35. La Jolla: Center for U.S.-Mexican Studies, University of California, San Diego.

———. 1988. *El reto.* México, D. F.: Editorial Diana.

Scherer García, Julio. 1986. *Los presidentes.* México, D. F.: Editorial Grijalbo.

Schmidt, Samuel. 1991. *The Deterioration of the Mexican Presidency.* Tucson: University of Arizona Press.

Scott, Robert E. 1964. *Mexican Government in Transition.* Urbana: University of Illinois Press.

Smith, Peter H. 1979. *Labyrinths of Power: Political Recruitment in Twentieth-Century Mexico.* Princeton: Princeton University Press.

———. 1992. The political impact of free trade on Mexico. *Journal of Interamerican Studies and World Affairs* 34 (1):1–25.

Spaulding, Rose. 1981. State power and its limits: corporatism in Mexico. *Comparative Political Studies* 14 (2):139–61.

Story, Dale. 1986. *The Mexican Ruling Party: Stability and Authority.* New York: Praeger Publishers.

Suárez, Luis. 1987. *Cárdenas: Retrato Inédito.* México, D. F.: Editorial Grijalbo.

Suárez Valles, Manuel. 1971. *Lázaro Cárdenas: una vida fecunda al servicio de México.* México, D. F.: B. Costa-Amic Editor.

Tannenbaum, Frank. 1956. *Mexico: The Struggle for Peace and Bread.* New York: Alfred A. Knopf.

————. 1974. *The Future of Democracy in Latin America: Essays by Frank Tannen-baum.* Ed. Joseph Meier and Richard Weatherhead. New York: Alfred Knopf.

Tardanico, Richard. 1980. Revolutionary nationalism and state building in Mexico, 1917–1924. *Politics and Society* 10 (1):59–86.

————. 1982. State, dependency, and nationalism: revolutionary Mexico, 1924–1928. *Comparative Studies in Society and History* 24 (3):400–23.

Teichman, Judith. 1988. *Policymaking in Mexico: From Boom to Bust.* Boston: Allen and Unwin.

————. 1992. The Mexican state and the political implications of economic restructuring. *Latin American Perspectives* 19 (2):88–103.

Townsend, William C. 1952. *Lázaro Cárdenas: Mexican Democrat.* Waxhaw, N.C.: International Friendship Publishers (2d ed., 1979).

Vasconcelos, José. 1963. *A Mexican Ulysses: An Autobiography.* Trans. Rex Crawford. Bloomington: Indiana University Press.

Vernon, Raymond. 1963. *The Dilemma of Mexico's Development: The Roles of the Private and Public Sectors.* Cambridge: Harvard University Press.

————, ed. 1964. *Public Policy and Private Enterprise in Mexico.* Cambridge: Harvard University Press.

von Sauer, Franz A. 1992. Measuring legitimacy in Mexico: an analysis of public opinion during the 1988 presidential campaign. *Mexican Studies* 8 (2):259–80.

Weber, Max. 1964. *The Theory of Social and Economic Organization.* Ed. Talcott Parsons. New York: Free Press (originally translated in 1947).

Weiner, Myron, and Samuel Huntington, eds. 1987. *Understanding Political Development.* Boston: Little, Brown and Company.

Weyl, Nathaniel, and Sylvia Weyl. 1939. *The Reconquest of Mexico: The Years of Lázaro Cárdenas.* New York: Oxford University Press.

Whitehead, Laurence. 1980. La política económica del sexenio de Echeverría: que salió mal y por qué? *Foro Internacional,* pp. 484–513.

Wilkie, James W. 1967. *The Mexican Revolution: Federal Expenditures and Social Change since 1910.* Berkeley: University of California Press.

————. 1970. *The Mexican Revolution: Federal Expenditures and Social Change since 1910.* 2d ed. Berkeley: University of California Press.

————. 1978. *La revolucion Mexicana: gasto federal y cambio social.* México, D. F.: Fondo de Cultura Económica.

Wilkie, James W., and Albert Michaels, eds. 1984. *Revolution in Mexico: Years of Upheaval, 1910–1940.* Tucson: University of Arizona Press.

Wilkie, James W., and Edna Monzón de Wilkie. 1969. *Mexico visto en el siglo XX: entrevistas de historia oral.* México, D. F.: Instituto Mexicano de Investigaciones Económicas.

Index

About the Author

DAN A. COTHRAN is Professor of Political Science at Northern Arizona University, where he specializes in Mexican and Latin American politics and comparative public policy.

ST. JOHN FISHER COLLEGE LIBRARY

0 1220 0035659 4

DATE DUE

143138

GAYLORD   PRINTED IN U.S.A.

JL 1281 .C7 1994
Cothran, Dan A.
Political stability and
 democracy in Mexico AHZ-6206